BASIC HOTEL FRONT OFFICE PROCEDURES

SECOND EDITION

BASIC HOTEL FRONT OFFICE PROCEDURES

SECOND EDITION

Peter Franz Renner

VNR VAN NOSTRAND REINHOLD
New York

Copyright © 1989 by Van Nostrand Reinhold

Library of Congress Catalog Card Number 88–14232
ISBN 0–442–27673–7

Printed in the United States of America

Van Nostrand Reinhold
115 Fifth Avenue
New York, New York 10003

Van Nostrand Reinhold International Company Limited
11 New Fetter Lane
London EC4P 4EE, England

Van Nostrand Reinhold
480 La Trobe Street
Melbourne, Victoria 3000, Australia

Nelson Canada
1120 Birchmount Road
Scarborough, Ontario M1K 5G4, Canada

16 15 14 13 12 11 10 9 8 7 6 5 4 3 2

Library of Congress Cataloging-in-Publication Data

Renner, Peter Franz, 1943–
  Basic hotel front office procedures.

  Index: p.
  1. Hotels, taverns, etc. I. Title.
TX911.R4 1988   647'.94   88–14232
ISBN 0–442–27673–7 (pbk.)

With special thanks to John Lindenlaub and Mike Coltman, who gave me my first opportunity to teach and stood by me through thick and thin.

PREFACE

In the short years since its first edition in 1981, this book has become *the* textbook for front-office procedures courses on three continents. It has been chosen by instructors in over 50 colleges, vocational schools, and government training programs to train more than 11,000 students.

Since then, several aspects of front-office operations have changed, while others remain the same. The most obvious example of change is the use of computerized equipment, from reservations to billing, and from switchboard operation to auditing and forecasting. While the first edition reserved a separate chapter for computer systems, this new edition treats them as natural aspects of the guest services cycle. The most prominent example of something that has *not* changed is the continued emphasis on customer relations: the clerk's primary responsibility to provide the best possible service to the traveling public.

Basic Hotel Front Office Procedures makes a unique contribution to the training literature, in that it emphasizes the methods and techniques of day-by-day front-office *operation*. It is not a book about front office or rooms department *management*. In addition to step-by-step descriptions of technical procedures, it explains practical interpersonal communication skills.

Each chapter is generously illustrated with forms, charts, and statistics. It clearly states the learning goals to be accomplished, includes appropriate examples of real-life situations and dilemmas facing the clerk, and concludes with a listing of key terms, discussion questions, and practical assignments.

Professional trainers have praised the book for its sound approach to training. Information is presented in clear steps, from simple to complex, from known to unknown, and from the general to the specific. As new concepts are introduced, they are linked to others presented previously, enabling the trainee to acquire information in a systematic manner. On-the-job training and classroom lectures and discussions can easily be integrated to create a complete training package.

Chapter 1 introduces the lodging industry as a vital component of the hospitality industry. It surveys worldwide chain affiliations and reviews the "best" hotels in the world. Organizational structures and job titles are explained, followed by detailed job descriptions for various front-office occupations.

Chapter 2 deals with manual and computerized reservations systems for individual and group bookings. Typical forms, charts, and procedures illustrate the reservations process from initial enquiry to day-of-arrival procedures. The concept of full-house management is given special emphasis.

Chapter 3 describes the steps in the rooming process, for arrivals with and without a reservation. Forms and charts illustrate the clerk's tasks of handling the initial contact, establishing credit, assigning rooms, quoting rates, and matching keys and mail. Selling techniques are emphasized throughout.

Chapter 4 explains basic front-office accounting functions and illustrates how computers handle billing and auditing procedures. The special duties of the cashier are detailed, including credit card processing, cash and check handling, account settlement, and end-of-shift tasks.

Chapter 5 addresses interpersonal communications skills, which desk clerks are expected to display at a high level of competence for most of their working day. Numerous techniques are explained to enable clerks to deal with criticism, compliments, and the everyday exchange of information. Special reference is made to complaint handling and telephone interactions.

Chapter 6 expands on the previous topics by giving a detailed account of how Transactional Analysis, or TA, can be applied in potentially difficult front office situations. Originally developed for therapeutic use and popularized in the 1970s, TA remains a practical, no-nonsense approach to problem solving and customer relations, and a useful framework for personal and professional development.

A *Glossary* of common hotel and front-office terminology completes the text, followed by two *Appendices*. The first covers the vital area of fire-safety procedures for employees and guests, and the second chronicles the history of American hotel keeping.

INSTRUCTOR'S MANUAL

A how-to-train guide has been developed by the author to accompany this text. It includes an industry-based skills chart, step-by-step lesson plans, a list of training films, and a collection of examination questions. For details, contact Peter Renner, Senior Partner, Training Associates Ltd., 2665 West 42nd Avenue, Vancouver, BC V6N 3G4, Canada.

CONTENTS

BASIC HOTEL FRONT OFFICE PROCEDURES

SECOND EDITION

CHAPTER ONE

WELCOME TO THE INDUSTRY

OBJECTIVES

The purpose of this chapter is to:

- Introduce the hospitality industry and its components.
- Explain organizational structures and titles.
- Provide job descriptions for front office employees.
- Describe types of chain affiliations.
- Review ratings for the ''best'' hotels.

INTRODUCTION

The term *hospitality industry* describes a wide range of business enterprises concerned with the transportation, feeding, entertaining, and housing of the traveling public. Airlines, bus companies, cruise lines, car rental agencies, amusement parks, tour operators, restaurants, bars, casinos, and hotels are all part of this industry.

The *lodging* or *hotel industry* is made up of companies that provide overnight accommodation to the traveling public, often in conjunction with food, beverages, entertainment, recreation, and meeting facilities. This book will use these terms interchangeably when referring to hotels, motels, motor hotels, resorts, convention or conference operations.

In a given *property*, several *operating departments* ensure that everything works more or less smoothly. Some of them deal directly with guests and are by tradition referred to as *front of the house* departments. Others provide indirect services and have become known as *back of the house* departments (Table 1.1).

1

Table 1.1
Operating Departments.

Front-of-the-House	Back-of-the-House
Door, bell, and valet attendants	Accounting
Front desk	Food preparation
Switchboard	Storage
Housekeeping	Dishwashing
Reservations	Security
Restaurants	Engineering/maintenance
Bars	Laundry
Banquet rooms	Personnel
Meeting rooms	Training
Recreational facilities	

This book deals with the work at the *front office* (also called the *front desk* or *reception*). Tracing each step of the guest service cycle—from initial reservations to the final check-out contact—it details the procedures and skills required by the staff to perform the following functions:

- Reservations: to receive, chart, store, and assign guest room reservations for individuals and groups.

- Information: to answer requests for information about rooms, hotel services, transportation, entertainment, and the surrounding community.

- Rooming: to match guests' needs to the rooms available; to handle the sale of rooms; to establish credit for incoming guests; to complete registration formalities.

- Guest accounting: to open and maintain proper accounts; to keep track of guests' charges and credits; to verify all transactions and compile management reports.

- Cashiering: to handle various settlement modes, including credit cards, cash, checks, foreign currency, and third-party billing.

- Concierge services: to provide guest services at the door, in the parking area, with luggage, and regarding special requests.

- Switchboard: to handle telephone traffic for guests and the rest of the operation; to provide wake-up and message services.

THE GUEST SERVICES TRILOGY

In a successful hotel enterprise, three parties are mutually dependent on each other: the customers, the owners, and the employees. One hotel corporation defines their roles as follows:[1]

''1. The *customers* [are] the reason-for-being of a business; [the aim] is to satisfy selected needs of targeted customers and in the process generate the revenues necessary to operate and make it worthwhile for owners and employees. A business is defined by the customers and needs it chooses to cater to. Without sufficient satisfaction of customer needs no business can grow and succeed.

2. The *owners* create and/or maintain the financial and material resources necessary for the creation of the products and services intended to satisfy the customers' needs. Without owners no business can be created or sustained.

3. The *employees* must provide the [human resources] and the technical knowledge required to produce and deliver the intended products and services in a way which not only satisfies the needs of the customers but also of the owners.''

The owners charge senior management personnel with the responsibility to satisfy the needs of these three players through the appropriate organizational structure and effective leadership. For day-to-day operations, senior managers delegate responsibilities for guest services and profitability to middle-management, supervisory, and front-line staff. This arrangement is similar in its top-down structure to a military chain of command. Common organizational structures are depicted in the following paragraphs; typical jobs are also described.

THE ORGANIZATIONAL STRUCTURE OF A HOTEL

In addition to the front/back of-the-house approach, a hotel's staffing structure can be viewed in terms of an organizational chart (Fig. 1.1). The chart shown here is based on a medium-sized operation and shows operating departments and common titles. There is great variance from hotel to hotel as to how titles and working relationships are assigned; there is no such thing as a standard organizational structure. For example, in some properties the executive housekeeper reports to the head of the rooms division, in others directly to top management. Similarly, the executive chef may be part of the food and beverage director's substructure or rank at the upper level of the chart and report directly to the general manager. A second chart (Fig. 1.2) is of special interest to newcomers to the industry. It illustrates management and operational positions according to six levels of professional expertise.

JOB TITLES AND FUNCTIONS

The *general manager* is in charge of the entire operation and is thus responsible for the overall performance of the hotel and its employees. Representing the ownership interests, this person directs the activities of all departments. Some

Figure 1.1
Organizational chart of a full-service hotel.

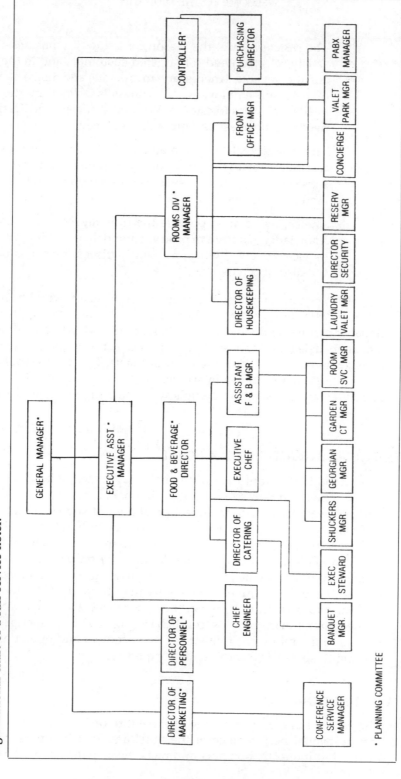

* PLANNING COMMITTEE

Courtesy of Four Seasons Olympic, Seattle, WA.

4

Figure 1.2
Organizational chart, arranged according to levels of professional development.

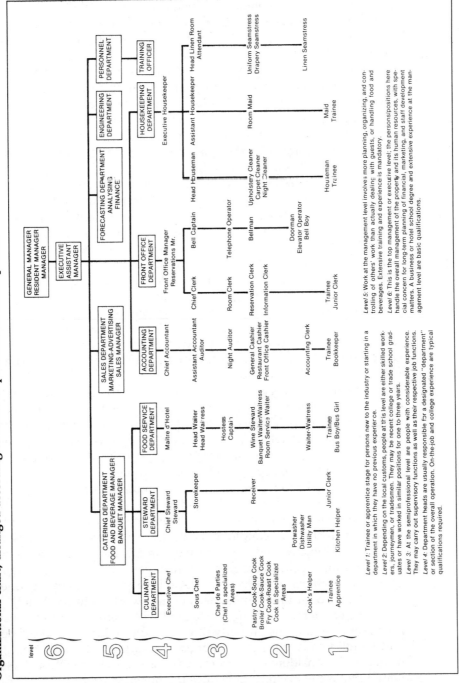

general managers are of the MBWA-type,[2] ''managing by wandering around,'' while others remain behind the scenes, delegating day-to-day supervision to a team of middle and junior managers. Most, to be effective, find that a combination of both styles is needed. The qualifications for becoming a GM have undergone considerable changes in recent years. As the U.S. economy shifted from an industrial to a service focus, so did successful hotel managers, changing from the traditional hands-on, roll-up-your-sleeves approach to a thinking-planning-scheduling one. One industry observer notes that *marketing* has taken over the U.S. lodging industry, that ''managers today deal with the market and its dynamics, not with ways to cut dining room food cost.''[3] Three employment advertisements illustrate how the qualifications required for hotel managers have changed over 20 years (Table 1.2).

The next person in line, the assistant to the chief, may carry the title of *executive assistant manager, resident manager,* or just *assistant manager.* This person is highly visible to staff and guests and takes an active role in the supervision of other managers and the functioning of all departments.

The *food and beverage,* or *F and B director* oversees the most labor-intensive part of the operation, handling everything from the purchase and receiving to the storing, preparation, and service of foods and beverages. Assisting this person may be a *catering manager, banquet manager, assistant F and B director, convention coordinator, restaurant manager,* or *bar manager.*

The *executive chef,* properly addressed as ''chef,'' is in charge of anything to do with food preparation and is assisted by a *sous chef* and a crew of specialist cooks and helpers. A *steward* handles the logistics of dish washing and the supply of cutlery, glasses, and china.

The *executive housekeeper* is responsible for the cleanliness and maintenance of all public areas, including lobbies, offices, guestrooms, and hallways. Subdepartments such as laundry, lost and found, valet services, and maintenance functions may also fall under this person's supervision. An *assistant housekeeper, room inspectors,* and *room attendants* or *room keepers* (occasionally called *maids*) make up the housekeeping staff. The personnel at the front desk work closely with the housekeeping crew, since both departments are charged with the responsibility for guest room sales and service.

The *engineer* looks after the maintenance and repair of the physical plant, which may include air conditioning, heating, elevators, refrigeration, lights, fire-fighting equipment, and anything mechanical. Large operations maintain their own painting, locksmithing, furniture repair, and carpentry departments. In smaller operations, the engineer has to be a jack-of-all-trades, one of the most important and, at times, most hard-to-find workers in the hotel.

The *director of marketing* is charged with generating new business for the hotel, representing the property through public relations and publicity activities, and handling advertising, promotion, and organization of special events. The desk staff is considered part of the in-house sales force. Typically, it is the marketing department which generates the business and the front-office crew that

Table 1.2
Three fictitious want ads showing how the qualifications for hotel general managers have changed over the years.

1965 General Manager	1975 General Manager	1985 General Manager Required
Fast-Growing Hotel Chain Looking For General Managers! Positions Available at Downtown and Resort Properties	*Aggressive Growth-Oriented Hotel Company Looking for General Managers*	*Assertive Market-Oriented Hospitality Company Looking for Entrepreneurial Managers*
Men applying must have: ☐ minimum five years in hotel operations with rooms-division orientation ☐ complete knowledge of hotel accounting and auditing techniques ☐ profit-orientation with strong skills in cost controls.	*Women or men applying must have:* ☐ minimum three years in the hotel industry (some operations experience useful) ☐ complete knowledge of the sales function ☐ profit orientation with good selling and public relations skills.	*Persons applying must have:* ☐ a minimum of five years in the lodging industry with three years direct involvement in marketing ☐ complete knowledge of demographic foot-printing techniques ☐ profit orientation with a yearning for statistics and econometrics.
Men applying should have: ☐ college degree ☐ some food and beverage training ☐ public speaking skills.	*Women or men applying should have:* ☐ BA in Business or Hotel Administration ☐ some food and beverage training ☐ some experience in advertising.	*Persons applying should have:* ☐ an MBA and specialization in travel economics or consumer research ☐ some food and beverage training ☐ some marketing experience.
Special attributes that will be considered: ☐ a CPA license ☐ playing a musical instrument ☐ sales-training courses.	*Special individual attributes that will be considered:* ☐ marketing degree ☐ EST training ☐ reasonably short hair.	*Special attributes that would be considered beneficial:* ☐ Nonsmoker interested in computer science ☐ a real estate license ☐ own a BMW or have run a marathon.

Source: U.S. Lodging Industry (Philadelphia, PA: Laventhal & Horwath, 1986), p. 6.

delivers the goods when the guests arrive. Assisting in the marketing department are *sales manager, public relations director,* and *sales representatives.*

The *controller* or *chief accountant* looks after all accounting functions, including payroll, banking, internal auditing, and various control functions. The desk staff works with the controller's staff to ensure that guest accounts are kept correctly, daily audit and management reports are prepared, and cashiering functions are completed. If the hotel uses computers extensively, a *systems supervisor* or *MIS* (management information systems) *supervisor* may be on the controller's staff.

The *personnel director,* also called the *director of human resources,* is responsible for the staffing element of the hotel: interviewing, selecting, recruiting, training, record keeping, and performance reviews. Labor relations, embracing collective bargaining, grievance, and disciplinary concerns also belong to this department's responsibilities.

The *rooms division manager* is the senior supervisor for that part of the hotel which handles the daily sales and service of guestroom business. A *front office manager* may be the next person in line. This person directly controls the activities of the desk clerks. The title of *assistant manager,* not to be confused with that of the hotel's executive assistant manager, is given to shift supervisors in charge of the desk. Working under the supervision of the front-desk manager are desk clerks, cashiers, concierges, door attendants, and bell attendants. To ensure that there is a senior person available at all times, some hotels create the position of *duty manager* or *manager-on-duty (MOD),* a title given on a rotating schedule.

At the desk itself, the functions of reservations, rooming, information, guest services, and cashiering are assigned to a group of employees. In a small property with 50 rooms and few additional departments, one or two persons can quite easily handle all front office functions; in a property of, say, 800 rooms and many service departments, several clerks divide the work among them. Such generalizations are tricky, as the number of employees in a hotel does not always reflect the number of rooms for sale. The standards and extent of service, the physical layout, and the labor cost are three other factors that contribute to the configuration. For instance, a small hotel with an emphasis on individualized service can employ as many people as a large property with less personalized service. Table 1.3 illustrates these contrasts.

For a full-service hotel, job descriptions for selected front office positions could read as follows:[4]

Desk Clerk

In some organization, this person is called a *desk attendant, receptionist,* or *rooms agent.*

Reports to: Front-office manager/assistant hotel manager.

Table 1.3
Number of employees per guest, by hotel type.

Type of hotel	Name and location	Number of guestrooms and suites	Number of employees	Number of employees for every guestroom
Resort	Turnberry Isle Yacht and Country Club, Miami, FL	118	650	5.5
	Resorts International Casino, Atlantic City, NJ	686	3746	5.5
	Ventanna Inn, Big Sur, CA	40	130	3.3
Highway	Sheraton Inn Hazlet, NJ	200	80	.7
	Ramada Inn Rochelle Park, NJ	176	145	.8
	Holiday Inn Holidome Dodge City, KS	110	115	1.0
Airport	Hilton Marina Hotel Miami, FL	500	307	.6
	Marriott Hotel Irvine, CA	504	500	1.0
	Sheraton Inn Newark, NJ	259	920	3.6

Source: *Lodging Hospitality*, August 1986.

Basic functions: In this organization, clerk handles rooming and cashiering duties.

- Welcomes and registers arriving guests.

- Presents statements and collects payment.

Responsibilities:

- Displays a friendly and professional manner in all dealings with guests, patrons, and other employees.

- Welcomes and registers hotel guests with an emphasis on fulfilling their requests.

- Follows special handling and credit procedures.
- Is familiar with room availability for current and future dates.
- Maximizes revenue and guest satisfaction by means of selling techniques.
- Selects and blocks rooms for arriving guests.
- Preregisters individuals and groups.
- Assists in escorting VIP and return guests to their rooms.
- Works closely with concierge staff to handle guest luggage and special requests.
- Follows through in rooming process by contacting guest by telephone to ensure satisfaction.
- Checks guest out according to set procedures.
- Makes change.
- Cashes checks.
- Exchanges foreign currency.
- Issues safety deposit boxes.
- Posts charges to guest accounts.
- Reconciles all cashier transactions at the close of shift.
- Coordinates and follows up with other departments to handle guests' special requirements.
- Handles and reports guests' problems and complaints.

Related responsibilities:

- Is cross-trained in the following departments: telephone, reservations, concierge, and housekeeping.
- Is capable of handling emergency procedures with professionalism.
- Performs tasks and projects assigned by supervisor.

Concierge

An expanded version of bell captain, in some operations the concierge is called *guest services host*. This person is called the *portier* in many European countries, or *head hall porter* in regions with a British tradition.

Reports to: Front office manager/assistant hotel manager.

Basic functions: To operate an efficient and effective concierge department, ensuring a high degree of guest satisfaction and return, in an atmosphere of hospitality. Does so in a dignified, positive, friendly manner and completes each guest request to the highest standard.

Responsibilities:

- Conducts him/herself in a professional manner at all times, reflecting the high standards of the company.

- Maintains a clean, well-groomed appearance in uniform; maintains a clean, well-organized work area.

- Assists guests at the concierge desk and over the telephone, prior to arrival, during their stay, and after departure.

- Keeps abreast of all events in the hotel by reviewing memos, messages, special-attraction lists, function sheets, arrival sheets, arrival/departure lists, etc.

- Maintains contacts with other businesses in the areas, including restaurants, airlines, ground transportation agencies, theaters, clubs, entertainment events.

- Maintains contacts with other concierges in the city and the company.

- Handles mail, messages, deliveries and rentals.

- Maintains an inventory of stamps and stationery and knows postage rates for domestic and foreign shipments.

- Handles and reports guests' complaints and problems.

- Performs or hires out secretarial work, such as photocopying, typing, and telexing, as requested by guests.

- Keeps current on all city attractions, transportation schedules, entertainment calendars, recreational charters and rentals, and related services to guests.

- Arranges and books tours and special attractions.

- Arranges services such as babysitting, shipping, courier dispatches, luggage repair.

- Supplies guests with emergency needs for toiletries, umbrellas, etc.

- Organizes and books onward travel arrangements.

- Ensures fast and correct service by bellstaff.

- Ensures fast and correct valet parking.

- Maintains a daily log book.

Bell Attendant

Bell attendant is a nonsexist job title for the customary *bellman;* in countries with a British tradition, the titles *porter* or *hall porter* may be used.

Reports to: Concierge.

Basic functions:

- Escorts guests to their rooms;
- Provides information on hotel services and room amenities;
- Maintains clean lobby area.

Responsibilities:

- Escorts guests to elevators and delivers luggage via service elevator.
- Places luggage in guestroom.
- Checks that guestroom is in good order (vacant and clean).
- Explains room features to guests, offers ice, and asks if pressing is required.
- Explains hotel services and food and beverage outlets.
- Transfers guests' luggage when room change is required.
- For checkouts, removes luggage from guestroom via service elevator.
- Assists concierge staff as needed.
- Remains at lobby post when not otherwise occupied.
- Relieves door attendant during meal breaks.
- Delivers guest messages on an hourly schedule.
- Delivers packages, mail, and flowers to guestrooms.
- Looks after flags as instructed by supervisor.
- Enters every service provided in a log book.
- Performs other duties as assigned by concierge.

Related functions:

- Will be cross-trained at the concierge desk.

CLASSIFICATION OF LODGING OPERATIONS

Hotel and motel operations can be classified in a number of ways: by extent of service (full-service, economy, resort, sports), by type of clientele (business, convention, family, singles), by location (airport, downtown, country), by size (small, medium, large), or by ownership (independent, chain, under contract). One trade magazine, *Lodging Hospitality*, groups hotels according to location: center city, resort, suburban, highway, and airport (see Table 1.3).

Many lodging enterprises belong to what is loosely called a *chain*, and they can be classified according to the nature of their affiliation. The most common kinds of chains are described here, using 1986–7 statistics.

A *franchise* involves a system in which the franchise owner grants another (a *franchisee*) the right to merchandize a product for a specific return. For hotel operations, the membership requirements differ widely, but they commonly include the following:

- A minimum number of rooms.
- Locations are carefully scrutinized.
- Architectural design must conform to a common standard.
- Specified services must be provided.
- Local management personnel must undergo a company training program.
- Standards are enforced regarding maintenance, staffing, service, price structure, and advertising.

An example of a typical franchise chain is Motel 6, Inc., made up of over 450 properties, all owned and operated by franchisees.

Another form of affiliation, *chain-owned*, refers to a string of operations owned and operated by one corporation. Red Roof Inns, Inc. is an example of such a chain. It owns and operates all of its 155 properties.

Chain-managed, on the other hand, is an arrangement whereby a company takes over the management of a hotel on behalf of the (often anonymous) owners. One such organization is Marriott Corporation, a chain of 156 properties, which manages hotels belonging to various owners under its ''Marriott Hotels and Resorts'' name.

A *referral group* consists of a number of hotels, independently owned and operated, that join under a common identity while maintaining their own. They do this for the following reasons:

- To operate a joint reservation system.
- To publish joint brochures.
- To share advertising expenses.
- To refer business to each other.
- To refer trained staff to each other.
- To combine their purchasing power.
- To maintain sales offices in major traffic centers.

For example, "The Leading Hotels of the World" is a referral chain of over 200 hotels. Founded in 1928, this group maintains headquarters in New York and reservations centers in 29 countries. Its catalogue lists hotels around the world under its own grouping:[5]

- City hotels.
- Warm-weather resorts.
- Cold-weather/ski resorts.
- Country hotels.
- Spas/health resorts.
- Golfing hotels.
- Tennis hotels.
- Historic landmarks.
- Yachting/boating resorts.

The term *chain* can be used whenever two or more properties do business under a common public identification. As the above definitions show, the term does not, by itself, tell who the owners are or how they are affiliated. This can be illustrated by a news report describing "one of the industry's largest real estate transactions,"[6] in which Holiday Corporation sold 21 hotels to a Chicago real estate company for $313 million in cash, while retaining a long-term contract to manage these properties. Trying to pin down a definition of a chain is further complicated by the practice of big names doing business under several identities. Three examples are Holiday Corporation, Ramada Inns, Inc., and the Radisson Hotel Corporation. As Table 1.4 illustrates, some of their properties are company owned, some franchised, and some under management contract. Table 1.5 provides an overview of the world's chain giants, including their total counts for rooms and properties.

THE WORLD'S BEST HOTELS

Another way to take an organized look at the hotel business is to see which are the best hotels. Lord Lichfield, an "acknowledged connoisseur of the superlative," asked 200 style-setters and experts to nominate their personal "bests" in places around the world.[7] "Best," according to Lichfield, "means the most commended or fitting; it is by no means the grandest or most expensive. It is a matter of avoiding mediocrity when there is an alternative." Table 1.6 is a summary of his findings.

Table 1.4
Three chains and their subsidiaries.

U.S. Lodging Chains	U.S. Properties		Status of Properties			Foreign Properties	
	Rooms	*Number of Properties*	*Company Owned*	*Franchised/ Licensed*	*Management Contract*	*Rooms*	*Number of Properties*
Holiday Corporation Memphis, TN							
Holiday Inns & Crowne Plazas	271,403	1,480	121	1,324	35	48,300	207
Embassy Suites	13,510	60	30	30	0	0	0
Hampton Inns	4,630	45	8	37	0	0	0
Residence Inns	8,668	69	34	42	0	0	0
Harrahs	2,868	4	0	0	0	0	0
Total	301,079	1,658	193	1,433	35	48,300	207
Ramada Inns, Inc. Phoenix, AZ							
Ramada Inns	67,229	455	14	441	3	2,449	18
Ramada Hotels	13,213	51	12	39	2	6,396	26
Ramada Renaissance Hotels	5,540	10	3	7	8	3,540	12
Total	85,982	516	29	487	13	12,384	56
Radisson Hotel Corporation Plymouth, MN							
Plaza Hotels	3,566	9	0	2	7	0	0
Suite Hotels	1,266	5	0	4	1	0	0
Hotels	7,154	26	0	12	14	3,806	19
Inns	3,484	14	1	10	0	0	0
Resorts	1,360	4	2	2	0	784	3
Total	16,830	58	3	28	22	4,590	22

Source: Lodging Hospitality, August 1986.

Another writer, Rene Lecler, claims to have visited 3,000 hotels in 103 countries. In the fifth edition of his "most idiosyncratic hotel guide in the world,"[8] he offers an annotated choice of the world's 300 best hotels. To him, "the personal touch rates very highly in hotels and there is no real substitute. For myself, above all, I admire . . . the professionalism of the man who has gone through the mill, learned and applied the right techniques . . . ."

Table 1.5
The world's largest hotel chains.

Rank	Organization	Rooms	Hotels
1	Holiday Corp. Memphis, TN, USA	318,608	1,685
2	Sheraton Corp. Boston, MA, USA	134,455	488
3	Hilton Hotels Corp. Beverly Hills, CA, USA	96,101	270
4	Ramada Inns, Inc. Phoenix, AZ, USA	96,000	570
5	Quality Inns Itl. Silver Springs, MD, USA	91,000	800
6	Trusthouse Forte Plc. London, England	73,381	750
7	Marriott Corp. Washington, DC, USA	65,072	147
8	Accor Paris, France	64,495	536
9	Imperial Group London, England	61,323	494
10	Balkantourist Sofia, Bulgaria	60,000	460
11	Club Mediterranée Paris, France	47,595	176
12	Days Inns of America Atlanta, GA, USA	46,000	325
13	Motel 6 Santa Barbara, CA, USA	45,000	401
14	Hyatt Hotels Corp. Chicago, IL, USA	44,000	80
15	Inter-Continental New York, NY, USA	35,770	96
16	Intourist Moscow, USSR	34,955	87
17	Hilton Intl. New York, NY, USA	34,774	90
18	Westin Hotels & Resorts Seattle, WA, USA	30,671	56
19	Econolodges of America Charlotte, NC, USA	28,383	359

Rank	Organization	Rooms	Hotels
20	Sol Hotels Palma de Mallorca, Spain	25,000	95
21	Prime Motor Inns Fairfield, NJ, USA	22,544	192
22	Raddisson Hotel Corp. Minneapolis, MN, USA	22,281	77
23	Wagons-Lits Hotel Div. Paris, France	21,209	160
24	Super 8 Motels, Inc. Aberdeen, SD, USA	20,247	323
25	Tokyu Group Tokyo, Japan	19,799	66

Source: ''H & RI Top 200,'' *Hotel & Restaurant International,* July 1986, pp. 62–76.

Table 1.6
World's Best Hotels

1
MANDARIN, Hong Kong
2
ORIENTAL, Bangkok
3
CONNAUGHT, London
4
CIPRIANI, Venice
5
CARLYLE, New York
6
BEVERLY WILSHIRE, Los Angeles
7
OKURA, Tokyo
8
HOTEL DU CAP, Cap d'Antibes
9
REGENT, Sydney
10
REGENT, Melbourne

Source: Lord Lichfield (ed.), *Courvoisier's Book of the Best* (London: Ebury Press, 1986) p. 188.

Three commercial organizations publish annual ratings of their "best" hotels:

Diamonds for excellence.

The American Automobile Association (AAA, or triple A) publishes over 25 million *TourBooks* and *Travel Guides* for 23 different regions every year. Featured in these publications are more than 22,000 classified and quality-rated lodging and dining places in the United States, Canada, and Mexico.

To be listed, an establishment is visited by a field representative and evaluated on its own merits; a multistoried downtown hotel receives the same attention as a small highway establishment or a remote resort; a local independent hotel the same scrutiny as a member of a national chain.

The evaluators follow a detailed inspection list and rate facilities and services on a scale from 0 to 5. A "diamond" ranking designates the degree of quality exhibited by each listed property. The diamonds stand for:

* Meets AAA basic requirements for facilities, services, and hospitality.

** Exceeds AAA minimum requirements in some categories.

*** Significantly exceeds AAA requirements in many categories. Offers very comfortable and attractive accommodations.

**** Exceptional: significantly exceeeds AAA requirements. Offers luxurious accommodations, as well as extra amenities. The management and staff, housekeeping and maintenance rank well above the average.

***** Renowned; awarded only to those exceptional properties widely recognized for marked superiority of guest facilities, services and overall atmosphere.

Of the nearly 20,000 establishments ranked, only 1 percent receive the coveted Five Diamond Award. A list of these properties follows:

Arizona Biltmore Hotel, Phoenix, Arizona

The Pointe at Squaw Peak, Phoenix, Arizona

The Pointe at Tapatio Cliffs, Phoenix, Arizona

Marriott's Camelback Inn, Scottsdale, Arizona

L'Ermitage, Beverly Hills, California

The Ritz-Carlton, Laguna Niguel, California

Fairmont Hotel and Tower, San Francisco, California

Four Seasons Clift Hotel, San Francisco, California

The Westin St. Francis, San Francisco, California

The Broadmoor, Colorado Springs, Colorado

Tall Timber, Durango, Colorado

C Lazy U Ranch, Granby, Colorado

Keystone Resort, Keystone, Colorado

Boca Raton Hotel & Club, Boca Raton, Florida

Hyatt Regency Grand Cypress, Lake Buena Vista, Florida

The Breakers, Palm Beach, Florida

The Ritz-Carlton, Buckhead, Atlanta, Georgia

The Cloister, Sea Island, Georgia

Halekulani Hotel, Honolulu, Hawaii

Westin's Mauna Kea, Kamuela, Hawaii

Hyatt Regency Maui, Lahaina, Hawaii

Stouffer Wailea Beach Resort, Wailea, Hawaii

The Ritz-Carlton, Chicago, Illinois

The Windsor Court Hotel, New Orleans, Louisiana

The Ritz-Carlton, Boston, Massachusetts

Alameda Plaza Hotel, Kansas City, Missouri

Marriott's Tan-Tar-A Resort, Osage Beach, Missouri

Harrah's Tahoe Hotel and Casino, Stateline, Nevada

The Helmsley Palace, New York, New York

The Westin Hotel Williams Center, Tulsa, Oklahoma

Salishan Lodge, Gleneden Beach, Oregon

Four Seasons Hotel, Philadelphia, Pennsylvania

The Adolphus, Dallas, Texas
Fairmont Hotel, Dallas, Texas

Inn on the Park, Houston, Texas
The Westin Galleria, Houston, Texas

The Mandalay Four Seasons Hotel, Irving, Texas

Commonwealth Park Hotel, Richmond, Virginia

Four Seasons Olympic Hotel, Seattle, Washington

The Greenbrier, White Sulphur Springs, West Virginia

The American Club, Kohler, Wisconsin

Four Seasons Hotel, Edmonton, Alberta

Four Seasons Hotel, Vancouver, British Columbia
The Mandarin, Vancouver, British Columbia

Four Seasons, Toronto, Ontario

Le Quatre Saisons, Montreal, Quebec
Ritz-Carlton Hotel, Montreal, Quebec

Acapulco Princess Hotel, Acapulco, Guerrero
Las Brisas, Acapulco, Guerrero

Camino Real, Mexico, D.F.

Behind the stars .

There is one award in North America, awarded annually to only a handful of properties, that sets its recipients apart from the rest of the industry. The Five-Star Award by the Mobile Travel Guide is based on a point system of site inspections. The Guide includes a cross-section of hotels, motels, resorts and restaurants, from the simple, clean, well-maintained operation achieving a 1-star rating to the elegant, full-service property warranting the coveted 5-star designation. In 1987, the top-ranking properties were:[1]

Motel

Quail Lodge, Carmel, CA

Salishan Lodge, Gleneden Beach, OR

Guest ranch

C Lazy U Ranch, Granby, CO.

Hotels

Bel-Air, Westwood Village, Los Angeles, CA

Four Seasons Clift, San Francisco, CA

The Stanford Court, San Francisco, CA

Harrah's Lake Tahoe, Stateline, NV

Williamsburg Inn, Williamsburg, VA

Carlyle, New York City

Grand Bay, Miami, FL

Hotels, cont'd

The Wigwam, Litchfield Park, AZ

Arizona Biltmore, Phoenix, AZ

The Pointe, Phoenix, AZ

Marriott's Camelback Inn, Scottsdale, AZ

Marriott's Rancho Las Palmas, Palm Springs, CA

Ritz Carlton, Laguna Niguel, CA

The Homestead, Hot Springs, VA

The Greenbrier, White Sulphur Springs, WV

Boca Raton Hotel & Club, Boca Raton, FL

The Breakers, Palm Beach, FL

The Cloister, Sea Island, GA

The Broadmoor, Colorado Springs, CO

Tall Timber, Durango, CO

Data for the *rating process* is collected from three sources: (1) each property is visited and inspected by a trained representative, who checks on the grounds, public rooms and sample guest rooms. (2) For potential 5-star operations, an additional anonymous visit is made by a senior inspector who stays with his or her party as a paying guest. (3) Every guide book, listing over 20,000 properties in the United States, includes a survey form on which travelers submit their evaluations. Such information is considered in the final rating process.

For five-star properties, special standards apply. Such a hotel stands in a very elite category, one in which the staff engages in tireless pursuit of excellence and perfection. Although there is no "typical" five-star hotel, since every one is unique, some common characteristics exist. Each offers a level of individual service with a superior standard of quality and elegance. The staff is clearly professional; their exceptional appearance, their articulate and knowledgeable approach to the guest reflect the quality of the establishment. Twice-daily housekeeping service is standard, including turn-down service. The lobby is a place of beauty, often displaying fine furnishings, antiques, and original works of art. Room service should be outstanding, and a superior restaurant, not necessarily a five-star, should be available. The grounds should be meticulously groomed and landscaped. The quality must be sustained continuously from year to year.

1. Mobil Travel Guide, Prentice-Hall Press, Deerfield, IL.

1. The American Automobile Association, pronounced ''AAA'' or ''triple A,'' rates the best hotels and resorts and gives its Five-Diamond Award (see box, ''Diamonds for Excellence'').

2. The Mobile Travel Guide selects its Five-Star Award winners (see box, ''Behind the Stars'').

3. *Institutional Investor* magazine polls 100 senior bankers, men and women who either head their institutions or are responsible for international operations, and asks them to rate leading hotels on a scale of 1 to 100.[9] The typical respondent spends 81 nights per year in a hotel, certainly a qualification for judging what is best in this class of hotels. The 1986 ranking shows that the top four hotels are in the Orient; the Vier Jahreszeiten in Hamburg, Germany, is the fifth; the Connaught in London is the top English hotel; the Carlyle in New York is the leading U.S. property; the Four Seasons in Toronto the winning Canadian hotel; and the Regent in Sidney the number one Australian. Table 1.7 gives the full list, arranged by world regions.

Table 1.7
The world's best hotels, by region.

Americas			Americas		
Regional Rank	Hotel	Global Rank	Regional Rank	Hotel	Global Rank
1	Carlyle New York	14	10	Park Lane New York	42
2	Four Seasons Washington, D.C.	15	11	Helmsley Palace New York	46
3	Stanford Court San Francisco	20	12	Regency New York	50
4	Ritz-Carlton Boston	21			
5	Ritz-Carlton Chicago	22	**Asia-Pacific**		
			Regional Rank	Hotel	Global Rank
6	Four Seasons Toronto	27	1	Oriental Bangkok	1
7	Pierre New York	33	2	Mandarin Hongkong	2
8	Madison Washington, D.C.	37	3	Okura Tokyo	3
9	Beverly Wilshire Los Angeles	39			

(continued)

Asia-Pacific

Regional Rank	Hotel	Global Rank
4	Regent Hongkong	4
5	Shangri-La Singapore	7
6	Peninsula Hongkong	9
7	Regent Sydney	12
8	Manila Manila	26
9	Imperial Tokyo	30
10	Regent Melbourne	32
11	Shilla Seoul	36
12	Mandarin Singapore	38

Europe

Regional Rank	Hotel	Global Rank
1	Vier Jahreszeiten Hamburg	5
2	Connaught London	6
3	Ritz Paris	8
4	Plaza-Athénée Paris	10
5	Claridge's London	11
6	Ritz Madrid	13
7	Dolder Grand Zurich	16
8	Berkeley London	17
9	Hassier Villa Medici Rome	18
10	De Crillon Paris	19
11	Imperial Vienna	23
12	Richemond Geneva	24
13	Bristol Paris	25
14	Vier Jahreszeiten Munich	28
15	Inn on the Park London	29
16	Baur au Lac Zurich	31
17	Breidenbacher Hof Düsseldorf	34
18	Sacher Vienna	35
19	Des Bergues Geneva	40
20	Maurice Paris	41
21	Grand Rome	43
22	Steigenberger Frankfurter Hof Frankfurt	44
23	Grand Stockholm	45
24	George V Paris	47
25	Dorchester London	48
26	D'Angleterre Copenhagen	49

Source: *Institutional Investor*, September 1986, p. 270.

KEY TERMS

Hospitality industry	Public relations
Lodging industry	Publicity
Front-of-the-house	Controller
Back-of-the-house	Systems supervisor
Organizational structures	MIS
General manager	Director of human resources
Executive assistant manager	Rooms division manager
Duty manager	Front office manager
MOD	Assistant manager
Resident manager	Desk attendant
Food and beverage manager	Receptionist
F & B	Rooms agent
Executive chef	Concierge
Sous chef	Franchise
Steward	Chain-owned hotel
Executive housekeeper	Chain-managed hotel
Engineer	Referral group
Director of marketing	Chain

NOTES

1. "The Dunfey Business Trilogy," *The Cornell Hotel and Restaurant Administration Quarterly*, May 1985, p. 145.

2. This term is used in *In Search of Excellence* (Thomas J. Peters & Robert H. Waterman, Jr., New York: Warner Books, 1982). Among successful MBWA managers they cite Edward E. Carlson, retired president of Westin Hotels and chairman emeritus of United Air Lines.

3. Robert Eaton, "The science of operating is yielding to the art of marketing," *U.S. Lodging Industry*, Philadelphia, PA: Laventhol & Horwath, 1986, p. 6.

4. Excerpted with permission from job descriptions used at the Newport Beach Four Seasons Hotel, Newport Beach, CA.

5. The Leading Hotels of the World, *1986 Catalogue*, New York, NY.

6. "H & R I Top 200." *Hotel & Restaurant International*, July 1986.

7. Lord Lichfield (ed.), *Courvoisier's Book of the Best*. London: Ebury Press, 1986.

8. Rene Lecler, *The 300 best hotels in the world*. Englewood Cliffs, NJ: Prentice-Hall, 1985, p. viii.

9. "The world's best hotels," *Institutional Investor*, September 1986, pp. 269–276.

DISCUSSION QUESTIONS AND ASSIGNMENTS

1. List the job titles for all employees in a lodging operation who (a) deal directly with guests, and (b) normally do not come into direct contact with guests. Do this for a city-center hotel, a resort hotel, and a highway hotel.

2. Using Table 1.2 as a guide, create similar advertisements for the positions of (a) desk clerk, (b) front office manager, and (c) night auditor.

3. Select a lodging operation in your community and prepare a fact sheet. It should contain this basic information:

   a. Name
   b. Address
   b. Chain affiliation
   c. Ownership
   d. Number of guest rooms
   e. Room rates
   f. Type of clientele
   h. Type of operation (use the classifications in this chapter)
   i. Recreational facilities available
   j. Proximity to other hotels and attractions
   k. Food and beverage outlets, operating hours, atmosphere
   l. Credit cards accepted
   m. Pet policy
   n. Banquet facilities

   Working alone or in a small group with other students, add to this list to arrive at a complete profile that would allow you to answer almost any question a guest might ask.

4. Make a list of the top ten or twenty lodging operations in your community. Show their name, chain affiliation, number of guestrooms, and rate range.

5. Determine your choice of "best hotel in the community." In writing, define what you mean by "best" and give a brief profile of the operation, its facilities, history, and operating philosophy.

6. Through personal interviews, develop a written profile of a general manager or department head of your choice. Explain why you selected this person, how the person reached his or her present position, and what his or her advice is to newcomers to the industry.

7. Select a different lodging operation from the ones you used in the previous assignments and find the information you need to draw up an organizational chart. Show the chart to a senior member of the management for verification. Explain to your study group how this chart differs from those shown in this chapter.

CHAPTER TWO

RESERVATIONS PROCEDURES

OBJECTIVES

The purpose of this chapter is to:

- Describe manual and computerized reservation systems.
- Show forms and charts used during the reservation process.
- List the day-of-arrival procedures at the front desk.
- Describe the handling of group bookings.
- Illustrate the concept of "full-house management."

INTRODUCTION

Guestrooms are a hotel's most perishable goods. A room not sold today is lost forever. In the cocktail lounge a bartender can store bottles not sold today for future sales; the rooms department does not have this flexibility. A room not sold is money not earned for the hotel. Expenses for maintaining the operation, however, continue to occur and must be covered. Figure 2.1 shows that full-service hotels obtain the lion's share of their revenue from room sales and spend about a third of their income on paying their employees. It is crucial that the front-office department have an efficient system to deal with reservations requests. The guest services cycle begins here.

Strong competition exists in the lodging market, and a well-functioning reservation systems is a must. A guest who experiences reservations difficulties will think twice (or not at all) about coming back to the same place. One disgruntled customer not only creates a loss of business by not returning, but may also spread the word to associates and friends, creating a dangerous ripple effect.

Figure 2.1
International hotels. Percentage distribution of revenue and expenses.

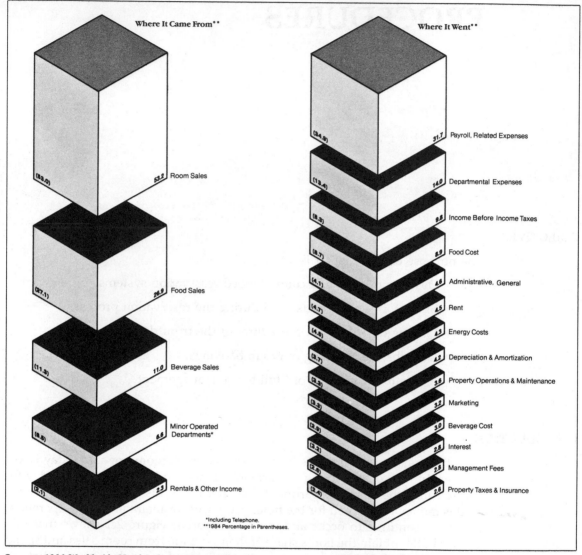

Source: *1986 Worldwide Hotel Industry* (New York: Horwath & Horwath International), p. 27.

However nicely decorated, conveniently located, efficiently managed, or reasonably priced an establishment is, if the front office does not function well and produce the promised accommodation, the reputation of the entire hotel will be harmed.

Small operations and those that have not switched to computers use a combination of cards and charts to organize their reservations traffic. While the application of computers is on the increase (see Table 2.1), an examination of the traditional reservations process, complete with cards and charts, will help you understand how the information is processed.

A reservation system must be able to handle the following functions:

1. Receive the request for a reservation.

2. Accept or deny the request.

3. Obtain pertinent data to handle requests accurately.

4. Add new reservations to those already in the system, and allow for easy access to the accumulated reservations.

5. Safeguard against people who make a reservation but do not arrive (no-shows).

6. Provide a detailed list of guests and their requirements on the day of arrival.

7. Support the front-office management's efforts to attain a full house.

The volume of reservation requests determines the amount of staff, space, and equipment required. All reservation-related activity should be routed through a designated reservations department. In a small operation, this could be part of the desk clerk's function, or handled by the manager and a secretary. As reservations traffic becomes more complex, a separate staff is needed: a *reservations manager* in a large property could supervise from two to ten people working on various aspects of reservations.

Table 2.1
Percentage of hotels using computerized reservations systems, by region.

United States	Canada	Caribbean	Middle East	Latin America
79.6	57.4	45.5	30.4	28.6

Asia	Australia	Continental Europe	Scandinavia	United Kingdom
42.9	49.2	60.0	52.6	65.5

Source: 1986 Worldwide Hotel Industry. New York: Horwath & Horwath International, 1986.

he Reservation Request

A prospective guest can obtain information about the hotel from a number of sources, including:

- Advertisements in magazines, newspapers, Yellow Pages.
- Direct-mail brochures.
- A travel agent or tour operator.
- A clerk from another hotel.
- Word-of-mouth referral from a fellow traveler.
- A mention in a guidebook.

Other business comes almost by chance, possibly because:

- The turnoff from the freeway leads to the hotel.
- The "Vacancy" sign caught someone's attention.
- The airport bus terminated in front of your hotel.
- The traveler recognized the chain's name and logo.

Table 2.2 presents market data for a worldwide sample of hotels, compiled by the accounting firm of Horwath & Horwath International.[1] The chart shows the composition of the hotels' markets and the sources of their reservations.

The way a reservation request reaches a hotel dictates how it is answered. Telegrams or a telephone call indicate an urgent request; courtesy and good business sense demand an immediate reply. Letters are acknowledged in writing if there is sufficient time before the arrival date. Corporate secretaries making reservations for their traveling employees (*corporate travelers*) and travel agents often use Telex.

Fig. 2.2 illustrates possible routes by which a traveler may contact a hotel for a reservation. *Hotels* within a given region (tourist area, proximity to airport) may operate a referral system among themselves even though they are not affiliated. *Travel agents* who arrange accommodations for their customers usually receive a 10 percent commission for every room or night that is booked through them. The service that the hotel gives the travel agent depends upon the agent's record of payment, cancellations, and no-shows. For *chain* referrals, travelers can call a toll-free telephone number or the number of a member hotel in their area to reserve space in any hotel of the chain. Some hotels employ *representatives* in major population centers. Airlines, car rental companies, cruise ship lines, and visitors information centers also offer reservation services.

A recent innovation is the automated reservation through *voice response units.* They allow a caller to make reservations by phone without talking to a person. A computer-generated voice responds to numbers keyed by the caller

Table 2.2
Market Data by region.

	All Hotels	Africa and the Middle East	Asia and Australasia	North America*	Europe	Latin America
Source of Business						
Domestic	50.2%	24.9%	49.2%	76.9%	42.1%	58.2%
Foreign	49.8	75.6	50.8	23.1	57.9	41.8
Total	100.0%	100.0%	100.0%	100.0%	100.0%	100.0%
Percentage of Repeat Business	40.0	36.9	38.2	45.2	34.9	46.3
Composition of Market						
Government Officials	7.1	9.2	5.7	8.7	3.4	4.8
Businessmen	38.3	39.9	38.5	34.9	39.4	48.5
Tourists (Individual)	20.4	13.6	23.2	23.0	20.3	22.9
Tour Groups	14.0	15.3	20.3	8.0	15.7	6.1
Conference Participants	10.5	5.2	5.7	16.0	12.1	6.2
Other	9.7	16.8	6.6	9.4	9.1	7.4
Total	100.0%	100.0%	100.0%	100.0%	100.0%	100.0%
Percentage of Advance Reservations	82.7	69.8	87.4	75.3	90.7	79.1
Compositions of Advance Reservations						
Direct	36.0	38.1	31.4	32.4	41.6	30.6
Reservation Systems	24.8	28.8	25.4	26.1	19.7	34.3
Travel Agents & Tour Operators	27.7	21.9	33.6	27.9	27.8	23.4
Other	11.6	11.2	9.6	13.6	10.9	11.7
Total	100.0%	100.0%	100.0%	100.0%	100.0%	100.0%

*Includes the United States, Canada, and the Caribbean.

Source: 1986 Worldwide Hotel Industry (New York: Horwath & Horwath International), p. 29.

on a Touch-Tone telephone. Telecommunications consultants claim that these machines can cut reservations labor costs in half.[2]

The American Express Assured Room Reservation Plan allows its members to use their credit cards to obtain guaranteed reservations. The cardmember calls

Figure 2.2
Reservation routes from potential guests to the property.

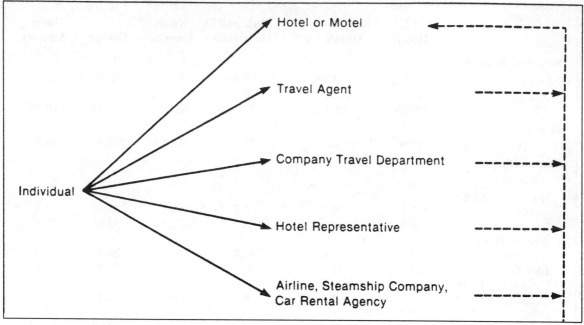

the hotel and requests an assured reservation, giving his or her American Express Card number. The requested location receives either a hard copy printout or a telephone reading that shows the arrival date, the room type, and the rate. On or before check-out time on the day of arrival, the registration folio is made out, the room number assigned, and the room held until check-out time on the following day.

To cancel, the cardholder has to telephone the reservation system or the property by 6:00 P.M. (4:00 P.M. for resorts) of the intended day of arrival. If the cardholder fails to cancel, a charge equivalent to one night's room charges is automatically made. On the other hand, if the person arrives and no room is available, the hotel must provide one night's stay at a comparable room at another establishment and transportation to the new hotel for free.

THE RESERVATIONS PROCESS

Once a reservation reaches the hotel, it must be accurately recorded and processed (Fig. 2.3). The procedures described here apply to most hotels. The manual procedures are described first, followed by a computerized reservation system.

Figure 2.3
The reservations process.

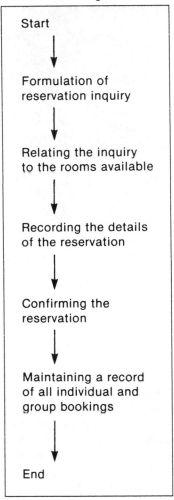

Start

Formulation of
reservation inquiry

Relating the inquiry
to the rooms available

Recording the details
of the reservation

Confirming the
reservation

Maintaining a record
of all individual and
group bookings

End

Adapted from M.L. Kasavana, *Hotel Information Systems* (Boston, MA: CBI Publishing Company), p. 181.

Accepting or Denying a Request

When receiving a request for a reservation, the clerk must be able to decide immediately whether to accept or deny it. A simple look-up must be available to show the hotel's reservations status for the next few months. Two common

Figure 2.4
Wall-mounted reservations chart.

Courtesy of Seattle Hyatt House, Seattle, WA.

methods are the chalkboard (Fig. 2.4) and the *space available sheet* (Fig. 2.5). They show, based on the reservations manager's calculations, the status for various room types (not actual room numbers): "Closed dates" are those for which no rooms are available. They are either blocked out visually or noted as "s/o": "sold out." A "go slow" warning, indicating an almost-full house, can be given for other dates. In such a case, only single reservations are to be accepted, and large bookings must be cleared with the person in charge. Other symbols can be used for other restrictions: no suites, deluxe only, no discounts, no king-sized beds, no package deals.

Accepting a Reservation

After determining the availability of rooms for the desired date, the clerks proceed to obtain more information on a *reservations card*. This could be one specifically designed for the hotel or purchased from a supplier (Figs. 2.6 and 2.7). The information needed includes:

Name.   Clarify exact spelling of first and last name as well as any title, such as Dr., Prof., or military, government, or church rank.

Figure 2.5
"Space available" sheet.

	1	2	3	4	5	6	7	8	9	10	11	12	13	14	15	16	17	18	19	20	21	22	23	24	25	26	27	28	29	30	31
JANUARY	1	2	3	4	5	6	7	8	9	10	11	12	13	14	15	16	17	18	19	20	21	22	23	24	25	26	27	28	29	30	31
FEBRUARY	1	2	3	4	5	6	7	8	9	10	11	12	13	14	15	16	17	18	19	20	21	22	23	24	25	26	27	28	29		
MARCH	1	2	3	4	5	6	7	8	9	10	11	12	13	14	15	16	17	18	19	20	21	22	23	24	25	26	27	28	29	30	31
APRIL	1	2	3	4	5	6	7	8	9	10	11	12	13	14	15	16	17	18	19	20	21	22	23	24	25	26	27	28	29	30	
MAY	1	2	3	4	5	6	7	8	9	10	11	12	13	14	15	16	17	18	19	20	21	22	23	24	25	26	27	28	29	30	31
JUNE	1	2	3	4	5	6	7	8	9	10	11	12	13	14	15	16	17	18	19	20	21	22	23	24	25	26	27	28	29	30	
JULY	1	2	3	4	5	6	7	8	9	10	11	12	13	14	15	16	17	18	19	20	21	22	23	24	25	26	27	28	29	30	31
AUGUST	1	2	3	4	5	6	7	8	9	10	11	12	13	14	15	16	17	18	19	20	21	22	23	24	25	26	27	28	29	30	31
SEPTEMBER	1	2	3	4	5	6	7	8	9	10	11	12	13	14	15	16	17	18	19	20	21	22	23	24	25	26	27	28	29	30	
OCTOBER	1	2	3	4	5	6	7	8	9	10	11	12	13	14	15	16	17	18	19	20	21	22	23	24	25	26	27	28	29	30	31
NOVEMBER	1	2	3	4	5	6	7	8	9	10	11	12	13	14	15	16	17	18	19	20	21	22	23	24	25	26	27	28	29	30	
DECEMBER	1	2	3	4	5	6	7	8	9	10	11	12	13	14	15	16	17	18	19	20	21	22	23	24	25	26	27	28	29	30	31

X - NO TWINS AVAILABLE
0 - NO DOUBLES AVAILABLE
I - NO SINGLES AVAILABLE

■ - CLOSED, NO SPACE AVAILABLE

35

Figure 2.6
Reservation form.

NAME		ARRIVAL TIME
		LENGTH OF STAY
TYPE OF ROOM		
SPEC. REQUESTS		
GUARANTEED ☐		6 P.M. ☐
REQUESTED BY		
PHONE		
COMPANY		
DATE	TAKEN BY	

20M-10-76

Address. A full mailing address is needed; box numbers are not enough. If there is a business or government affiliation, that address must also be obtained in full.

Arrival date. Use the format customary at the hotel, either 5/20/8– or 20 May 198–.

Departure date. Spell out the same way as arrival date. If the caller is uncertain of the exact departure date, put down an approximate date.

Times of arrival and departure. These are needed by the desk and the housekeeping department to anticipate high and low periods of business. They are particularly important if they fall outside the normal range.

Means of transport. This information is useful in determining the status of suspected no-shows. A flight number helps to find out if a guest is delayed

Figure 2.7
Reservation form.

Four Seasons Hotel
NEWPORT BEACH

RESERVATIONS

ARRIVAL DAY / DATE _____

DEPARTURE DAY / DATE _____

GROUP NAME _____

SOURCE CODE_____

ROOM TYPE _____

NAME _____
　　　　　(LAST)　　　　　　　　(FIRST)

FIRM_____

ADDRESS _____

_____

IN PARTY _____

RATE _____

☐ GUARANTEED　　　☐ 6 PM

GTD TO: _____

SPECIAL SERVICES: _____

CALLER _____

PHONE (　　　) _____

CONFIRMATION ☐ YES ☐ NO

RES. TAKEN BY _____

DATE RES. TAKEN _____

COMMENTS _____

_____

_____

_____

_____

_____

_____

Courtesy of Four Seasons Hotel, Newport Beach, CA.

because a flight is late in arriving. A ''by car'' arrival can be affected by poor weather conditions or closed roads.

Rate. Distinguish between ''rate requested'' and ''rate confirmed.'' The first reflects what the caller has requested, the latter what has been promised: they are not always the same. For example: A caller asks for a mininum rate. The clerk responds, ''Our rates range from $60 to $95 in our standard rooms. We'll do our best to accommodate you at or near our lowest rate.'' Avoid confirming the absolutely lowest rate, just in case there is no room available in that group when the guest arrives. If the caller insists on a specific amount, acknowledge the request and note it as ''confirmed rate'' on the card. It will have to be honored upon arrival, regardless of what rooms are vacant.

Special rates may also apply to certain calls. In a hotel that frequently handles group bookings, clerks are instructed to ask routinely, ''Do you belong to a group?'' Asking this question ensures that blocks of rooms ''on hold'' are correctly assigned to the people for whom they are intended. In hotel jargon, reservations are thus "picked up." If, on the other hand, a reservation request is not linked to the group block, the guest could miss out on the special group rate or even be refused a reservation should the hotel be sold out. Group organizers, too, must know how many rooms have been picked up. When a room is assigned to a group member, a notation is made on both the group booking chart and the individual reservation card.

Guests may also be booking one of the *plans*, including the American Plan (room, breakfast, lunch and dinner) or the Modified American Plan (room, breakfast, and one other meal). This applies mostly in resort hotels or to bookings based on a special package brochure.

Reservation status. Use the terms "advance payment," "guaranteed payment," "late arrival," "6:00 P.M. arrival," "part of a group booking," "convention," etc.).

Special requests. Note special requests, such as children's bed to be put in the room, extra quiet room, not on the south side, wheelchair guest, VIP, requests a room with a view.

Classification. For a variety of reasons, management may be interested in the marketing mix of its customers. In this case, customers are number-coded on the reservation form according to certain classifications. The following are examples:

1. Corporate traveler.

2. Transient traveler.

3. Package group.

4. Airline employee or delayed passenger.

5. Government employee (special rate).

6. Central reservations office.

7. American Express Assured Reservation.

8. Walk-in.

When asking for all of this information, the clerk must quickly and politely establish control over the conversation. People who are accustomed to making hotel reservations anticipate most of the questions and are usually prepared to give all necessary details. Those less familiar with the procedures need to be prompted courteously. A well-managed reservations request should take two or three minutes to complete, not more.

Once all details are obtained, the clerk repeats the key details to the caller to ensure their correctness. Some customers request a written confirmation, and hotels send them routinely as long as there is enough time available before arrival. Figures 2.8, 2.9, and 2.10 are examples of different forms in use.

Figure 2.8
Multipurpose reservation confirmation. Top section copies through to attached folio, registration form, and room/information slip.

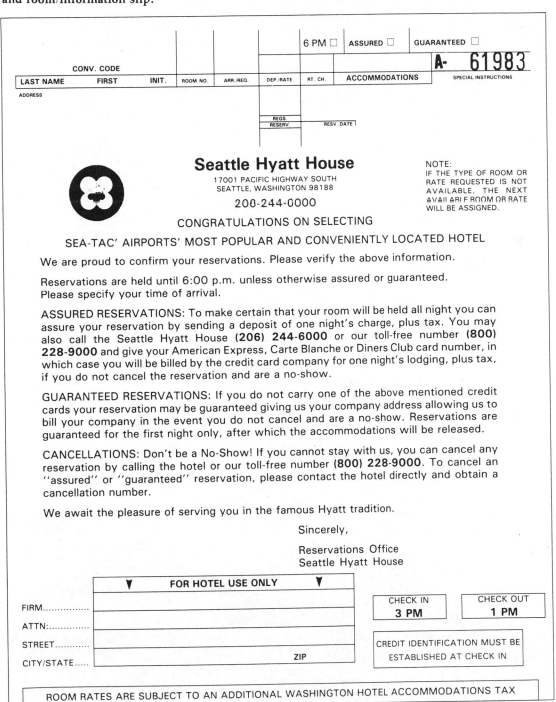

	CONV. CODE						6 PM ☐	ASSURED ☐	GUARANTEED ☐
LAST NAME	FIRST	INIT.	ROOM NO.	ARR./REQ.	DEP./RATE	RT. CH.	ACCOMMODATIONS		SPECIAL INSTRUCTIONS
ADDRESS									

A- 61983

REGS.
RESERV.   RESV. DATE

Seattle Hyatt House
17001 PACIFIC HIGHWAY SOUTH
SEATTLE, WASHINGTON 98188

200-244-0000

NOTE:
IF THE TYPE OF ROOM OR RATE REQUESTED IS NOT AVAILABLE, THE NEXT AVAILABLE ROOM OR RATE WILL BE ASSIGNED.

CONGRATULATIONS ON SELECTING

SEA-TAC' AIRPORTS' MOST POPULAR AND CONVENIENTLY LOCATED HOTEL

We are proud to confirm your reservations. Please verify the above information.

Reservations are held until 6:00 p.m. unless otherwise assured or guaranteed.
Please specify your time of arrival.

ASSURED RESERVATIONS: To make certain that your room will be held all night you can assure your reservation by sending a deposit of one night's charge, plus tax. You may also call the Seattle Hyatt House **(206) 244-6000** or our toll-free number **(800) 228-9000** and give your American Express, Carte Blanche or Diners Club card number, in which case you will be billed by the credit card company for one night's lodging, plus tax, if you do not cancel the reservation and are a no-show.

GUARANTEED RESERVATIONS: If you do not carry one of the above mentioned credit cards your reservation may be guaranteed giving us your company address allowing us to bill your company in the event you do not cancel and are a no-show. Reservations are guaranteed for the first night only, after which the accommodations will be released.

CANCELLATIONS: Don't be a No-Show! If you cannot stay with us, you can cancel any reservation by calling the hotel or our toll-free number **(800) 228-9000**. To cancel an "assured" or "guaranteed" reservation, please contact the hotel directly and obtain a cancellation number.

We await the pleasure of serving you in the famous Hyatt tradition.

Sincerely,

Reservations Office
Seattle Hyatt House

▼   **FOR HOTEL USE ONLY**   ▼

FIRM...............

ATTN:.............

STREET...........

CITY/STATE.....   ZIP

| CHECK IN | CHECK OUT |
| 3 PM | 1 PM |

CREDIT IDENTIFICATION MUST BE ESTABLISHED AT CHECK IN

ROOM RATES ARE SUBJECT TO AN ADDITIONAL WASHINGTON HOTEL ACCOMMODATIONS TAX

Courtesy of Seattle Hyatt House, Seattle, WA.

Figure 2.9

Reservation confirmations generated by a computer. Top: reservation guaranteed by a deposit; middle: reservation guaranteed by a credit card; bottom: reservation not guaranteed.

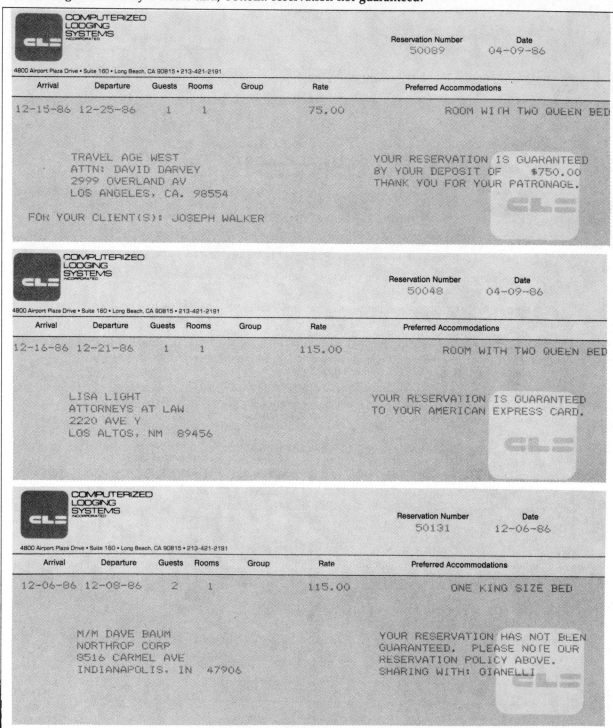

Figure 2.10
Simplified confirmation form.

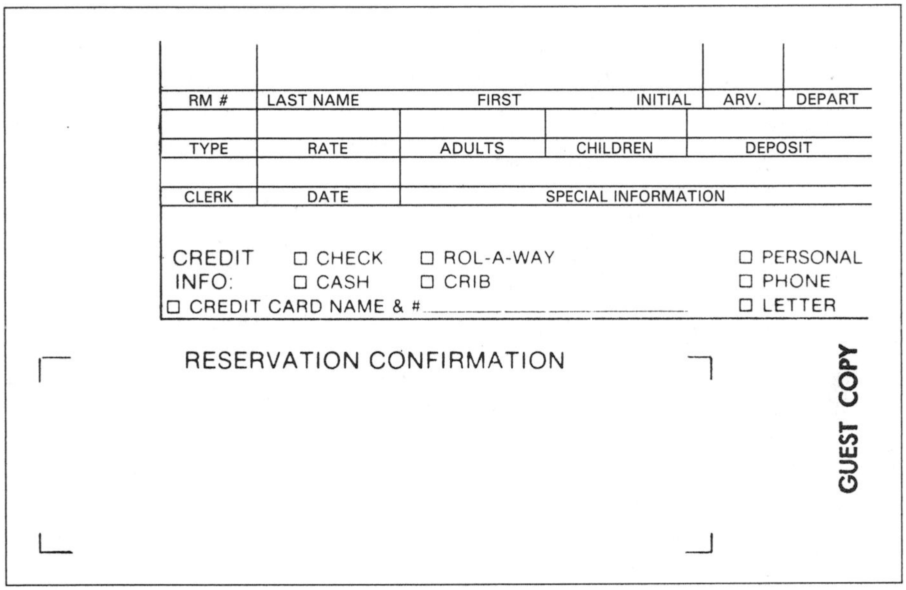

RM #	LAST NAME	FIRST	INITIAL	ARV.	DEPART

TYPE	RATE	ADULTS	CHILDREN	DEPOSIT

CLERK	DATE	SPECIAL INFORMATION

CREDIT   □ CHECK   □ ROL-A-WAY   □ PERSONAL
INFO: □ CASH   □ CRIB   □ PHONE
□ CREDIT CARD NAME & #_____   □ LETTER

RESERVATION CONFIRMATION

GUEST COPY

Computer Networks

A hotel that belongs to a referral network may receive reservations via a computer network. One look in the Yellow Pages of the telephone book reveals a list of such networks under the heading "Out of Town Reservations." Potential guests are encouraged to call a toll-free number to reach a central reservation office for the chain. Operators have immediate access to the room status of all properties involved and can determine what types of reservations can be accepted for a certain hotel. Once accepted, the reservation is relayed to the property by means of a teleprinter. The information arrives at the reservations office in abbreviated form similar to that shown in Figure 2.11.

Denying a Reservation

When the request for accommodations has to be denied, the caller must be informed immediately. The clerk should not stop here; obviously, this person has made some effort to obtain accommodations at the hotel, and the sales opportunity is still there. Suggesting alternate dates, types of rooms and rates other than those requested, or even trying to find a room in a neighboring hotel can result in either a booking at the hotel, or, at least, a very good impression of the clerk's helpfulness. This may cause the person to return to the hotel at a later

Figure 2.11
Sample Telex message advising hotel of reservation.

1	HSW Y 435 G DECEMBER 15 1200
2	SOLD 1S INT DECEMBER 17 RT $80.00
3	TIMMONS MS V PTY OF 1
4	ARR BY 6 PM
5	2038 WEST FIFTH AVE SAN DIEGO CA 73530
6	BKED BY PTY
7	757 925 3148

Explanation:

1. NAME of property abbreviated; file CODE for this reservation; INITIAL of clerk who took the reservation; DATE and TIME when reservation was accepted.

2. The "message" in this case is that a room was SOLD for 1 night SINGLE; DAY of arrival; RATE confirmed at $44.00.

3. NAME of party. NUMBER of people in the party.

4. Arrival TIME.

5. ADDRESS of party.

6. WHO booked the reservation.

7. Permanent CODE for this reservation for reference purposes.

date. Reasons for denying the reservation, other than "sold out," should not be given. If circumstances require a written response, the hotel will probably send a standard letter. Often, hotels keep waiting lists, and denied reservations are contacted as rooms become available.

Charting the Reservations Data

A hotel with limited reservation volume may use a simple *reservation journal*, not more than one page for each day, showing all relevant data regarding expected guests listed for each arrival date (Fig. 2.12). Such a system works with up to ten reservations per day, or until the page is full. After that, it becomes unreliable.

A more efficient way to store and display reservations data is by means of a *reservations chart* (Fig. 2.13). As reservations are received, the data are transferred from the reservations card to a chart. It shows the rooms in the hotel listed by number and type (room 101, for example, is a twin-bedded room with a bath). Along the top are written the days of the month. Typically, three months are displayed at a time; as one month comes to an end, another one is started.

Figure 2.12
Reservation journal.

ROOM RESERVATIONS

DAY_____ DATE_____ 19 ___

LINE NO.	HOW MADE			NAME	HOUR OF ARRIVAL	NO. IN PARTY	KIND OF ROOM	RATE	ROOM ASSIGNED
	LETTER	WIRE	VERBAL						
1					A.M. P.M.				
2					A.M. P.M.				
3					A.M. P.M.				
					A.M.				

Reservation cards intended for days beyond these three months are kept in a simple filing system under a monthly heading. As a new month becomes available on the chart, the cards are pulled and the information entered on the chart.

Chart entries are made in light pencil or erasable pen to allow for alterations in cases of cancellation or such changes as length of stay or number of

Figure 2.13
Reservation chart, by room number.

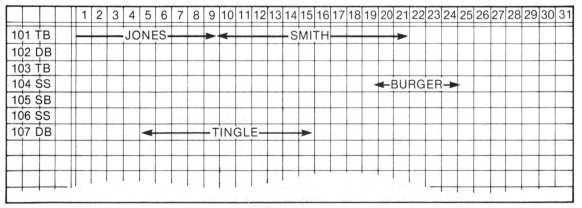

people in the party. This system can be customized to suit most operations. Special color entries could denote special rate bookings; weekends and high season periods could be flagged, and out-of-order rooms blocked. The beauty of this system is its simplicity. The casual visitor to any back office, expecting sophisticated computers, would be surprised to find, in many operations, a battered but well-functioning charting device. To quote one reservations supervisor, ''Charts don't have power failures.''

One staff member should be designated to do the charting. This ensures uniformity of entries and reduces the chances that entries are overlooked or duplicated. This person should also initial the reservations card as soon as the pertinent data have been transferred and write or stamp a code, such as ''c'' or ''charted,'' on the card. Charted cards are filed according to arrival date, in alphabetical order.

Changes to a Reservation on File

If changes are necessary, a *reservation change form* (Fig. 2.14) is completed and attached to the original reservations card. The chart is adjusted, and date and initials are written on the card to document the changes.

For a cancellation, the clerk pulls the card, makes the notation of ''cancelled'' on it, and stores the card at the back of that day's reservations. Keeping cancelled reservations on file can be useful, since the traveler may still arrive and expect a room. Had the card been destroyed, the rooming clerk would have had no record to demonstrate to the guest that the reservation had been held but was cancelled on a certain date on the instructions of a certain person.

Walk-in guests must also be added to the chart so that the number of rooms available is shown accurately. All check-ins without reservations are therefore listed on the *no reservation lists* (Fig. 2.15), which is given to the reservations clerk.

The Density Chart

The chart just described has some limitations. It requires one line per room, each dedicated to a room by number, with the guest names written beside them, lined up for the days of intended occupancy. But what would happen, for instance, if Mr. Jones, expected to check out of room 101 on the ninth (see Fig. 2.13), wants to stay a little longer? What would happen to our promise to Mr. Smith? A simple modification to the chart avoids this dilemma and makes the chart suitable for twice the volume. The modified chart (Fig. 2.16), called a density chart, has no room numbers, only numbers of *room types*. The sample here shows 136 double-bedded rooms, 77 queen-sized and 89 king-sized bedrooms, 3 parlors, and a number of suites. Charting is even simpler than before. As a type of room is requested, the highest number on the chart is crossed out, always leaving the count of rooms in a category clearly visible.

Figure 2.14
Reservation change or cancel slip.

```
┌─────────────────────────────────────────────────────┐
│          RESERVATION CHANGE OR CANCEL                 │
│                                                       │
│   Name                                                │
│   ─────────────────────────────────────────────      │
│   Res. Date                                           │
│   ─────────────────────────────────────────────      │
│   To                                                  │
│   ─────────────────────────────────────────────      │
│                                                       │
│   ─────────────────────────────────────────────      │
│                                                       │
│   Clerk:              Date                            │
│   ─────────────────────────────────────────────      │
│   Remarks:                                            │
│   ─────────────────────────────────────────────      │
│                                                       │
│   ─────────────────────────────────────────────      │
│                                                       │
│   ─────────────────────────────────────────────      │
│                                                       │
│   ─────────────────────────────────────────────      │
│   Completed by                                        │
│   ─────────────────────────────────────────────      │
│                                                       │
└─────────────────────────────────────────────────────┘
```

Charting a Group Booking

The new chart also permits the blocking of group bookings. They are indicated by the group's code, in this case 102. Twenty-two rooms are reserved for this group for Friday and Saturday nights. As group members make their reservations, clerks cross out one group block after another.

Reservations Correspondence

Letters, memos, or tour operators' lists relating to reservations must be filed for quick access. One method is to keep the reservation correspondence filed in four categories:

1. Inquiries only.
2. Future bookings.
3. Past bookings.
4. Group bookings.

Figure 2.15
"No reservation" list.

NO RESERVATION LIST

Date_____

Room No.	NAME	Departure Date	Room No.	NAME	Departure Date

Figure 2.16
Reservation chart, by type of room.

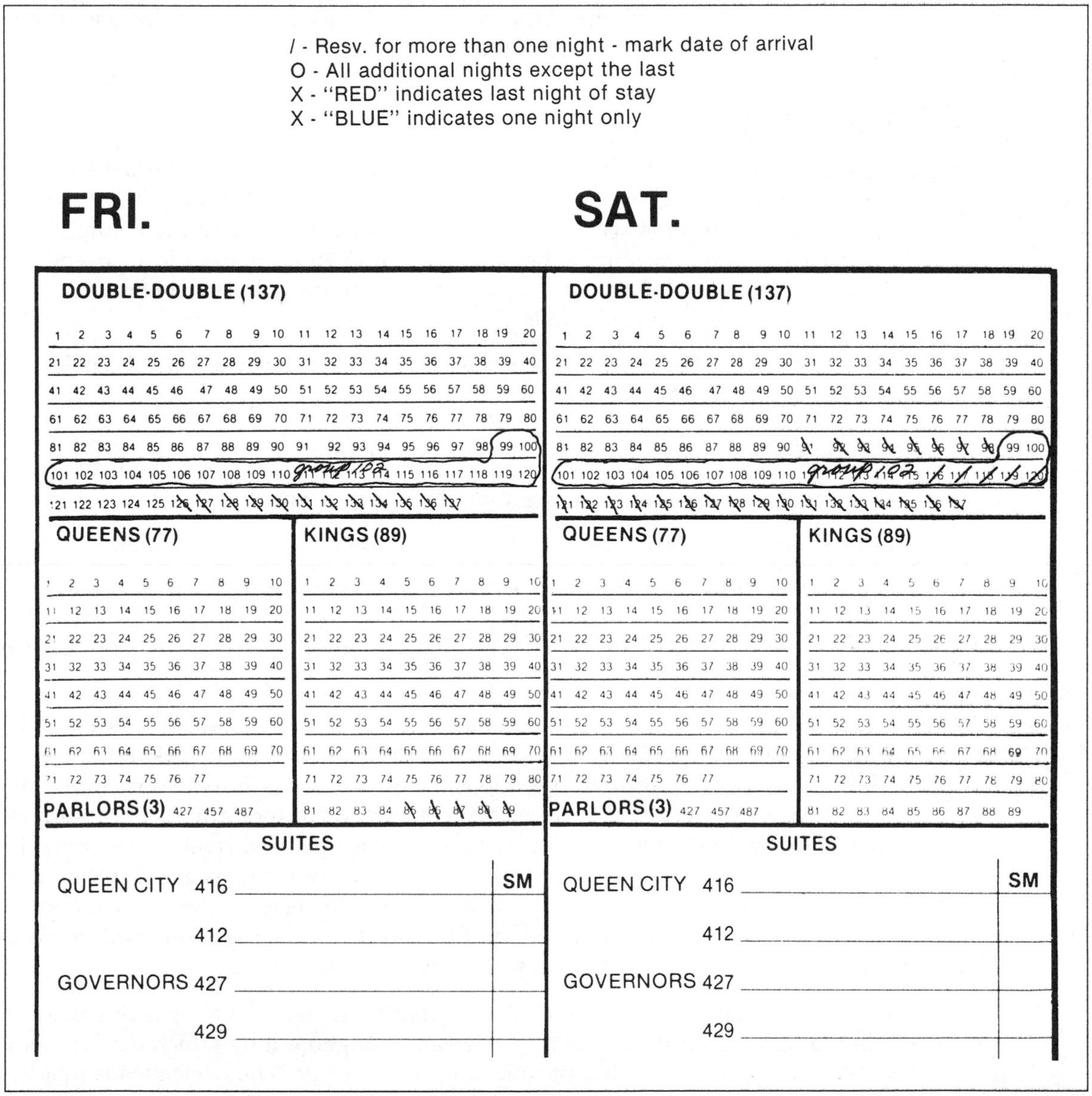

/ - Resv. for more than one night - mark date of arrival
O - All additional nights except the last
X - "RED" indicates last night of stay
X - "BLUE" indicates one night only

FRI.

DOUBLE-DOUBLE (137)

1 2 3 4 5 6 7 8 9 10 11 12 13 14 15 16 17 18 19 20
21 22 23 24 25 26 27 28 29 30 31 32 33 34 35 36 37 38 39 40
41 42 43 44 45 46 47 48 49 50 51 52 53 54 55 56 57 58 59 60
61 62 63 64 65 66 67 68 69 70 71 72 73 74 75 76 77 78 79 80
81 82 83 84 85 86 87 88 89 90 91 92 93 94 95 96 97 98 99 100
101 102 103 104 105 106 107 108 109 110 111 112 113 114 115 116 117 118 119 120 (group 102)
121 122 123 124 125 126 127 128 129 130 131 132 133 134 135 136 137

QUEENS (77)

1 2 3 4 5 6 7 8 9 10
11 12 13 14 15 16 17 18 19 20
21 22 23 24 25 26 27 28 29 30
31 32 33 34 35 36 37 38 39 40
41 42 43 44 45 46 47 48 49 50
51 52 53 54 55 56 57 58 59 60
61 62 63 64 65 66 67 68 69 70
71 72 73 74 75 76 77

PARLORS (3) 427 457 487

KINGS (89)

1 2 3 4 5 6 7 8 9 10
11 12 13 14 15 16 17 18 19 20
21 22 23 24 25 26 27 28 29 30
31 32 33 34 35 36 37 38 39 40
41 42 43 44 45 46 47 48 49 50
51 52 53 54 55 56 57 58 59 60
61 62 63 64 65 66 67 68 69 70
71 72 73 74 75 76 77 78 79 80
81 82 83 84 85 86 87 88 89

SUITES

QUEEN CITY 416 ____ SM
412 ____
GOVERNORS 427 ____
429 ____

SAT.

DOUBLE-DOUBLE (137)

1 2 3 4 5 6 7 8 9 10 11 12 13 14 15 16 17 18 19 20
21 22 23 24 25 26 27 28 29 30 31 32 33 34 35 36 37 38 39 40
41 42 43 44 45 46 47 48 49 50 51 52 53 54 55 56 57 58 59 60
61 62 63 64 65 66 67 68 69 70 71 72 73 74 75 76 77 78 79 80
81 82 83 84 85 86 87 88 89 90 91 92 93 94 95 96 97 98 99 100
101 102 103 104 105 106 107 108 109 110 111 112 113 114 115 116 117 118 119 120 (group 102)
121 122 123 124 125 126 127 128 129 130 131 132 133 134 135 136 137

QUEENS (77)

1 2 3 4 5 6 7 8 9 10
11 12 13 14 15 16 17 18 19 20
21 22 23 24 25 26 27 28 29 30
31 32 33 34 35 36 37 38 39 40
41 42 43 44 45 46 47 48 49 50
51 52 53 54 55 56 57 58 59 60
61 62 63 64 65 66 67 68 69 70
71 72 73 74 75 76 77

PARLORS (3) 427 457 487

KINGS (89)

1 2 3 4 5 6 7 8 9 10
11 12 13 14 15 16 17 18 19 20
21 22 23 24 25 26 27 28 29 30
31 32 33 34 35 36 37 38 39 40
41 42 43 44 45 46 47 48 49 50
51 52 53 54 55 56 57 58 59 60
61 62 63 64 65 66 67 68 69 70
71 72 73 74 75 76 77 78 79 80
81 82 83 84 85 86 87 88 89

SUITES

QUEEN CITY 416 ____ SM
412 ____
GOVERNORS 427 ____
429 ____

Courtesy of Seattle Hyatt House, Seattle, WA.

If the reservations office is closed after hours, or located away from the desk, all correspondence pertaining to a day's reservations should be moved to the front office. This allows the clerks to check the documentation in case of disputes, missing details, or other unusual situations.

The Problem of No-Shows

Filling the house to the maximum presents a daily challenge, especially if those who have made a reservation fail to arrive (*no-shows*). Had they informed the hotel of their intention well in advance, the room allocated to them could have been sold to walk-ins. Since they did not call, a room is held in vain and the result is a loss of revenue. Lodging operators routinely protect themselves from such mishaps, by doing the following:

- They impose limits on the time to which a reservation will be held.
- They ask for advance payment in cash or by credit card.
- They request that payment be guaranteed.
- They take more bookings than they have rooms.

Sometimes these measures are taken alone, other times in combination.

Time limit. Most hotels, when accepting a reservation, make it clear that they will hold it only until a certain time, generally between 6:00 and 7:00 P.M. After that, they are not obligated to honor the reservation, but will of course do so if a vacancy exists.

Advance payment. A second precaution against no-shows is to ask for a deposit, or advance payment, usually equal to the amount of the first night's stay. The no-show guest forfeits the deposit, and the hotel is paid for the empty room. Incidentally, the advance-payment method offers guests an assurance that the room will be waiting, regardless of their time of arrival. At the time the deposit is received, a voucher is written out. Its three copies are distributed as follows: the top copy is mailed to the guest as a receipt, the second copy is attached to the reservations card, and the third copy is filed in a control file in case of cancellations or changes to the reservation.

Guaranteed payment. Individuals, corporations, and travel agencies who do volume business with a hotel may have an arrangement by which a reservation is taken in good faith, without time limit or a deposit. The basic idea is that the hotel will keep the room for an arrival at any time and that, in turn, a bill will be sent to the originator of the reservation should a no-show occur. However, many hotel operators are reluctant to collect on no-shows for fear of appearing penny-pinching. They would rather not collect this debt than spoil future reservations from a steady source. A large number of customers avoid paying the amount owed by providing elaborate explanations for the no-show, expecting the hotel to withdraw the invoice. A collection rate of about 10 percent is considered good. One hotel recorded the following collection pattern:[3]

46% No response whatsoever.

18% Guest claims reservation had been cancelled.

5% Mail was returned, no such address.

4% Guest actually stayed in the hotel, but was still billed.

4% Guest stayed, but on a different day than shown on the reservation.

2% Guest was told that there was no reservation waiting.

2% Guest forgot to cancel.

1% Reservation was not to be guaranteed.

8% Assorted other reasons.

Overbooking. By anticipating the number of no-shows and other factors affecting occupancy statistics, desk staff can greatly increase the number of sold rooms at any given time. There are, for instance, people who do not arrive as expected; others leave earlier than expected; still others extend their stay beyond the reserved period (*stayovers*). This presents a kaleidoscope of arrivals, departures, and in-betweens. Hotels try to anticipate these changes with the practice of *overbooking:* accepting more reservations than there are rooms available. For instance, in a 100-room hotel that uses a seven percent overbooking practice, the following situation could arise:

40 rooms occupied.

2 rooms out-of-order.

An additional 65 reservations would be accepted, adding up to a total of 107.

Should all the guests with reservations arrive and all present occupants stay, there would be seven annoyed people lined up at the front desk. Hotels overbook to the extent of 5 to 15 percent, while airlines have been known to do so at a rate of over 20 percent. The public is becoming less tolerant of this practice and is beginning to react to it. In part, this change stems from a much-publicized case in which Ralph Nader, the consumer activist, sued an airline for $1.5 million for failure to honor his confirmed reservation.

In some states, government agencies have the right to ask hotels for their reservations figures to ascertain whether overbooking is occurring. Hotels in Hawaii have issued public statements that condemn the practice of overbooking. Some managers do not allow overbooking at all, but rely on an approach of customer education by explaining to the reservation-seeker the conditions under which the reservation is accepted (time limits, deposits). People who do not show are sent a reminder (''We held a room for you and missed you. Please stay with us on your next trip and let us know when you change your plans'').

Day-of-Arrival Routines

Unless this is part of the night clerk's duties, the early-morning clerk or front-office manager follows a routine in preparation for the day's business:

1. Moves today's reservations to the desk and arranges them in alphabetical order on the reservations rack.

2. Checks for any special request. These might be guests that were promised a specific room, location, rate, or type of accommodation. Early in the morning, as vacancies become apparent, a specific assignment is made: rooms are indicated by number on the reservations form, and appropriate blocks are made on the room rack. Certain guests may be scheduled for special attention. Group bookings are color coded for easy identification.

3. Makes a count of all remaining reservations by type of room.

4. Makes a count of all rooms in each category on the room rack:

   • How many rooms are vacant.

   • How many are expected to become vacant.

5. Determines the number of rooms available for walk-ins by computing expected arrivals, present vacancies, and expected check-outs on the following night.

6. Informs the other clerks, housekeeping staff, and reservations people of the room count and how many, if any, walk-ins are to be accepted.

7. Throughout the day, updates information by checking and recalculating the numbers. For example, departures may be slower or faster than expected, cancellations or reservations might be coming in, and walk-ins might be registering. The situation will fluctuate, depending upon the pattern of guest movements. By keeping the figures up-to-date, over-selling or underselling can be avoided. If several clerks work at a busy desk, communication can at times be hectic as events change quickly. A *sell sheet* (Fig. 2.17) can be placed behind the front desk, to quickly note walk-ins and last-minute cancellations, both of which influence rooms status directly.

Blocking Group Bookings

Certain groups are offered a special rate and a block of rooms. This may involve a conference, convention, sales meeting, training seminar, travel group, or other

Figure 2.17
Sell sheet.

Date_____   Target Number_____

Walk-ins

1	2	3	4	5	6	7	8	9	10
11	12	13	14	15	16	17	18	19	20
21	22	23	24	25	26	27	28	29	30
31	32	33	34	35	36	37	38	39	40
41	42	43	44	45	46	47	48	49	50
51	52	53	54	55	56	57	58	59	60

Cancels

1	2	3	4	5	6	7	8	9	10
11	12	13	14	15	16	17	18	19	20

Instructions:

This form is to be used when the possibility of a sell-out exists. For each unscheduled check-in, mark the lowest numbered available box using the following codes:

Same Day Reservations . . . . R
Walk-ins . . . . W
Unscheduled stay-overs . . . . S

For cancellations use lower boxes and the following codes:

Cancels C
Unscheduled check-outs . . . . U

Periodically subtract total cancellations from total walk-ins.

gathering. The arrangements are usually made by the sales department in conjunction with the reservations manager. Once the number of people expected and the room rates are determined, the following procedures are followed:

   1. A group of rooms is blocked off on the reservations chart, with the group indicated by a code number.

2. Reservation forms are made available for the group members, with instructions to contact the hotel directly by a certain cutoff date.

3. When all blocked rooms have been booked, no further reservations are accepted unless an additional block is arranged.

4. Any rooms not booked by the deadline are released for general use.

5. A *group booking sheet* (Fig. 2.18) is maintained in conjunction with the reservations chart (Fig. 2.16) to show group blocks for each month. This sheet serves two basic purposes. First, it permits a reservations clerk to quickly check for and accept a group booking. Second, it permits management to control group bookings. Hotel managers are careful not to deny a room to a regular customer in favor of a group booking.

COMPUTERIZED RESERVATIONS

Of all hotel operations, reservations are most often associated with computers. As Table 2.1 shows, computerized systems are widely accepted in the United States, and their use increased by 20 percent in just two years.[4] Hoteliers in Canada, Europe, and the rest of the world tend to depend on manual systems, as the typical property there is smaller than in the U.S. When electing to computerize, hotel owners have two routes available: They can purchase an in-house system or join a reservations system operated by referral chains and transportation companies.

Basically, computer-assisted reservations systems involve the five phases shown in Figure 2.19. Reservations data are kept in computer files, requiring fewer labor hours and providing higher accuracy than manual systems. The computer stores thousands of reservations, and an operator can retrieve them in seconds, using a keyboard and display screen. The system automatically sorts and updates all records and related files and prints confirmations on high-speed line printers.

Several firms market hotel computers. The CLS Reservation System permits booking of individuals and groups using a single screen.[5] Space availability can be checked and bookings made for any future date, various summary reports can be generated to assist management in scheduling and forecasting, and confirmations and registration cards can be printed automatically. Basic reservations functions begin with a *menu* (Fig. 2.20), from which clerks select specific functions. A few are discussed here.

Individual and Group Reservations

Reservations clerks may enter, review, modify, query, cancel, and delete future bookings. Future space availability can be checked for any date, rooms can be blocked, and VIP and repeat requests can be posted. For multiproperty systems,

Figure 2.18
Monthly group booking sheet.

MONTH YEAR

DATE	CONV	GROUP NAME	RATE	1	2	3	4	5	6	7	8	9	10	11	12	13	14	15	16	17	18	19	20
4/2/89	348	INTERNATIONAL TRAINERS	40-44						45	45													
4/2/89	349	NABISCO	38-44								70	100	100	70									
4/3/89	350	INT. ACCOUNTANTS															22	22					
				1	2	3	4	5	6	7	8	9	10	11	12	13	14	15	16	17	18	19	20

Figure 2.19
Flow chart of computerized reservations process.

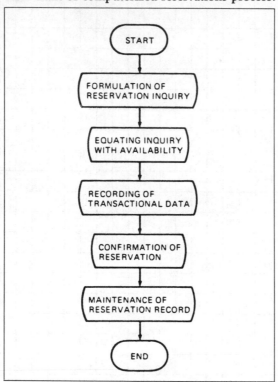

Source: M. Kasavana, *Hotel Information Systems* (Boston,
MA: CBI Publishing), p. 181.

reservations may be transferred from one hotel to another. Clerks may also book
blocks of rooms by room type or as "run of the house" (i.e., any room in the
hotel); the system keeps track of the rooms blocked as reservations are booked.

VIP Guest History

Each guest identified as a VIP will automatically be added to the guest history
system upon checkout. A "picture" is taken of the guest's folio, along with
information on length of stay, total room charges, food and beverage and other
charges. Clerks can check to see if a person has stayed at the hotel during the
last two years; obtain a summary of previous revenue and room preference patterns; and request lists, mailing labels, and reservations printouts. The guest
history function also handles automatic re-reservations. In multiple-property
systems, all members have access to all records.

Figure 2.20
Reservations menu.

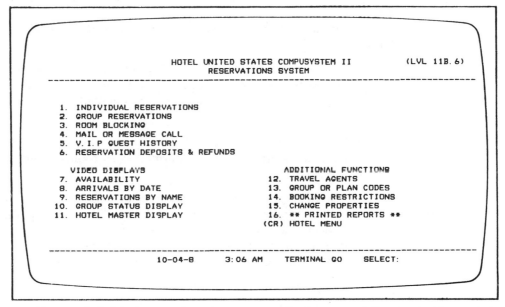

Availability Displays

Several types of screens are available to review availability of rooms before accepting a reservation:

- Today's date, including house counts.

- Future date, with no limitation on years in the future.

- Graphic analysis of net rooms to sell for up to 18 days on one screen.

- Blocked rooms in the future.

- Occupancy information for a single unit up to a year in the future.

Other Displays

Arrivals by date. Gives clerks a quick look at all guests arriving, on any date, arranged alphabetically.

Reservations by name. Displays all reservations fitting a specific name limit, such as all those beginning with ''BER,'' for any date or a specific date.

Group status display. Any group block may be examined on the screen, showing rooms held, rooms booked, net rooms remaining, as well as potential and actual revenue.

Information is also available through a *report menu* (Fig. 2.21), which includes:

- *Room availability reports* (Fig. 2.22), which can be done according to type of rooms sold, guaranteed reservations, and nonguaranteed reservations. They are shown in graph or detailed breakdown from 1 to 365 days.

- *Group status report* (Fig. 2.23), which displays group reservations by arrival date and with such information as rooms reserved, booked, and unsold by type.

- *Blocked rooms report* (Fig. 2.24), which shows each room number with an 11-day spread, beginning with the starting date entered by the clerk. Beneath each date, the report shows whether the room is presently blocked for a future reservation, presently occupied or a due-out, or in conflict between a guest and a blocked reservation.

Figure 2.21
Reports menu for reservation system.

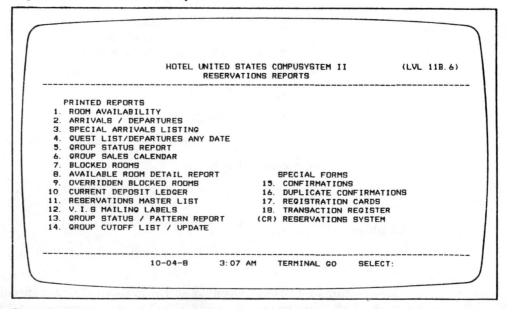

Figure 2.22
Room availability report.

C. L. S. DEMO HOTEL   PAGE: 2   DATE: 12-05-86

ROOM AVAILABILITY REPORT - THROUGH 12-31-86
INCLUDING BLOCKED ROOM DETAIL
AS OF 12-05-86   9:49 AM

ROOM 0610 (EXECCHRIS NAYLOR   ARRIVING 120786 FOR 2 DAYS (1) ROOMS IN BLOCK.

MONDAY   DATE: 12-08-86   TOTAL ROOMS: 85   SOLD: 56   AVAILABLE: 20   % OCCUPANCY: 77 %

TYPE:	KING	QUEN	DBDB	PRLR	EXEC	BLK	WAIT
TOTAL:	22	17	22	12	13	0	0
SOLD:	3	1	1	0	1	0	0
RES GNTD:	5	11	4	0	2	0	0
RES NON-G:	7	11	15	3	1	0	0
AVAIL:	7-	6-	2	8	9	0	0

ROOM 0102 (EXECCYDEL INY   ARRIVING 120886 FOR 5 DAYS (1) ROOMS IN BLOCK.
ROOM 0210 (EXECTONY DZECK   ARRIVING 120686 FOR 10 DAYS (1) ROOMS IN BLOCK.
ROOM 0407 (QUENGLORIA FINNAIR   ARRIVING 120886 FOR 2 DAYS (2) ROOMS IN BLOCK.
ROOM 0506 (KINGMARK KOENIG   ARRIVING 120686 FOR 4 DAYS (1) ROOMS IN BLOCK.
ROOM 0610 (EXECCHRIS NAYLOR   ARRIVING 120786 FOR 2 DAYS (1) ROOMS IN BLOCK.

TUESDAY   DATE: 12-09-86   TOTAL ROOMS: 86   SOLD: 60   AVAILABLE: 26   % OCCUPANCY: 70 %

TYPE:	KING	QUEN	DBDB	PRLR	EXEC	BLK	WAIT
TOTAL:	22	17	22	12	13	0	0
SOLD:	3	1	1	0	1	0	0
RES GNTD:	21	11	0	15	3	1	0
RES NON-G:	1	0	15	3	1	0	0
AVAIL:	3-	5	6	8	10	0	0

ROOM 0102 (EXECCYDEL INY   ARRIVING 120886 FOR 5 DAYS (1) ROOMS IN BLOCK.
ROOM 0210 (EXECTONY DZECK   ARRIVING 120686 FOR 10 DAYS (1) ROOMS IN BLOCK.
ROOM 0407 (QUENGLORIA FINNAIR   ARRIVING 120886 FOR 2 DAYS (2) ROOMS IN BLOCK.
ROOM 0506 (KINGMARK KOENIG   ARRIVING 120686 FOR 4 DAYS (1) ROOMS IN BLOCK.

WEDNESDAY   DATE: 12-10-86   TOTAL ROOMS: 86   SOLD: 64   AVAILABLE: 22   % OCCUPANCY: 74 %

TYPE:	KING	QUEN	DBDB	PRLR	EXEC	BLK	WAIT
TOTAL:	22	17	22	12	13	0	0
SOLD:	3	1	1	0	1	0	0
RES GNTD:	20	11	8	1	1	0	0
RES NON-G:	13	1	8	1	1	0	0
AVAIL:	14-	4	13	9	10	0	0

57

Figure 2.23
Group status report.

GROUP / CONVENTION STATUS REPORT

FROM TOP TO END OF FILE

RESERV CODE	RES DT	NAME	GROUP	AGENT	ARRV. DATE	DAYS	ROOM TYPE	QUAN	RATE	ROOMS COMMITTD	PICK-UP	UNUSED
G1011	04/15/86	HAWAIIAN HOLIDAYS,	GROUP		12-03-86	2	BLK	1	65.00	10	9	1
G1017	04/15/86	US STEEL,	STEEL		12-04-86	3	BLK	1	60.00	22	21	1
G1004	04/14/86	MERLE NORMAN,	MERLE		12-05-86	2	BLK	1	65.00	12	11	1
G1014	04/15/86	IBM COMPUTERS,	IBM		12-05-86	2	BLK	1	65.00	25	24	1
G1053	09-08-86	TEST GROUP RESERVATION,	G1053		12-05-86	2	BLK	1	0.00	1		
G1070	12-02-86	VICTOR EQUIPMENT CO,	G1070		12-05-86	2	BLK		0.00			
G1009	04/15/86	HUGHES AIRCRAFT,	AIR		12-06-86	3	BLK	1	85.00	10	9	1
G1024	04/15/86	MATSON SHIPPING,	SHIP		12-06-86	2	BLK	1	70.00	27	26	1
G1020	04/15/86	NORTHROP CORP,	NORTH		12-07-86	2	BLK	1	60.00	10	9	1
G1012	04/15/86	ERNST & WHINNEY INC,	ERNST		12-09-86	2	BLK	1	90.00	30	29	1
G1013	04/15/86	HONDA MOTORS,	HONDA		12-10-86	5	BLK	1	75.00	20	19	1
G1018	04/15/86	PLAZA CLUB,	PLAZA		12-11-86	5	BLK	1	80.00	15	14	1
G1001	04/14/86	MATTEL TOYS,	MATTL		12-12-86	5	BLK	1	110.00	20	19	1
G1010	04/15/86	HERBALIFE INC,	HERB		12-16-86	3	BLK	1	85.00	18	17	1
G1022	04/14/86	MCDONALDS CORP,	MCD		12-16-86	2	BLK	1	100.00	34	33	1
G1002	04/14/86	XEROX CORPORATION,	XEROX		12-17-86	2	BLK	1	75.00	10	9	1
G1000	04/14/86	CALIFORNIA TEACHERS,	TEACH		12-20-86	15	BLK	1	70.00	15	14	1
G1056	12-01-86	THE ANYBODY GROUP,	GROUP		12-20-86	3	BLK		0.00	1		
G1006	04/15/86	VOLKSWAGON OF AMER,	VOLKS		12-25-86	15	BLK	1	80.00	25	24	1
G1057	12-01-86	DIANE'S GROUP, * CXLD *	DIANE		12-25-86	3	BLK		0.00			
G1056	12-01-86	ESR,	G1066		12-26-86	3	BLK		0.00			
G1007	04/15/86	C ITOH ELECRONICS,	CLS		12-29-86	2	BLK	1	75.00	1		1
G1015	04/15/86	HERTZ CORP,	TEST		12-31-86	1	BLK	1	60.00	22	21	1
G1068	12-01-86	ESR,	G1068		03-27-87	9	BLK	1	0.00	15	14	1
G1042	08-20-86	TEST, * CXLD *	BALL		05-11-87	1	BLK		0.00	1		

TOTAL FILE TRANSACTIONS: 25

Figure 2.24
Blocked rooms report.

C. L. S. DEMO HOTEL — PAGE: 1 — / MES. Rep - 7 / — DATE: 12-05-86

B L O C K E D   R O O M S   R E P O R T

ROOM #	12-05-86	12-06-86	12-07-86	12-08-86	12-09-86	12-10-86	12-11-86	12-12-86	12-13-86	12-14-86	12-15-86
0101 DBDB	OCCUPD	OCCUPD	OCCUPD	OCCUPD	OCCUPD	OCCUPD	OCCUPD	DUEOUT			
0104 DBDB											
0106 DBDB	OCCUPD	DUEOUT							50056	50056	50056
0107 QUEN											
0116 DBDB											
0201 DBDB	OCCUPD	DUEOUT									
0202 EXEC	OCCUPD	OCCUPD	OCCUPD	OCCUPD	OCCUPD	OCCUPD	OCCUPD	OCCUPD	OCCUPD	OCCUPD	OCCUPD
0203 PRLR	OCCUPD	OCCUPD	OCCUPD	OCCUPD	OCCUPD	OCCUPD	OCCUPD	OCCUPD	OCCUPD	OCCUPD	DUEOUT
0204 KING	OCCUPD	OCCUPD	OCCUPD	OCCUPD	OCCUPD	OCCUPD	OCCUPD	OCCUPD	DUEOUT		
0205 KING		50540									
0206 DBDB											
0207 QUEN	OCCUPD	DUEOUT									
0208 KING											
0209 PRLR											
0210 EXEC		50061	50061	50061	50061	50061	50061	50061	50061	50061	50061
0211 PRLR											
0212 EXEC											
0215 KING											
0301 DBDB	OCCUPD	DUEOUT									
0302 KING											
0303 KING	OCCUPD	DUEOUT									
0304 DBDB	DUEOUT										
0305 QUEN	OCCUPD	DUEOUT									
0306 EXEC											

- *Special arrival* lists for subgroups such as VIPs only, guaranteed only, special requests only, direct bill only, share-withs only, wait-listed only, or all arrivals.

- *Reservations master list* will generate a report or sets of baggage or mailing labels for selected reservations or all reservations for the hotel. Reports may be generated by reservation number, in alphabetical order, by arrival date, or by group members only. This feature also prints a list of deposits still on file from cancelled reservations, as well as reservations for which deposits have not been received.

- *Confirmations* and *registration cards* can be printed at any time but are routinely generated during the night audit.

Benefits of Computerized Reservations

Customers, staff members, and management benefit from a computer-assisted system. It processes information faster and more accurately than a manual system does. Inquiries from potential guests and their agents can be handled more efficiently, management has access to better forecasts and summaries, and the staff is able to pay greater attention to the guest. Ideally, this should improve profitability, customer satisfaction, and the quality of work.

A word of warning is necessary, however: avoid the ''It's the computer's fault'' trap when dealing with guests. The computer is just a tool for providing the best possible service to every guest. In the final analysis, the human contact makes the difference, not the machine.

FULL-HOUSE MANAGEMENT

A key goal of rooms management is to achieve a high occupancy rate, or a full house, for as many nights as possible. Many hotels reach 100 percent occupancy on certain nights (the Hale Koa Hotel in Honolulu did it on a year-round basis in 1986), but industrywide, the figures are less impressive (Table 2.3). Many hotels reach such a level on certain nights, but industrywide the picture looks less dramatic (Table 2.3). To work toward maximum possible occupancy rate, the front office crew must follow a systematic room sales approach. It requires a good understanding and frequent monitoring of market trends, seasonal influences, and guest arrival and departure patterns. To discuss full house management concept, several terms must be understood:

Occupancy percentage: An expression of the degree to which available rooms were sold in a given period, expressed by the following formula:

$$\frac{\text{Rooms occupied}}{\text{number of rooms available for sales}} \times 100 = \text{Occupancy percentage}$$

Turn-away: To refuse walk-in business because rooms are not available.

Table 2.3
Worldwide occupancy statistics, by region.*

	United States	Canada	Caribbean	Middle East	Asia	Australia	Continental Europe	United Kingdom
Annual room occupancy	65.6 %	67.8	54.0	56.9	65.7	67.6	68.6	64.6
Number of guests per room	1.34	1.5	1.91	1.19	1.28	1.56	1.37	1.32

*All figures are medians

Source: 1986 Worldwide Hotel Industry (New York: Horwath & Horwath International).

Walk-in: A guest who comes to the hotel without a reservation; a guest who simply walks into a hotel seeking accommodation for the night.

Stay-over: A guest who was expected to check out on a certain day but remains in the hotel beyond the stated day of departure.

Cancellation: A reservation that is cancelled in time for the room to be reallocated.

Due-outs: Guests who are expected to depart from the hotel on a given day or during a given time period.

How important is it to achieve a full house? Could one not just work until as many rooms as possible have been sold for any given night? Such questions are valid and reflect a healthy caution toward pushing for a full house, possibly at the cost of turning away a guest with a reservation. Many managers insist that no guest should ever be turned away; at the same time they frown upon rooms left unsold when there are enough travelers to fill them. The front desk staff is caught in the middle. The factors influencing the reservation and occupancy situation are many, and most are impossible to control. Here are the major ones:

- Guests leave before their stated departure date.

- Due-outs decide to stay longer.

- Expected walk-ins do not materialize.

- Certain rooms are put out-of-order for emergency repairs.

- Transportation systems change guests' arrival patterns (airline strikes, cancelled flights, missed connections).

- Weather conditions affect the departure and arrival patterns of guests traveling by private vehicle or public transport.

Aside from the human dilemma, there is of course the business side. Table 2.4 illustrates how potential room revenue is lost when a hotel or motel does not reach full occupancy. This chart depicts lost revenue for one night only, when in reality an operation may have ten, twenty, or more nights per year in which rooms remain vacant. To calculate the total lost revenue for 30 nights, the dollar amount lost for one night is multipled by 30. If, for instance, a hotel has 200 rooms and reports a 98 percent occupancy for a night, and has an average room rate of $50, then the lost revenue for that night alone is $200. When multiplied by 30, this amounts to $6,000 in lost revenue. A 98-percent occupancy rate is considered exceptionally high, with many operations aiming quite optimistically for a 60-percent rate on an annual basis (and contrasted with the statistics in Table 2.3). Aside from the increased rooms revenue, additional guests also generate food and beverage revenue for restaurants, coffee shop, cocktail lounge, and room service, thus adding to the profitability of the other departments.

Robert Brymer, a professor of hotel management, proposes several measures to achieve full-house status.[6] An accurate record of reservations, no-shows, and cancellations must be kept after every night. Over a period of time, this will indicate a trend from which one can predict future no-shows and cancellations. Brymer's chart (Fig. 2.25) shows how such a traffic record can be maintained. The percentage of no-shows and cancellations is computed on the number of rooms due to be occupied by reservations. In addition, a forecast is made as accurately as possible of the arrival and departure patterns of customers. Alongside this information is the number of walk-ins, due-outs, and stay-overs. These tabulations, together with an estimation of the influence of other variables (weather, out-of-order rooms, etc.) provides for a fairly realistic forecast of the reservations pattern. It may take a year or more to establish reliable statistics that reflect seasonal fluctuations, but most of the general indicators will become apparent after a few weeks of record-keeping.

Here is an example based on a 200-room hotel: On the night of May 21, the front-office manager has forecast an occupancy of 180 rooms. On May 22, there are 100 scheduled check-outs, leaving 80 rooms as carryover from May 21. There are also 120 reservations due to arrive that day. Therefore, the carryovers and expected arrivals will provide for a 200-room occupancy for May 22. From previous records, the following traffic pattern is known:

15%   No-shows and cancellations

10%   stay-overs, estimated from previous records to be 10 percent of the scheduled number of due-outs

0%   Anticipate variables. For this day, none are assumed to affect the hotel's rooms business.

Table 2.4
Room revenue lost in one night by not attaining 100 percent occupancy

Average Rate	Number of Rooms in Hotel																			
	100		200		300		400		500		600		700		800		900		1000	
	Percentages of Occupancy Near 100%																			
	98	99	98	99	98	99	98	99	98	99	98	99	98	99	98	99	98	99	98	99
	Dollar Amount in Room Revenue Lost																			
$30	60	30	120	60	180	90	240	120	300	150	360	180	420	210	480	240	540	270	600	300
$35	70	35	140	70	210	105	280	140	350	175	420	210	490	245	560	280	630	315	700	350
$40	80	40	160	80	240	120	320	160	400	200	480	240	560	280	640	320	720	360	800	400
$45	90	45	180	90	270	135	360	180	450	225	540	270	630	315	720	360	810	405	900	450
$50	100	50	200	100	300	150	400	200	500	250	600	300	700	350	800	400	900	450	1000	500
$60	120	60	240	120	360	180	480	240	600	300	720	360	840	420	960	480	1080	540	1200	600
$70	140	70	280	140	420	210	560	280	700	350	840	420	980	490	1120	560	1260	630	1400	700
$80	160	80	320	160	480	240	640	320	800	400	960	480	1120	560	1280	640	1440	720	1600	800
$90	180	90	360	180	540	270	720	360	900	450	1080	540	1260	630	1440	720	1620	810	1800	900
$100	200	100	400	200	600	300	800	400	1000	500	1200	600	1400	700	1600	860	1800	900	2000	1000

Source: Adapted from an article published in the August 1976 issue of *The Cornell Hotel and Restaurant Administration Quarterly;* reproduced by permission of the Cornell School of Hotel Administration. © 1976.

Figure 2.25
Daily rooms-traffic record.

DATE	Total No. of Reservations	Transient Reservations		Group Reservations		Total No. of No-shows and Cancellations	Percentage of No-shows and Cancellations
		No-shows	Cancellations	No-shows	Cancellations		
JAN. 4	202	8	10	5	7	30	15%

NUMBER OF WALKINS			NUMBER OF DUE-OUTS	NUMBER OF STAYOVERS			
Transient	Group	Total		Transient	Group	Total	Percentage of Due-outs
22	2	24	119	11	1	12	10%

Adapted from an article originally published in the August 1976 issue of *The Cornell Hotel and Restaurant Administration Quarterly*; reprinted by permission of the Cornell School of Hotel Administration, © 1976.

Given this information, one can now determine how many, if any, walk-ins to accept. A few simple calculations reduce the guesswork:

Number of reservations × Estimated percentage
of no-shows and cancellations = Estimated no-shows and cancellations

Number of stay-overs ± Anticipated variables = Number of estimated additional/fewer rooms occupied

Estimated no-shows + Cancellations − Estimated additional/fewer rooms occupied = Number of reservations acceptable over the original number

Therefore:

$120 \times .15 = 18$ expected no-shows and cancellations.

$10 + 0 = 10$ estimated additional rooms occupied by stay-overs.

$18 - 10 = 8$ reservations to be accepted above the original 120.

This example demonstrates how accurate records on reservations traffic helps front-office personnel attain a high percentage of occupancy.

KEY TERMS

Rooms revenue	Turn-away
Corporate traveler	Requested/confirmed rate
No-show	Stay-over
Reservation system	Reservation status
Advance payment or deposit	Cancellation
Reservation department	Reservation chart
Guaranteed payment	Due-out
Hotel representative	Walk-in
Overbooking	Occupancy rate
American Express Assured Room	Pick-up (of group reservations)
Group booking	Blocked rooms
Room status	Guest history
Full-house management	Confirmations
Space-available sheet	Run of the house
Walking a guest	Menu (on computer screen)
Reservation card	

NOTES

1. *1986 Worldwide Hotel Industry*, New York: Horwath & Horwath International, 1986, p. 29. The statistics result from an annual survey of approximately 1,000 hotels with an average of 150 to 300 rooms, 67 percent occupancy rates and US$ 45 room rate.

2. "Foreword," *1986 Worldwide Hotel Industry*, New York: Horwath & Horwath International, page 5.

3. Seattle Hyatt House, Seattle, WA.

4. "Lodging's 400 Top Performers," *Lodging Hospitality*, August 1986, p. 68.

5. CLS (Computerized Lodging Systems), Long Beach, CA, is a pioneer supplier of technology to the industry. Over 400 CLS systems, of which this reservations system is one, have been installed in the United States, Canada, Europe, and Latin America. CLS products are marketed in conjunction with the NCR Corporation.

6. R. A. Brymer, "Full House Management," *The Cornell Hotel and Restaurant Administration Quarterly*, August 1976, pp. 34–38.

DISCUSSION QUESTIONS

1. Why are guest rooms a hotel's "most perishable goods"?

2. Describe the positive effects an efficient reservations system has on a hotel's operating performance.

3. List the components of a reservations system and explain the function of each one.

4. Explain the steps in the American Express Assured Room Reservation Plan.

5. What does the space-available sheet tell you? What are its limitations when dealing with reservation requests?

6. When denying a reservation, you have an excellent sales opportunity for your establishment. How do you take advantage of it?

7. Design a reservation form. It must be suitable for taking reservations over the telephone and must be easily filed and retrieved. You will be asked to explain how your form meets these requirements.

8. What are the consequences of clerks forgetting to fill out the no-reservation list?

9. Critique the group booking sheet in this chapter. List its strengths and weaknesses, and draw up an improved sheet if possible.

10. Using Brymer's full-house management approach, calculate how many, if any, reservations or walk-ins to accept for the following situation:

    You are responsible for room sales in a 250-room property. On the night of October 4, the forecast shows an expected occupancy of 175 rooms. On October 5, there are 120 scheduled check-outs. There are 108 expected reservations for that day. Therefore, the carry-overs and the expected arrivals will provide for what percentage occupancy for the October 5?

You may assume the following arrival and departure patterns:

12 percent no-shows and cancellations.

10 percent of the scheduled number of due-outs as stayovers.

In addition, housekeeping reports that four rooms will be out-of-order for renovations.

ASSIGNMENT

Assume the role of someone looking for information on future room booking with a hotel in your area; think of making a reservation for a visiting relative. Contact the operation in person or over the telephone and inquire about rates, vacancies, and booking procedures. Plan to ask for a special request, such as an extra-large bed, pet policy, transportation to and from the airport, late arrival, or special diet.

Record your impressions of the interaction: How helpful was the hotel staff? What would make you decide either to book or not book with this establishment? What suggestions do you have for desk personnel that might lead to an improvement of their service?

Bring your written notes to the next class. You may be asked to make a brief presentation.

CHAPTER 3

ROOMING PROCEDURES

OBJECTIVES

The purpose of this chapter is to:

- Describe the steps in the rooming process.

- Describe room sales techniques.

- Explain rooming procedures for guests with and without reservations.

- Illustrate the forms and charts used.

- Show how to establish credit for new guests.

- Outline the tasks performed by bell attendants.

- List special room rates and plans.

- Describe the procedures for overbooking.

INTRODUCTION

Rooming procedures are at the core of the clerk's work; they demand the utmost ability to communicate, persuade, plan, think—and to do all that under pressure and with a genuine desire to be of service. At its simplest, *rooming* is the task of assigning a number of people to a given number of rooms until the house is full. But, unlike the ticket sales at a theater box office, hotel room sales is a complex task. This chapter explains the steps in the rooming process (Fig. 3.1) and outlines the clerk's responsibilities along the way. The traditional sequence is described in detail, followed by an explanation of the use of computers.

Figure 3.1
The rooming process.

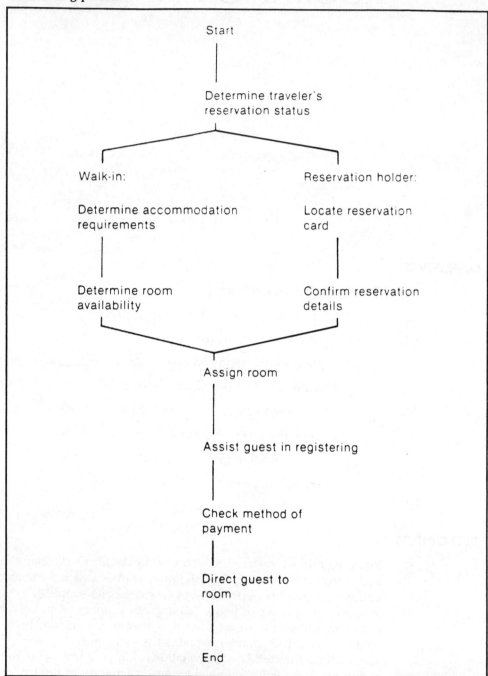

GREETING THE GUEST

Both friendliness and indifference are contagious. Guests begin their relationship with the hotel long before they arrive at the desk. After all, it is the guest who makes the first important moves, selecting the hotel over all others, making a reservation, taking the trouble to travel to the property, and quite possibly waiting in line to be served.

The first persons to contact the incoming guest, after the attendant at the door, are likely to be desk clerks. *They represent the entire hotel.* The initial impression they make greatly influences guests' perceptions of the entire operation. A guest who is positively impressed at the desk carries that impression to the next encounter with a hotel employee, be it the bell attendant who shows the room, the telephone operator who assists with a long distance call, the room-service waiter who delivers the evening snack, or the bartender serving the predinner cocktail. A guest met with indifference and poor service at the desk, however, will be on guard when dealing with other employees and may transfer resentment from one encounter to the next.

The Importance of the Desk Clerk, or, Has Nothing Changed in 66 Years?

''In my opinion, the clerk can easily help make or destroy the popularity of this house. It is of vital importance that the clerk have personality, one that is pleasing and appeals to the general public. It is really necessary that he should know each person that comes into the hotel. He should always have a pleasant word, smiles and extend to the guest who has just arrived as many courtesies and favors as it is possible for him to extend, making the guest feel that he is really receiving something more than he pays for.''

> Anonymous general manager, quoted in *The New York Hotel Review,* March 3, 1923.

''The desk clerk is a very important person. He is the first person to meet you when you walk into a hotel. He greets you with a big smile, he is in charge of keys, messages and mail. His primary mission, however, is to inform you that you do not have a reservation.''

> Shelly Berman, comedian

''What is the contribution of the desk clerk, you ask? I will tell you this much that I know to be true. If the beginning of the guest stay starts out well, it will many more times than not end well.''

> Randolph Guthrie, general manager,
> Shangri-La Hotel, Singapore

Regardless of how busy the clerk is, she must make every effort to develop the guest–hotel relationship in the best possible direction. She greets the guest with a friendly ''Good afternoon, sir'' or ''Good evening, madam,'' and ''Welcome to the Plaza. May I help you?'' A genuine, unforced smile and direct eye contact must be the rule, not the exception. If the clerk is busy on the telephone or at the computer terminal, she turns to the guest and says, ''I will be with you in just a moment, sir.'' She then disengages herself from that task as quickly as possible and gives full attention to the new arrival. She may ask the guest if he has had a pleasant trip (flight, ride, walk, etc.), while concentrating on the task at hand: to determine the guest's needs, match them to the hotel's services, and keep check-in time to a minimum.

MARKETING SKILLS

The clerk must be a sales representative at all times. Even when providing information to people who are not guests, he is *selling* the hotel by leaving a favorable impression in their minds. When it comes to the assignment of rooms, his skills are truly put to the test. To do so, clerks, like sales personnel in other businesses, must have a thorough knowledge of the product they sell. They must have at their fingertips the details of the hotel's policies, procedures, rates, and services. Figures 3.2, 3.3 and 3.4 are examples of selling tools a clerk must be familiar with. Here are some questions, quite typical of the ones guests ask of desk clerks throughout the day:

- Do you have a restaurant (cocktail lounge, coffee shop)?
- What are its hours?
- Do you have an entertainer?
- What are the show times?
- Do we have to dress up?
- What are the menu offerings?
- Is there a children's menu?
- Do we have to make a reservation?
- What recreation facilities do you have?
- How far do we have to go? Can we rent equipment?
- What are your rooms like?
- Is there a view?

Figure 3.2
Hotel floor plan.

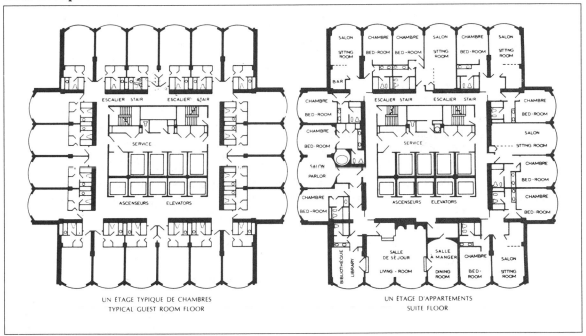

Courtesy of Canadian Pacific Hotels.

- How noisy, quiet, close to the pool, next to each other, are the rooms?
- Do you have rooms that are connecting (next to the elevator, near the exercise room)?
- What provisions have been made for persons with walking disabilities?
- Why is one room more expensive than the other?
- Does the room have a shower, a bath, or a combination? Are the beds long (wide, soft, hard)? How many pillows are there? Is there room for a crib (extra bed)?
- What is the difference between a studio and a suite?
- What is your pet policy? Are there kennels nearby?
- What about children? Are there special rates?
- Can you arrange for a sitter? Do you have a playroom?

Figure 3.3
Hotel fact sheet.

THE FOUR SEASONS
Vancouver, British Columbia, Canada

ADDRESS:
FOUR SEASONS HOTEL
791 West Georgia Street
Vancouver, BC V6T 2T4

Telephone: (604) 689–9333
FAX number: (604) 684–4555

LOCATION:
At Pacific Centre, corner of Howe and West Georgia Streets, across the street from the Vancouver Art Gallery. Within walking distance of Gastown, Robsonstrasse and theatres.

RATING
AAA/CCA Five Diamond, Mobile Four Star.

TRANSPORTATION
Taxi stand at door. Complimentary limousine in the downtown area.

ROOMS
385 Rooms, including 19 large one/two bedroom suites, 2 executive split level suites, 45 Deluxe Four Seasons suites. Individually controlled air conditioning and heat, bathrobes, hairdryers, miniature bars, remote colour T.V. with movie and sports channels, telephone in bathroom, digital clock radio in all rooms.

RESTAURANTS/LOUNGES
Chartwell—Elegant dining for lunch and dinner.
The Harvester—cafe style informal dining, breakfast, lunch, and dinner.
The Garden Lounge—Light luncheon menus, cocktails, background piano music each evening.
Terrace Bar—Intimate lobby bar.
Room Service—24 hours—full menu offered.

SERVICES
Gift shop and newsstand. Immediate access to Pacific Centre shopping complex, 300 shops and boutiques and two major department stores. 24 hour concierge, 24 hour valet and dry cleaning, twice daily maid service, complimentary shoe shine.

RECREATION
Indoor/outdoor pool, whirlpool, outdoor hot tub and sun deck, saunas, video exercises, Paramount fitness gym and Precor exercise equipment. Aerobic classes daily.

CONFERENCE & BANQUET FACILITIES
Park Ballroom accommodates 450 persons for meals, 600 for meetings. Le Pavilion, 120 for meals, elegant setting. Gold Plate service and choice of menu offered in this special room. Nine other rooms accommodating 20 to 180 for meeting and meal functions.

PETS
Accepted on leash. Not allowed in dining rooms, lounges, swimming pool area.

PARKING
Indoor parking

CHURCHES
All denominations within walking distance of hotel.

ELECTRIC POWER
110 volts—60 cycle A.C.

CREDIT CARDS
Four Seasons, American Express, VISA, En Route, Diners, Master Card, Carte Blanche.

CHECK OUT
1:00 P.M.

CANCELLATION POLICY
Cancellations must be received before noon on expected arrival date. If cancellation of a *guaranteed* reservation is not received before 6 p.m. on the day of arrival, the hotel will charge for one night's accommodation.

TOLL FREE RESERVATIONS
In Canada—1-800-268-6282
In United States—1-800-332-3442
In Toronto—445-5031
In Frankfurt—251060
In London—834-4422
In Paris—42566617
Elsewhere contact your local Air Canada, Japan Airlines or UTELL International reservations office.

Courtesy of Four Seasons Hotel, Vancouver, BC.

Guest services are continually expanding as hotels make efforts to stay competitive (Fig. 3.5); clerks must know the details of each. Questions may also be asked about other operations in the chain, the city, or the district where the hotel is located, and about shops, government offices, hospitals, entertainment and sports facilities, sights, tours, and transportation in the area. The clerk must be able to respond with confidence, but should not hesitate to admit, ''I am afraid I don't know the answer, but I'd be glad to get the information for you.''

Upselling Rooms

To some guests, the cost of the room is a concern. The experienced clerk can tactfully size up the guest and make diplomatic offers that respond to the guest's needs. Sometimes a guest stipulates a rate directly: ''At your lowest rate, please,'' or, ''I'd like your $45 special I saw advertised at the airport.'' Others only hint at their wishes: ''We had really hoped to stay in a small hotel near the

Figure 3.4
Jogging guide.

JOG TO
UNION SQUARE
Approximately 1 mile

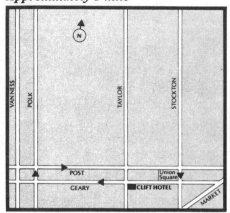

Start at the Clift Hotel, Taylor and Geary, proceed west on Geary to Polk; proceed north on Post to Powell; proceed south on Powell to Geary; proceed west on Geary and return to the Hotel.

JOG ON
NOB HILL
Approximately 1½ miles

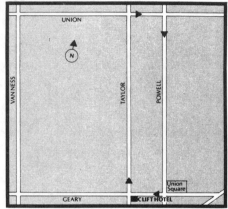

Start at the Clift Hotel, Taylor and Geary, proceed north on Taylor to Union; proceed east on Union to Powell; proceed south on Powell to Geary; proceed west on Geary and return to the Hotel.

(Only for skilled runners prepared for San Francisco's hills.)

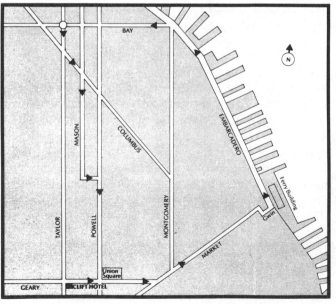

JOG AT THE
EMBARCADERO
Approximately 4 miles

Start at the Clift Hotel, Taylor and Geary, proceed east on Geary to Market; proceed east on Market to the Embarcadero; proceed north on Embarcadero to Bay; proceed west on Bay to the Taylor Street cable car turn-around. Take the Powell Street cable car back to Powell and Geary and proceed west on Geary to return to the Hotel.

Courtesy of Four Seasons Clift, San Francisco, CA.

Figure 3.5
Percentage of hotels offering selected guest services.

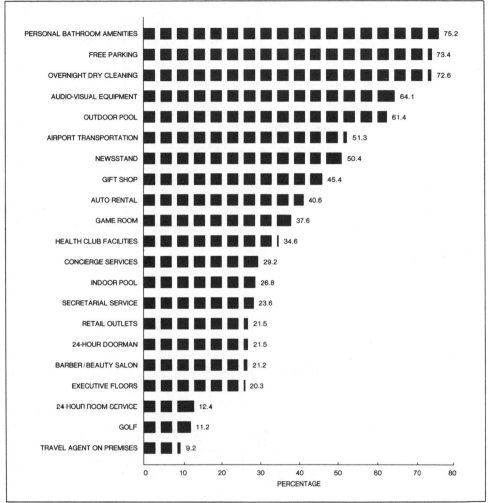

Source: *1986 U.S. Lodging Industry* (New York: Laventhol & Horwath), p. 56.

coastal highway, but they were all booked.'' In any case, the clerk must listen carefully, offer a choice of rates, and show how price relates to value.

Novice clerks may find it difficult to relate to such rates as $50 or a $100 for a single room. (Figure 3.6 shows the average room rates charged by U.S. properties.) Guests usually anticipate what the rates will be as long as they fit the reputation, location, and general standard of the operation. Should they find the rates unreasonable, they have the choice of leaving and finding more suitable offers elsewhere.

Figure 3.6
Rate card.

	SINGLE	DOUBLE
Moderate Rate	*$140*	*$160*
Superior Rate	*$155*	*$175*
Deluxe Rate	*$170*	*$190*
Four Seasons Room	*$190*	*$210*
Deluxe Four Seasons Room	*$210*	*$230*
Executive Suite	*$250*	*$250*
Parlor and One Bedroom Suite from	*$390*	*$390*
Parlor and Two Bedroom Suite from	*$530*	*$530*

Room rates effective June 1, 1986. All rates subject to city room tax and change without notice. Our checkout time is 1:00 pm. For toll free reservations: (800) 268-6282

Four Seasons Hotel
NEWPORT BEACH

690 Newport Center Drive
Newport Beach, California 92660
Telephone: (714) 759-0808
Telex: 183127 FS Hotel NPBCH

Courtesy of Four Seasons Hotel, Newport Beach, CA.

Table 3.1
Average annual room rate, by location and size of property.

	By location of property			
Center City	**Suburban**	**Airport**	**Highway**	**Resort**
$62.62	52.81	51.12	41.69	58.21
	By size of property			
Under 150 rooms	**150–299 rooms**	**300–600 rooms**	**Over 600 rooms**	
45.03	49.67	65.33	80.30	

All figures are medians in US dollars

Source: 1986 U.S. Lodging Industry (New York: Laventhol & Horwath), pp. 41 and 50

The clerk should be confident and businesslike when making suggestions. Rarely does a clerk quote a minimum rate. The preferred approach is to provide guests with a choice of rates, often starting with a high one and working down. At the same time, emphasis is placed on the value the guest is being offered, not just the price. The clerk paints a mental picture of the room and its features, its relative advantages, and special features.

Here is a summary of some key upselling techniques. More are found in the Box, ''Upselling Rooms.''

1. Know the product.

2. Control the encounter. Ask specific questions, such as, ''We have a quiet double room on our Silver Floor. Is that suitable for you?'' Avoid vague, open-ended questions, such as ''What kind of a room are you looking for?''

3. Sell high, but avoid high-pressure selling techniques.

4. Always quote the full rate plus tax.

5. Turn a negative aspect of a room or rooming situation into an advantage for the guest. For example, a room without a view becomes a ''quiet room.'' A room near the elevator or near the busy pool may be noisy, but it is ''handy'' and ''easily accessible if you plan to do much swimming.''

6. Sandwich the price between descriptive phrases. For example, ''One of our extra-large rooms at $75 plus tax, overlooking the park.'' Or quote the price of more than one room, giving the guest a choice, ''We still have double rooms for $60, but the ones with the new minibar are $75.''

Upselling Rooms.

Mark Gordon, an experienced front office and general manager, trains his staff in three nonpressure selling techniques.[1] They are especially effective in inducing guests to accept medium-priced and deluxe rooms instead of minimum-rate accommodations. His techniques are:

The Choice-of-Doors Technique

The clerks gives the guest a choice of rate categories and asks, ''Which would you prefer?'' No pressure is applied, the guest does that all by herself. People tend to avoid extremes and are likely to select the middle choice. Thus, a guest being offered a room rate of $40, $55, or $85 will most likely go for the $55 room, even if she had planned on the lowest rate.

The Door-in-the-Face Technique

This approach has to be handled with tact and without pressure. It can result in drastic increase of the average rate per occupied room. Clerks start from the top down, quoting the highest-priced room in the category the guest wishes. A single guest may be offered a ''deluxe room on our Gold Floor, with patio and sitting room at a rate of $145.'' The guest may accept this room or ask for something ''less pricy,'' at which point the clerk quotes the next rate down, say the ''deluxe room on the Silver Floor, with king-size bed and a view of the park, at $110.'' By comparison, this room still appears of above-average quality but considerably less expensive than the previously quoted one. According to the theory of reciprocity, many guests will be convinced that after rejecting the highest rate, accepting the middle-rate room is a rational compromise.

The Foot-in-the-Door Technique

This technique is based on the notion that people who have already agreed to one proposition will quite easily agree to another one. The clerk taking a reservation over the phone or selling a room over the counter can use this by saying, ''We are holding a single room in the East Wing for you, Mr. Walton. For an extra $20, you can have a deluxe room in our new Lakeside Wing,'' or, ''for $35 per person you can take advantage of our weekend package, which includes the champagne breakfast in your room, plus dinner for two in the Redwood Room.'' The guest can simply say ''no, thank you'' or accept the upsale suggestion.

Upselling is not a game or a way to squeeze extra dollars out of unsuspecting travelers. It should be part of a professional receptionist's and guest services representative's repertoire. It should be seen as one more way to (a) provide better service to the guests by offering choices, and (b) increase rooms revenue for the hotel.

---

1. Marc Gordon, ''Upselling Rooms: 3 Effective Techniques,'' *Lodging,* January 1986, pp. 64–65.

7. Ask for the sale. Once all the information has been presented to the guest, the clerk must gently, but resolutely, close the sale. ''If that is a suitable choice, may I ask you to sign the registration card?'' is an effective way to move negotiations to a close.

8. Listen to guests' conversational comments, such as, ''Wow, what a hot day. I could do with something cool.'' They will help to determine their needs better and to sell other services of the hotel: ''Our outdoor pool and bar are still open.''

9. Sell the whole hotel by making suggestions for dinner (''Just dial 5 on your room phone to make a reservation''), or for drinks in the lounge (''The new entertainer is fantastic!), or for recreational facilities (''There is no charge for the use of the sauna and weight room'').

10. Try to anticipate the guest's needs and offer services, suggestions, and assistance.

ROOM ASSIGNMENT

Before assigning a room to anyone, the clerk needs to know if the guest has a reservation. Phrases like ''Are we expecting you?'' or ''Are we holding a reservation?'' quickly help to determine the reservations status, without putting those without a reservation on the spot. Depending on the reply, the ensuing steps differ, as shown on in Figure 3.1. Each is described in the following paragraphs.

Before proceeding though, a warning: Always check for possible reservations before checking in a guest. What would happen if a person is checked in as a *walk-in*, ignoring the reserved room? The new guest takes a room from the ''vacant'' inventory, while the clerk continues to hold a ''reserved'' room. Should the house fill up, walk-ins may be turned away, rooms remain unsold, and income is lost to the hotel. This can be prevented by routine checks of outstanding reservations against all registered guests.

Full House

If there is no suitable vacancy, the clerk should express regret, explain that the hotel is fully booked, and offer assistance in locating accommodation elsewhere. Efficient clerks are in touch with similar hotels in the area and know the vacancy situation there. By making a telephone call, you can often provide alternative arrangements and leave the traveler with a positive impression of your hotel.

Interhotel room-status systems are in use in many areas. Participating hotels are shown on an indicator board that can be accessed by the desk staff in each property. Light signals are used to show room status:

Panel lit up: No vacancy

Panel not lit: Rooms available

Light flashing: Limited vacancy, please telephone first for details.

To ensure that all front-office personnel are kept continually informed of room status within the hotel, a sign may be placed behind the desk in full view of the staff, giving "full," "sell," or similar messages that are helpful to the clerk responding to a walk-in situation (Fig. 3.7). The sign "No Discounts Available" means that the house is almost filled, that people prepared to pay the full rates are likely to walk in before the end of the day, and that, therefore, no special discounts for airline and company employees can be accepted.

Walk-ins

Before offering a room to a walk-in, the clerk must determine the guest's requirements:

- What type of room is desired?

- How many people are in the party?

- What is their anticipated length of stay?

- What rate is acceptable?

Based on the answers to these basic questions, the clerk matches rooms available to the customer's wishes. Asking the questions is essential; assuming you know the answer may cause embarrassment. For example, just because a couple is seeking accommodation, the clerk must not assume that they are looking for a double room. They may have traveled on the same flight or come in the same taxi, but their arrival at the desk together was mere chance. They are definitely looking for separate accommodation. Even if they are traveling together, they may wish separate rooms or possibly twin beds, not a double bed. Similarly, they may have three children and a dog waiting in the car or be the advance party for three couples traveling in a passenger van. By obtaining the basic facts first, the clerk maintains control and is able to provide good service.

A quick glance at the *space available sheet* provides a summary of future bookings, and a visual inspection of the *room rack* shows the status of each room for the coming night. Together, this information allows for prompt guest service.

Guests with a Reservation

If the guest says, "I have a reservation," the clerk locates and removes the card from the reservation rack, or calls up the information on the computer screen. A scan for special notations may reveal special requests, such as specific room types or number, extra pillows, flowers, cot in the room, VIP treatment, or bill-

Figure 3.7
Signs informing clerks of current reservation status.

Courtesy of Seattle Hyatt House, Seattle, WA.

ing instructions. If the hotel maintains a *guest history file*, additional details may be available to guide the room assignment.

Before the clerk selects a room for the guest, the specific room requirements must be confirmed: type of room and rate, number of people in the party, length of stay, and extras. Although this information may already be on file, it must be checked with the guest. Requirements may have changed since the reservation was made; the clerk must ensure that the guest receives exactly what is needed. "We are holding a double-bedded room for you in our south wing, Mrs. Rogers. Your expected check-out date is the twenty-second. Is that correct?"

ASSIGNING A ROOM

Room assignment is the matching of a guest's needs with the hotel's available space. As soon as all facts are determined, the clerk *blocks* the room on the rack by placing a temporary *flag* (a brightly colored card) into the appropriate pocket of the room rack. This prevents another clerk from selling the same room to another guest. In due time, the flag will be replaced with a slip showing the guest's name.

REGISTERING A GUEST

The guest now fills out a *registration card* that provides the hotel with the basic details to close the contract. The registration cards shown here are a sampling of the most common types, each serving a different purpose. Figure 3.8 includes a duplicate that, when completed, is given to the guest. In Figure 3.9, the registration card is part of the guest folio. The top section is prepared before the guest's arrival and requires only a signature. The card in Figure 3.10 was prepared in advance by the hotel's computer system.

Once the guest has signed in, the clerk:

- Verifies the spelling and pronunciation of the guests's name: ''Thank you very much, Mr. Zwierzewicz. Did I pronounce that correctly?''

- Uses the guest's name in addressing the guest. In the case of a returning guest or one with a reservation, clerks can begin using the name much earlier, avoiding the impersonal ''Sir'' or ''Madam.''

- Checks the legibility of both the name and address.

- Notes the presence of the guest's signature, which might be required to compare signed charges from restaurants and the cocktail lounge.

- Fills in any hotel details, such as room number, rate, number of guests, clerk's initials or name, departure date, and folio number.

- Stamps the date and time of registration, using a special imprinter (Fig. 3.11).

- Works quickly and accurately, so as not to detain the guest.

OBTAINING CREDIT INFORMATION

Traditionally, hotels gave accommodation to anyone who showed up at the desk, was appropriately dressed, had baggage, and behaved in a manner acceptable to the clerk or the manager. This practice continues, in principle, but hotels have, by necessity, become more assertive in requiring credit information from the guest before check-in. Giving a room to a stranger really means extending temporary credit; in that way, the registration card can be considered an application for credit. Most people are honest and intend to pay for all the services and goods they receive during their stay. Some are less honest and may intend to defraud the hotel. It takes very little to run up a sizable bill and quietly depart (*skip*). Assume, as an example, a room rate of $75 per night, add to that charges for dinner, long distance calls, drinks, and laundry services, and the $150 to $200 mark is quickly crossed. For this reason, most establishments expect guests to prove their creditworthiness before receiving a room key.

This credit check is done either at registration time or when the reservation is taken. In either case, it must be done tactfully: nobody likes their honesty

Figure 3.8
Registration card: the top portion stays at the desk, the bottom copy is given to the guest.

ORIGINAL

Sheraton-Landmark
SHERATON HOTELS & INNS. WORLDWIDE
1400 ROBSON,
VANCOUVER, B.C., CANADA
V6G 1B9
TELEPHONE   TELEX
(604) 687-0511   04-55495

THIS SIDE FOR OFFICE USE ONLY

NAME _____
PLEASE PRINT

STREET _____

CITY _____
PROVINCE OR STATE

FIRM _____

PHONE (RES.) _____ (BUS.) _____

SIGNATURE _____

MAKE OF CAR _____ LIC. No. _____

ON CHECKING OUT, MY ACCOUNT WILL BE SETTLED BY

☐ CASH   ☐ COMPANY
☐ CREDIT CARD _____

RES. ☐
NO RES ☐
TRAIN ☐
PLANE ☐
CAR ☐
TRAVEL AGT. ☐
RET. GUEST ☐

WE HAVE REGISTERED YOU AS

M _____

ROOM _____

RATE _____

GUESTS _____ CLERK _____

FOLIO No. _____

DEPARTURE _____

PREPAYMENT _____

NOTICE TO GUESTS
THE MANAGEMENT IS NOT RESPONSIBLE FOR MONEY,
JEWELRY, OR OTHER VALUABLES UNLESS DEPOSITED
IN VAULT PROVIDED FOR THAT PURPOSE.

CHECK OUT TIME 2:00 P.M.

100M-6/78

DUPLICATE

Sheraton-Landmark
SHERATON HOTELS & INNS, WORLDWIDE
1400 ROBSON,
VANCOUVER, B.C., CANADA
V6G 1B9
TELEPHONE: TELEX:
(604) 687-0511   04-55495

WELCOME GUEST:

WE SINCERELY HOPE YOUR STAY WITH US WILL BE
A PLEASANT ONE. PLEASE FEEL FREE TO CALL
UPON US FOR ANY ASSISTANCE YOU MAY REQUIRE.
OUR OPERATOR IS ON DUTY AT ALL TIMES.

FOR INFORMATION REGARDING PRIVATE BANQUETS
AND OTHER FUNCTIONS PLEASE CONTACT OUR
BANQUET MANAGER.

UPON RETIRING. WE SUGGEST THAT YOU DEPRESS
THE CENTRE PORTION OF THE DOOR KNOB TO
SECURE THE NIGHT LOCK.

WE TRUST YOU WILL HAVE AN ENJOYABLE STAY.

THE MANAGEMENT.

WE HAVE REGISTERED YOU AS

M _____

ROOM _____

RATE _____

GUESTS _____ CLERK _____

FOLIO No. _____

DEPARTURE _____

PREPAYMENT _____

NOTICE TO GUESTS
THE MANAGEMENT IS NOT RESPONSIBLE FOR MONEY,
JEWELRY, OR OTHER VALUABLES UNLESS DEPOSITED
IN VAULT PROVIDED FOR THAT PURPOSE.

CHECK OUT TIME 2:00 P.M.

Courtesy of Sheraton Landmark Hotel, Vancouver, BC.

Figure 3.9
Guest folio with registration card attached.

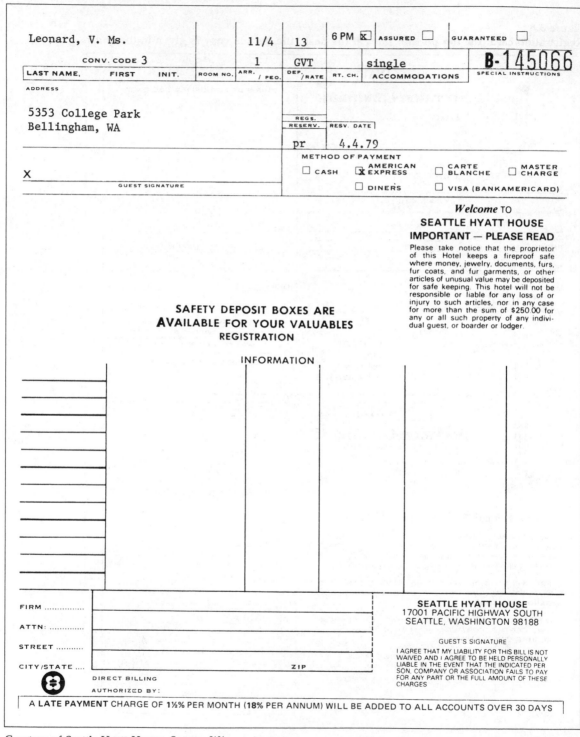

Courtesy of Seattle Hyatt House, Seartle, WA.

Figure 3.10
Computer-generated registration card.

Room Number	Room Type	Room Rate	# Guests	Arrival Date
1023	KING	90.00	1	12-06-89

Account No.	Resv. Status	Group/Plan	# Nights	Departure Date
50136	NONGTD		2	12-08-89

Name
SAINTSBURY, DAWN M.

☐ Business ☐ Residence

Address		Telephone
2665 WEST 42ND AVE.		604-263-5555

City	State	Zip Code
VANCOUVER	BC	V6N 3G4

Company/Group
HOURGLASS COMMUNICATIONS   CANADA   State

Make/Model of Car	License Number

Travel Agent	Advance Deposit
	.00

Signature   Service Rep. I.D.
X

1 ROOM(S)

Upon Checking Out My Account Will Be Settled By:
☐ VISA   ☐ Diners/Carte Blanche
☐ Mastercard   ☐ Cash
☐ American Express ☐ Other: _____

I agree that my liability for this bill is not waived and I agree to be held personally liable in the event that the indicated person, company or association fails to pay for the full amount of the charges.

COMPUTERIZED LODGING SYSTEMS INCORPORATED

4800 Airport Plaza Drive • Suite 160 • Long Beach, CA 90815 • 213-421-2191

COMPUTERIZED LODGING SYSTEMS INCORPORATED

4800 Airport Plaza Drive • Suite 160 • Long Beach, CA 90815 • 213-421-2191

Guest Name   SAINTSBURY, DAWN

Room Number	Room Rate	# Guests	# Nights	Departure Date
1023	90.00	1	2	12-08

PLEASE NOTE:

A safe deposit box is available for the protection of your valuables. The hotel's liability is limited pursuant to general business law.

Please notify a front desk service representative if there is any error in this record of your registration. We want to make certain that your name and room number are correct so that your mail and messages can reach you promptly.

EXPRESS CHECK-OUT SERVICE

If you presented a credit card upon registration, you may simply sign below and leave this card with a front desk service representative to receive Express Check-Out Service. You will be billed through your credit card company and an itemized statement of your account will be mailed to you immediately at the address shown on your registration card.

We are pleased to offer this service to you, and hope that you find it a convenience.

I hereby authorize this establishment to charge my designated credit card account directly for all charges I incur during my stay.

Signature
X

Figure 3.11
Time- and date-stamping machine.

Courtesy of New World Harbourside Hotel, Vancouver, BC.

questioned. Phrases like "How do you intend to settle your account, Mrs. Simpson?" or "If I may have your credit card now, I can make a note of the number and it will speed up your check-out on Thursday, Mr. Whittle," will bring a reasonable response to a reasonable request. The clerk should follow the company's rules in this matter and consult his supervisor if a guest refuses to provide the information.

The majority of travelers carry some kind of credit card. Even people who dislike credit cards carry them while they travel. It is becoming more and more difficult to rent a car, purchase an airline ticket, or check into a hotel without such a card.

Processing a Credit Card

When the guest hands you her credit card at check-in time, the card is immediately imprinted on the charge slip and on the back of the registration card, and the slip is attached to the back of the guest account just started. As soon as possible, a credit card authorization is obtained for an anticipated spending amount and recorded on the back of the folio (Fig. 3.12). For a guest registering for three nights in a $65 per night room, a $400 authorization might be requested from the credit card company. This allows for the $195 room charge, taxes if applicable, and likely charges for restaurant, bar, laundry, telephone, and other services the guest might use while staying. (For details on credit card processing, see Chapter 4).

Figure 3.12
Credit authorization on the back of a guest folio.

DATE	NAME	CARD NO.	AMOUNT	APPROVED VAL. CODE	MJR. OK

CHECK HISTORY			
DATE	AMOUNT	AUTHORIZED BY	CASHIER

ROOMING THE GUEST

Once the registration card is signed and credit details settled, the guest is *roomed*. This is the beginning of the stay, and it should be a further opportunity to make the guest feel at home and comfortable with the facilities and services of the hotel. Some hotels present guests with a copy of the registration card, which acts as a receipt and formalizes the arrangement just concluded (Fig. 3.9). Another version, called a passport (Fig. 3.13) has a copy of the registration card stapled on the inside and is given to the guest with the words, "Here is your passport for use during your stay with us, Mr. Wooster. In it you will find useful information about all the facilities at your disposal and a list of telephone numbers if you need assistance or require a service. We also ask you to show this passport when you charge for services in the dining room or lounges. It identifies you as a registered guest." The form in Figure 3.14 is an envelope that contains the room key and messages for a preregistered guest. The top section will serve as a check-out form for the guest who wishes to leave without being detained at the desk.

Increasingly, hotels give guests the choice of using the services of the bellman or carrying their own luggage. ("Bellman" is the traditional job title and reflects that the work is typically done by men. The title "bell attendant" is the nonsexist alternative in North America; in Great Britain the job has always been "hall porter".) In the latter instance, the guest is given the room key and rooming slip and is directed to the elevator. If the bellman assists in the rooming ("Would you like me to ask Mike to help you with your luggage, Mrs. Yearsley?"), he should be ready for the call and be at the desk when requested. Some desks have a buzzer or bell to summon such help, but the traditional call is "Front, please." This reflects the custom of giving the call to the bellman next in line, avoiding preferential treatment for potential "good tippers." (The contrasting call for "last, please" asks for the attendant last in line and involves a task not directly related to a waiting guest. Such tasks could include moving luggage from one room to another, inspecting a room for readiness, delivering a message, or paging a manager.)

The bell attendant is told to "Please show Mrs. Yearsley to suite 229," or, in the case of the returning guest, "Mike, please welcome Mr. Kluckner back to the Four Seasons." Such introductions prevent a guest being shown to the wrong room, possibly with the someone else's luggage. Whatever is said, however, must be said in a low voice so as not to compromise the guest's security and confidentiality.

The bell attendant is an extension of the front office; he completes the rooming procedure initiated by the desk clerk. Upon receiving the key, he:

- Addresses the guest by correct name.

- Makes sure that the key is for the assigned room.

- Asks the guest how many pieces of luggage there are and whether they are all in the lobby (or in the car, or due to arrive from the airport).

Figure 3.13
Guest passport, front and back view.

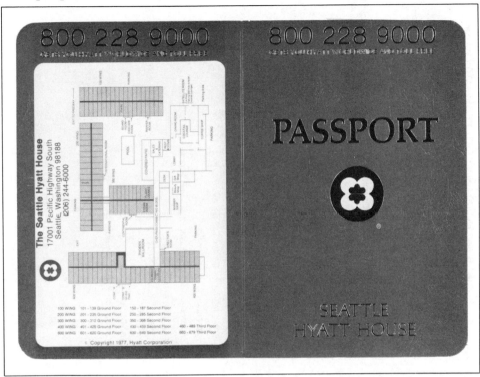

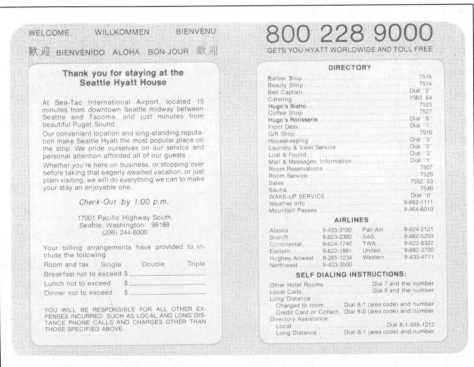

Courtesy of Seattle Hyatt House, Seattle, WA.

Figure 3.14
Rooming envelope for a preregistered guest.

Aloha, and welcome to the Sheraton-Waikiki Hotel.

We hope that you will enjoy your stay with us on the beach at Waikiki and that you will make use of the many fine facilities of the Sheraton-Waikiki Hotel. Charges for meals or entertainment at all of the Sheraton Hotels in Waikiki may be billed to your room.

Again, welcome to Hawaii, our beautiful 50th State, and thank you for selecting the Sheraton-Waikiki Hotel.

Mahalo,

THE STAFF AND MANAGEMENT
SHERATON-WAIKIKI HOTEL

RENNER, MR PETER   1 07/17
07/13
1 LM
21, OR, 99   95.00   SW-0488

You have been pre-registered into
room 2009
Here is your key and any mail or messages.

Sheraton Waikiki Hotel
P.O. Box 8559 / 2255 Kalakaua Avenue / Honolulu, Hawaii 96815
Telephone: (808) 922-4422

IMPORTANT
THE SHERATON WAIKIKI HOTEL OFFERS THE CONVENIENCE OF IN ROOM "SAFEKEEPERS"™ OR FREE OF CHARGE SAFE DEPOSIT BOXES FOR STORAGE OF YOUR VALUABLE ITEMS.

DINING AND ENTERTAINMENT AT THE SHERATON WAIKIKI

THE HANOHANO ROOM

High above the incandescent Waikiki skyline, take in the panoramic view of Diamond Head, Pearl Harbor and Waikiki Beach. Dine on gourmet cuisine from our extensive Continental dinner menu or enjoy buffet breakfasts and our spectacular Sunday Brunch buffet. Breakfast 7 a.m.-10:30 a.m. Sunday Brunch 8:30 a.m.-2 p.m. Dinner 6 p.m.-10:30 p.m. Cocktails 4 p.m.-12 Mid-Nite.

SAFARI STEAK HOUSE

Exotic Africa awaits you here. Gourmet Prime Rib and great seafood combinations and tempting desserts. Also an elaborate salad bar. Open nightly for dinner. Dinner 6 p.m.-10:30 p.m.

KON TIKI RESTAURANT and LOUNGE

Begin your evening in the Kon Tiki Lounge with an exotic selection from our drink menu featuring over 70 potent Polynesian mixtures. Then take a grass shack elevator to our restaurant - a tropical setting of splashing waterfalls and verdant plants. Here you'll dine on the finest Chinese, Polynesian, and Continental cuisine. Dinner 5:30 p.m.-10:30 p.m. Cocktails 5 p.m.-12 Mid-Nite.

THE OCEAN TERRACE

Informal dining featuring local delicacies as well as all-American selections. At dinner, mellow Hawaiian music by strolling musicians. Our superb buffets at breakfast, lunch and dinner offer a seemingly endless variety of choices. Breakfast 6 a.m.-11:30 a.m. Lunch 11:30 a.m.-3 p.m. Dinner 5:30 p.m.-9:30 p.m.

THE OAHU BAR

Sunset cocktails by the sea. Enjoy lively entertainment and dancing. Open 11:30 a.m.-1 a.m.

KAU KAU SNACK BAR

A snack shop dedicated to quality and fast, friendly service. Breakfast 5 a.m.-11 a.m. Lunch and dinner 11 a.m.-2 a.m.

SAND BAR

Poolside on Waikiki Beach.

Courtesy of Sheraton Waikiki Hotel, Honolulu, HI.

- Escorts guests to their car to transport luggage.

- Assists guest with parking arrangements.

- Escorts the guest to the room and opens the door of the room (after first knocking to make sure the room is empty).

- Enters the room before guests to glance around the room and check its readiness. If it is occupied or not in order, he asks the guest to remain in the hallway while he checks with the desk for a different room.

- Invites the guests to enter the room.

- Distributes the luggage according to the guest's wishes, and points out features of the room, such as air-conditioning unit, heating, television, radio, house phone, and directory.

- Leaves the key and wishes the guest an enjoyable stay.

- Does not hang around for a tip; if a tip is offered, he accepts it in a businesslike manner and puts it away.

- Returns to his post in the lobby.

Upon his return to the lobby, he signs a logbook or what used to be called the *bellman call sheet* (Fig. 3.15). A basic job description of the bell attendant is given in chapter 1.

COMPLETING THE FORMS

As the guest leaves the desk, forms must be completed to start the accounting cycle. If the guest has sent a deposit, an account card, or *folio*, may already have been made out (see Fig. 3.9) and be waiting in a section of the *bucket*. The bucket is the special holder in which guest accounts stand upright (Fig. 3.16). If the hotel uses a posting machine, the folio will have two or three slips attached to the top (Fig. 3.17). The first slip (*the room slip*) goes into the appropriate pocket of the room rack; the second, (*the information slip*) is sent to the switchboard. If the hotel keeps an information rack (other than the one at the switchboard), a third slip, an information slip, is filed there. Once the slips are distributed and the folio started, the folio is stamped and filed in the bucket, together with the registration and reservation cards, in order of room number.

The following information is typed at the top of the guest account (and simultaneously copied to the slips fastened underneath):

- Room number.

- Last name.

- Gender.

Figure 3.15
Bellman call sheet.

BELLMAN CALL SHEET

DATE_____ 19_____

WATCH_____ SHEET NO._____

ROOM NO.	BELLMAN NO.	SERVICE PERFORMED	TIME LEFT	TIME RETURNED

Checked By_____
BELL CAPTAIN

FORM NO. 1028 INSCO

Courtesy of Wilcox International, Chicago, IL.

Figure 3.16
Guest folio rack, or *bucket*.

Courtesy of Seattle Hyatt House, Seattle, WA.

- Initials.
- Check-in and check-out dates.
- Number of guests.
- Rate.

Below this is printed:

- Guest's street address.
- Clerk's initials.
- Typist's initials.
- Reservation/no reservation (R/no R).

And below this:

- City.
- State or province.
- Company name.

Figure 3.17
Guest folio with two slips.

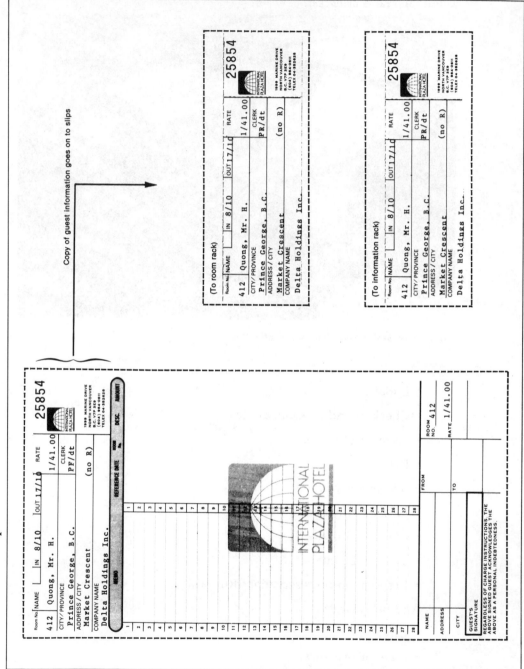

Courtesy of Plaza International Hotel, North Vancouver, BC.

Here are some examples of rate notations:

Standard: No Reservation

101 Tingle, M/M J. 70 Richmond Park Road Sheffield, Yorkshire S13 8HQ England	8-17/12	2/85.00	No R.	PF/dt

Special Rate for Travel Agent

424 Ford, Mrs. L. 65 Fifth Avenue Dearborn, MI 23009	4-11/12	1/58.50	TA	MF/f

Special Rate for Commercial Traveler

222 Ferguson, Ms. M. 7 Main Street Morristown, NJ 08353 Winger Realty	15-19/12	1/62.50	COMM	g/h

Family Rate

282 Kluckner, M/M K. and Sara-Jane 4656 West 42nd Avenue Vancouver, BC V1N 3E7	4-8/12	3/76.00	FAM	r/f

Two People Splitting the Room Rate

434 McNeil, C. Dr. 94 Osler Street Vancouver, BC B7C 3H9	15-17/12	2/41.00 @ 2 accounts	B/s

In this case two accounts are made out, two information slips are sent, and both slips are folded in half and put into the room-rack pocket, names showing.

Room Rate as Reserved not Available

222 Burgermeister, M/M G.H. Diedesfelder Strasse 10 6800 Mannheim, W. Germany Brentano Design Co.	13-21/12	2/71.50 Q	B/s

If a guest was promised a rate no longer available, it should still be honored. A "Q" (for quoted) is placed next to the rate.

Explanation of Abbreviations:

> M/M: Mr. & Mrs.
>
> 8–17/12: Arrive December 8, depart December 17.
>
> 2/85.00: two guests in room for $85.00.
>
> PF/dt: two sets of clerks' initials, the first for the one who handled the rooming, the second for the one who completed the paperwork.
>
> No R: walk-in; no reservation.
>
> TA: referred by travel agent, commission to be paid.
>
> COMM: member of a commercial traveleres' association, entitled to discount.
>
> FAM: special family rate.
>
> Q: rate as quoted, which is lower than the posted rack rate.

Even if the desk is busy, the clerk must try to complete accounts and slips as soon as possible after the guest checks in. The reasons for the urgency? Charges may be incurred by the guest almost immediately, and they will have to be posted to an account. The switchboard may receive important telephone calls for the guest within minutes of arrival and up-to-the-minute information must be on file. Also, if they are not recorded right away they may not get posted, resulting in an embarrassing phone call to the guest to confirm the original quote or other charges.

THE HOUSEKEEPER'S REPORT

This inventory of the rooms is taken by the *room attendants* (traditionally referred to as maids). It describes the status of each room: either occupied, vacant, on-change, or check-out (see below). A first report is usually prepared early in the morning and a second one late in the afternoon. Three copies are completed: one stays with the housekeeper, the second is sent to the front desk, and the third one, as a control copy, to the manager or accountant.

Occupied means that the room is rented; either guests are in the room, or luggage and personal belongings are present. *Vacant* means that the room is not occupied and that it is clean and ready for occupancy. *On change* or *check-out* signify that the room is unoccupied but has not been made up. When the room attendant goes into each guest room, she quickly surveys the room, determines its status, and makes the appropriate entry on the report.

Sample reports are shown for a large and a small hotel: Figure 3.18 is one typical of a 200-or-more-room hotel. A code is entered next to each room number ("O" for occupied), another for check-outs that have not been made up ("C/O"), and the space left blank for a vacant room. The code "OOO" (out-of-order) describes rooms that are vacant but not for sale. Reasons for OOO status could be a major cleaning or renovation work, damaged furniture or fixtures—features of the room that are not expected to be fixed in time for the coming night. A similar, but simpler *maid's report* (Fig. 3.19) requires the insertion of the room numbers with a corresponding indication of each room's status.

When the report arrives at the desk, it is time-stamped, then compared with the room rack. Each room on the rack is checked against the status on the report. If, for example, a room shows "occupied" on the rack but "vacant" on the report, an investigation is necessary. These steps might be taken:

1. The bucket is checked to see whether the guest account for this room is still there. Perhaps the guest has checked out, and someone forgot to make the changes on the room rack.

2. If this is not the case, the housekeeping department is informed and another check requested. It might turn out that the room is indeed occupied and a mistake was made by the original checker. It could also be that a guest arrived after the completion of the report: this could, however, have been determined by checking the check-in time stamped on the occupant's registration card.

3. Many managers require that a *discrepancy report* (Fig. 3.20) be sent to the housekeeping department, indicating any differences between the report and the room rack. This provides for a record of the problem, a recheck, and the eventual solving of the puzzle.

4. If housekeeping cannot clear up a discrepancy, it must be reported to a senior clerk or front-office manager for further action. It could be that the vacant room should still be occupied, as suggested by the active account still in the bucket. It may turn out that the guest left without settling the account. Someone who does that, with the intention to defraud the hotel, is referred to as a *skip*.

5. If the rack shows the room as occupied but the room is vacant, and the bucket holds no guest account, closer checking of yesterday's check-outs may reveal that the guest left a day ago and someone forgot to pull the slip out of the room rack. This one is called a *sleeper*, most likely a source of lost revenue to the hotel and, in the case of a presumed full house, a guest turned away the previous night.

Figure 3.18
Housekeeper's report.

HYATT REGENCY VANCOUVER

V - 66
2 - 73

Total Rooms Occ ______________

Expected Check Outs __________

Expected Arrivals ______________

HOUSE KEEPER'S REPORT

Date ______________

Time ______________

401	501	601	701	801	901	1001	1101	1201	1401	1501	1601	1701	1801
402	502	602	702	802	902	1022	1102	1202	1402	1502	1602	1702	1802
403	503	603	703	803	903	1003	1103	1203	1403	1503	1603	1703	1803
	504	604	704	804	904	1004	1104	1204	1404	1504	1604	1704	1804
	505	605	705	805	905	1005	1105	1205	1405	1505	1605	1705	1805
	506	606	706	806	906	1006	1106	1206	1406	1506	1606	1706	1806
	507	607	707	807	907	1007	1107	1207	1407	1507	1607	1707	1807
	508	608	708	808	908	1008	1108	1208	1408	1508	1608	1708	1808
	509	609	709	809	909	1009	1109	1209	1409	1509	1609	1709	1809
	510	610	710	810	910	1010	1110	1210	1410	1510	1610	[illegible]	1810
	511	611	711	2315	2415	2515	1111	1211	1411	1511	3015	3115	
	512												
1916		2116	2216	2316	2416	2516	2616	2716	2816	2916	3016	3116	3216
1917	2C17	2117	2217	2317	2417	2517	2617	2717	2817	2917	3017	3117	3217
1918	2C18	2118	2218	2318	2418	2518	2618	2718	2818	2918	3018	3118	3218
1919	2C19	2119	2219	2319	2419	2519	2619	2719	2819	2919	3019	3119	3219
1920	2020	2120	2220	2320	2420	2520	2620	2720	2820	2920	3020	3120	3220
1921	2021	2121	2221	2321	2421	2521	2621	2721	2821	2921	3021	3121	3221
1922	2022	2122	2222	2322	2422	2522	2622	2722	2822	2922	3022	3122	3222
1923	2023	2123	2223	2323	2423	2523	2623	2723	2823	2923	3023	3123	3223
1924	2024	2124	2224	2324	2424	2524	2624	2724	2824	2924	3024	3124	3224
1925	2025	2125	2225	2325	2425	2525	2625	2725	2825	2925	3025	3125	3225

IDENTIFY BY COLOUR

BLUE — Occupied Room
RED — Expected Check Out
BLANK — Vacant

Courtesy of Hyatt Regency, Vancouver, BC.

Figure 3.19
Maid's report.

MAID'S REPORT						
			DATE _____			
		NAME _____				
ROOM	A.M.				P.M.	
	Occup'd	Vacant			Occup'd	Vacant

Figure 3.20
Discrepancy report.

Discrepancies

DATE_____

ROOM #	HOUSEKEEPING	RACK	RACK RE-CHECK	DEPOSITION

Check-Outs

ROOM #	HOUSEKEEPING	RACK	RACK CHECK-OUTS	COMMENTS

Additional notations used on the housekeeper's report include:

Slept out. *Slept out* (SO) denotes an occupied room that has not been slept in. The explanation for this may be found in a number of scenarios. It could be that the guest, after prepaying when checking in, does not bother to check out when departing. As a result, the folio remains in the active file and the room rack shows the room as occupied. Occasionally a guest leaves the hotel for a day and asks that the room be kept until her return. In this case, the room is empty, but it remains "occupied" on the rack and the regular room charge is added to the guest's account.

A third situation may reveal a possible *skip*. The room is empty, the rack shows "occupied," and the folio lists an accumulation of charges and no billing or charge instructions. This guest, it appears, has skipped out without intending to pay. This case should be referred to the duty manager or senior clerk immediately.

Double-locked. *Double-locked* (DL) indicates that the room was security-locked by the guest from the inside and that the room attendant was unable to enter the room with the normal passkey.

Do not disturb. *Do not disturb* (DND) means the guest put a ''Do Not Disturb'' sign on the door, preventing a visual check of the room. If DND or DL appears on the evening report again, the manager may be called to investigate.

SPECIAL ROOMING SITUATIONS

Did Not Stay

Occasionally, a guest wishes to depart soon after having checked in (*did not stay;* DNS). Staff should ascertain the reasons and attempt to resolve the problem, if possible. If the room has not been used, no charge will be made. The switchboard is informed and asked to remove the guest's name from the information rack, the room rack is altered to show the room as vacant again, and the folio, registration form, and reservation cards are voided with the letters DNS. Some managers insist on being informed of all DNS's as a way to spot potential guest services problems. They also wish to prevent dishonesty by clerks who show a folio as DNS, collect the money from the departing guest, and have the room made up by a collaborator in the housekeeping department.

Did Not Arrive (DNA)

Sometimes a guest with a reservation does not arrive as planned (DNA). If, at the end of a day, reservation cards are still in the reservation rack, the clerk should:

1. Check the information rack to see if the guest already checked in.

2. Check the arrival date, since the card might have been misfiled.

3. If the guest was expected to come by air, check with the airline for possible delays.

4. Attach a time-stamped reservation (if the reservation was guaranteed or the deposit paid) to the folio and add the notation DNA. The cashier and night clerk will handle it.

5. Note DNA on reservation card, and store for easy access. Occasionally, the guest arrives a day later, thinking that the reservation was made for that day. Having a record of the DNA helps resolve the situation should no vacancy exist the next day.

Registered but Not Assigned

A guest who is *registered but not assigned* (RNA) is one who arrives in the morning, when rooms are not available. Such a guest is asked to sign the registration card but is not roomed. The registration card is kept at the desk, inscribed with the letters RNA. As soon as the right room becomes available, the registration card, room rack, and folio are updated. The guest is roomed upon return to the desk.

Advance Payment

In everyday commerce, we are frequently asked to pay before consuming the goods; seeing a play or boarding a plane are two examples. We then have the choice of not paying and foregoing the service. This practice is not uncommon in hotels whenever the traveler presents a credit risk. Innkeepers have traditionally retained the right to refuse service for reasonable causes, and "unable to pay" is such a cause. Credit cards of course take care of this eventuality, but the occasional traveler either prefers to deal in cash only or is unable to produce an acceptable alternative.

If a hotel demands payment in advance, the clerk should tell the guest politely, collect the amount for one night's accommodation, issue a receipt, and treat the guest with the same professional attitude as any other guest. After check-in, all cashiers (front desk, dining room, cocktail lounge) are informed of a *COD* (cash on delivery) situation; this guest is required to pay directly for any services consumed, other than those for which prepayment has been obtained.

To avoid embarrassing confrontations, this COD status should be made clear to the guest at time of check-in. Subsequent attempts by the guest to charge for services should be politely refused. Repeated attempts must be reported to the manager on duty.

No Information

Certain guests request that no information regarding their presence in the hotel be given to callers. This may apply to honeymoon couples and celebrities who do not want to be disturbed. The "no info" notation must be clearly marked on the slips so that both room clerk and switchboard can respond appropriately. The response "not registered at all" is sometimes used.

Very Important Persons (VIP), Special Attention Guests (SPATT), Distinguished Guests (DG)

These designations on a reservation form alert the desk clerk and others, especially housekeeping and room service staff, that the person referred to is to be given certain special treatment.

SPECIAL RATES

Room rates are set by management and listed in government and promotional literature. They may not be altered by the clerk. They are indicated on the room rack (thus called *rack rates*) and deviations are allowed only for clearly defined exceptions. While they differ from one operation to another, their abbreviations and definitions are similar.

Government Rates

Government rates (GVT) are flat rates quoted for government employees traveling on business.

Corporate Rates

Corporate rates (CORP) are guaranteed ''not-to-exceed'' rates for members of certain organizations.

Commercial rates

Commercial rates (COMM) are reduced rates given to members of the Commercial Travelers Association or other organizations that have entered into a discount scheme with the hotel.

Airline Rates

Airline rates are reduced rates given to airline personnel, not airline passengers; company ID is required.

Day Rate

Day rates (DAY) are applicable to the use of a guest room for a portion of the day only, usually between 10:00 A.M. and 4:00 P.M.

Complimentary Rates

Complimentary rates (COMP) are applicable to guests who are given a room free of charge by the hotel.

Weekly Rates

Weekly rates are special rates given by some hotels to people staying for a week or longer, sometimes applied by charging for six nights and giving the seventh ''on the house.''

Figure 3.21
Advertisements for package plans.

Some Enchanted Island. The Sagamore.

Just the two of you. Alone in the private luxury of a suite at The Sagamore. The flames in the fireplace cast a warm glow in the room. The champagne is perfectly chilled. The night is yours. Whatever you're looking for, you'll find it at The Sagamore—especially romance.

Classic Romance Package
$195*
3 days/2 nights

• Suite with fireplace • Breakfast tea & dinner daily • Champagne and chocolates upon arrival • Complimentary drink coupons • Indoor swimming, tennis, racquetball, health spa and more. When weather permits, cross country skiing and ice skating. Downhill skiing at nearby Gore Mountain. Transportation available.

For reservations see your travel planner or call toll-free
1-800-358-3585

Per person, double occupancy. Arrival day. Package subject to availability. Rates subject to change. Taxes and gratuities not included. Offer good through April 30, 1987.

CONDOMINIUMS FOR SALE. A limited number of 2-bedroom units with full hotel facilities are available. Sale on terms in offering plan. Call (518) 644-2092.

THE SAGAMORE
AN OMNI CLASSIC RESORT
ON LAKE GEORGE AT BOLTON LANDING, NEW YORK 12814

Spend the weekend in ... *Style*

For only
$54.00*
per person, per night, based on double occupancy.

You want to be a part of it. New York, New York. And you can do it in style for just $54.00 per person, per night, based on double occupancy.

A deluxe guest room in the heart of Manhattan with free valet parking, of course. And to make it special, you'll find fresh flowers upon arrival, Godiva chocolates and a chilled bottle of champagne. Save the champagne for later, and come down to the lounge for a welcome cocktail on us. And each morning awaken to a complimentary full American breakfast.

Just outside our door there's some of the world's best shopping and entertainment. But you needn't venture out unless you want to, because you'll find two excellent restaurants and a lavish Sunday brunch with an international theme all right here.

Weekends at Halloran House. We don't compromise our style, so why should you?

Halloran House

525 Lexington Avenue, New York, New York 10017 212-755-4000
U.S.: 800-223-0939   Canada: 800-854-3355
*Effective through May 31, 1987. Exclusive of applicable taxes. Subject to availability.

106

Family Rates

Family rates (FAM) are special rates for families who have children under a certain age staying in their parents' room.

Package Plans

Some hotels offer *plans,* quoting a package price for the room and certain meals (Fig. 3.21). The most common examples are:

Figure 3.21 (*Continued*)

It's not just another hotel.
It's another era.

The Princess. A charming, century-old, truly Bermudian
hotel reigning over Hamilton Harbor. Just minutes
to downtown Hamilton with its wonderful collection of duty free shops, sumptuous restaurants
and entertaining nightlife.

$82.50
per person/double occupancy

THE *Princess*
Hamilton, Bermuda

For information and reservations contact your
travel agent or call **800-223-1818;**
in New York State **800-442-8418;**
in New York City **212-582-8100**

Effective for occupancy April 1 thru November 30, 1987. Subject to availability. Meals, tax and gratuities additional.
Represented by Princess Hotels International, Inc.®

European plan. The European plan (EP) includes the rate for the room only. This term is used mainly by travel agents when quoting a straight overnight rate.

American plan. The American plan (AP) includes the price of the room and three meals: breakfast, lunch, and dinner. Resorts use this plan extensively.

Modified American plan. The modified American plan (MAP) includes the room plus breakfast and dinner; guests are free to make their own luncheon arrangements.

HANDLING OVERBOOKING

Toward the end of a given day, it may become obvious that the hotel is over-booked: more reservations are on file than there are rooms vacant. The clerk must carry out certain procedures to determine the exact number and nature of overbookings:

1. Check for reservations with a time limit (such as 6:00 P.M. arrival); if the limit has been passed, these can be pulled, time-stamped, and held on file without legal or moral obligation to fulfill them.

2. Check the arrival date: perhaps some are misfiled and meant for a different day.

3. Check with the switchboard: perhaps some guests with reservations are already in the hotel. If they are, the clerk time-stamps and attaches the reservation card to the registration card in the bucket.

4. Check the spelling of names on the reservation cards against similar ones already registered. This may flush out duplicates.

5. Check to see if there are any rooms out-of-order, not made up, for house use, or in a similar condition that could be readied on an emergency basis. These rooms could be offered to the guests at reduced rates.

6. Check the room rack for blocks to see if they coincide with the reservations still on file or if someone checked a guest into a room different from that previously assigned.

7. Check with comparable hotels in the neighborhood to see if guests could be relocated (or *walked*) there.

Walking a Guest

Occasionally, a guest arrives with a confirmed reservation, only to be told ''We are sold out.'' This situation may be the exception, rather than the rule in most hotels, but the clerk must be able to face it proactively. This means to be pre-pared, to anticipate the steps to follow, and to create a backup system. Take a case of a guest arriving at 8:30 P.M. with a 6:00 reservation. It will be an unenviable task to convince her that the room was held until 7:00 P.M. and that by now the house is full. In effect she is told that it is her own fault that she is without a room. Even with very careful wording, the guest may respond with, "I thought a reservation meant a reservation! What kind of hotel are you running here, anyway? I want to speak to the manager." Or take another case, in which the hotel's overbooking gamble backfired and five guests with reservations, guaranteed by credit cards, are waiting, but only two rooms remain vacant.

Walking in Style

Hotels must take the "walking" of guests very seriously and establish clear procedures. Front-office staff in a first-class hotel might be given these guidelines:[1]

1. Some persons must not be walked. These include returning customers, celebrities, and anyone whose arrangements require his or her presence in the hotel.
2. If you must relocate anyone, do so early in the evening, between 6:00 and 8:00 P.M., rather than late at night.
3. The guest should be inconvenienced as little as possible.
4. A management staff member must look after the guest. This may be a senior manager on duty, an assistant manager, or the front-desk manager.
5. Explain the situation briefly, extend sincere apologies, and explain the alternative arrangements.
6. The guest and luggage are taken by limousine to a hotel of similar quality where advance reservations have been secured.
7. Flowers or fresh fruit are sent to the guest's room at the other hotel.
8. The guest must be telephoned upon arrival at the new hotel to ensure that the arrangements are satisfactory. Messages and phone calls must be forwarded.
9. Appropriate departments must be informed of the relocation. These include switchboard, concierge, and reservations.
10. The guest must not be charged for the room. Hotels usually extend a special rate to each other's relocated guests.
11. If the guest had a reservation for two nights, the hotel must make every effort to have her return to the original hotel the next day. Upon return, the original rate prevails.
12. If the guest is staying for only one night, a letter of apology is sent by the general manager, including an invitation to the guest to return.
13. If at all possible, the management staff member who looks after the relocation in the evening should be there in the morning to greet the guest when she returns to the hotel.
14. Record the details of the relocation in the front-office log. The general manager will want to know the details the next day.
15. Any "walk" sent to the hotel from another hotel should be upgraded and given special attention.

[1] Fashioned after the policy at the Four Seasons Clift Hotel in San Francisco.

The novice clerk will be well advised to call in a senior front-desk staffer: a senior clerk, assistant manager, duty manager, owner, or front-office manager. That person is introduced to the guest by title and name to make it clear that she is talking to someone in authority. The gesture further communicates the seriousness of the situation as far as the hotel is concerned.

Depending on company policy, alternate arrangements can be made at a hotel nearby and transportation arranged (see the Box, "Walking in Style"). If company policy does not allow the hotel to pay for the guest's stay in another hotel, providing free transportation and sending a follow-up letter or telephone call from the manager may repair any damage to the hotel's name. Whoever arranges for the walk also arranges that messages, telephone calls, or mail be sent to the new hotel; switchboard and bell staff are informed as well so that anyone looking for the guest can find her at the new address.

Refusing accommodation to a guest who holds a confirmed reservation can have serious side effects from a legal and public relations standpoint. Managers, therefore, want to be informed of every relocation. Figure 3.22 is a guest relocation report, which requires reason for the relocation and an indication of the guest's reaction. This report, ideally, will result in a letter of apology from the manager to the guest and an invitation to "stay with us on your next visit to our city."

Twelve Common Errors in Rooms Department Operation

A study of the operation of hotels and motels[1] revealed the most common errors the front-desk staff makes. They are listed here, together with the author's comments.

1. *A guest arrives with a confirmed reservation, but no rooms are available.* This relates to full-house management and overbooking and is an everyday problem as the desk staff attempts to fill the house and compensate for no-shows.
2. *A guest arrives with a confirmed reservation, but the clerks cannot find the reservation.* Rooms are available, however, and the guest checks in. This problem situation can be turned into a smooth check-in if the clerk can think on the spot, play down the missing paperwork, offer the guest a room, and attempt to locate the registration later.
3. *The desk clerk is impolite.* There is absolutely no excuse for this, however busy or tired the staff may be.
4. *The bell attendant or guest is given the wrong key and must return to the desk.* This can be avoided by the clerk examining the key as it is handed over. A verbal "Here is your key to room 1209" aids in the verification. The bell attendants must be trained to routinely confirm the room number before leaving the lobby.
5. *Check-in or check-out lines are too long.* Prepared registration cards, an up-to-the-minute knowledge of the rooms status, and teamwork behind the desk are the key to making long lines shrink quickly.

(continued)

Figure 3.22
Guest relocation report.

GUEST RELOCATION REPORT

NAME OF HOTEL: _____   DATE: _____

HOTEL ROOMS WERE PAID FOR BY THE HOTEL FOR THE FOLLOWING GUESTS:

NAME OF GUEST & TIME OF ARRIVAL	COMPANY	RELOCATION (Hotel)	TYPE OF RES. (Assured, Gtd.)	*REASON WALKED	**GUEST REACTION

ORIGINAL – Retain for hotel file
YELLOW   – Send to Hyatt Hotels Corporate office
            Attention: Rooms Division Director

*Sales pick-up greater than block; miscount; low no-show; computer error (explain)
**Irate; accepted situation; other

Courtesy of Seattle Hyatt House, Seattle, WA.

111

6. *"Hold for arrival" mail is not delivered.* This can be overcome through a two-step procedure: (1) Mail and messages arriving before the guest are placed in alphabetical order, marked "arriving on (date)," and a cross-notation is placed on the reservations card. (2) When the guest checks in, the clerk spots the notation and hands the item to the guest.

7. *The guest's credit is not verified and bills cannot be collected.* The establishment of guest credit is an integral part of the check-in procedures. No guest should be roomed unless this step is completed satisfactorily. In case of doubt, the clerk must consult with the supervisor.

8. *Luggage is sent to the wrong room.* Desk clerks and door and bell attendants work hand-in-hand in processing luggage from the door to the room. Names and room numbers must be verified at every step.

9. *Rates quoted by travel agents do not match those cited by the hotel when the guest checks in.* The quoted rate, if it is in writing from a travel agent, should be honored.

10. *Employees are not aware of guest services.* As primary sales representatives, desk clerks must be familiar with the details of laundry, valet, room service, transportation, recreation, and so forth, and be able to advise and "sell" the guest whenever appropriate.

11. *Rooms are not properly cleaned.* Quality performance in the first place and thorough checking by supervisory staff afterwards are the only way this can be avoided. Any guest comments alluding to guestroom problems must be forwarded to the executive housekeeper.

12. *Room attendants fail to report room deficiencies,* such as missing amenities, nonfunctioning TV, plugged drain, inadequately stocked minibar, incomplete cleaning. Clerks also hear of problems, either by direct complaints, requests for room change, or incidental conversation of the "how are you enjoying your stay" type. Any problem pertaining to the quality of services and facilities must be investigated and reported to people who can fix it. A log entry and follow up are essential.

[1]"50 Common Errors in the operation of hotels and motels," *Quality Assurance II.*

This and other quality assurance articles are available from the Educational Institute, The American Hotel & Motel Association, 1407 South Harrison Road, East Lansing, MI 48823.

PREREGISTRATION

For convention and tour groups, as well as return customers, some hotels arrange for preregistration of guests. From the information on file, a registration card is typed up for each guest. The arriving guests need only sign their card; room and folio number are added by the clerk. Figure 3.14 shows a preregistration envelope given to a returning guest. The following steps describe a typical group registration:

1. Group bookings are usually made well in advance. The tour guide, travel agent, or convention organizer provides the hotel with a guest list, containing names, desired types of room (singles, doubles, twins, etc.).

2. On the morning of arrival, rooms are blocked off on the room rack, and keys are sorted.

3. Either individual or group registration cards are made out, so that guests need only sign their names when they arrive.

4. If group billing is to be used, an account is opened; no individual charges will be allowed.

5. If requested, individual accounts are opened, and information and room rack slips are made ready.

6. On arrival, a separate counter (or table) is set up in the lobby, away from the main desk to minimize traffic congestion.

7. Upon arrival of a tour, the escort comes to the desk, signs on behalf of the group, or takes the list for signatures to the bus.

8. Each guest receives an envelope with a note saying something like, ''Welcome to the Park International Hotel,'' a key, charge instructions, tour or convention details, map of the city, and so forth.

9. Bell attendants stand by to take guests and their luggage to their rooms in small groups. (Rooms should have been blocked in a way that keeps the members of the group close together.)

10. The switchboard is informed of the arrival by either individual slips or a tour list.

11. Departments that are affected by the arrival of the group are informed. They may be banquets, restaurants, room services, housekeeping, recreation facilities, cashiers, and security.

SAFEKEEPING OF GUEST PROPERTY

At any time during a stay, a guest may request the use of a safety deposit box. Some hotels offer in-room safes, either free of charge, coin operated, or charged electronically to the guest's account. Other properties provide, as they are required to do by most state and provincial laws, a safety deposit box near the front desk. Guests are issued a key, which, in conjunction with a front office master key, opens and locks their individual steel box. The guest signs a safe deposit agreement (Fig. 3.23), which spells out the procedures for use and surrender of the box.

Figure 3.23
Safe deposit agreement.

SEATTLE HYATT HOUSE

SAFE DEPOSIT AGREEMENT

Date _____ 19 ___

Safe Box No. _____

Guest Name _____ Room No _____

PRINT LAST NAME FIRST

Permanent Address _____

THE USE OF THIS SAFE DEPOSIT BOX IS SUBJECT TO THE RULES PRINTED BELOW

1. Safe deposit boxes are available only to registered guests of The Seattle Hyatt House and to those persons approved by such guests and whose signature appears below on this safe deposit agreement. Where the use of a safe is authorized in the name of two or more persons, it is deemed to be under the control of each of them as fully as if it were in his name alone. Either may have access alone or may surrender the safe.

2. The Seattle Hyatt House is hereby released from any liability whatever arising from the loss of the key or the presentation thereof by a person other than one authorized herein. Safe deposit keys must be surrendered at the time of checkout. A charge of $50.00 will be made for a key lost or carried away and not returned. Liability is limited to $500.00 for loss by theft or otherwise where such items are delivered for deposit in the hotel safe or other depository, unless there is a special agreement in writing to the contrary.

3. A safe deposit box will be considered abandoned if the key is not surrendered at the time of checkout or within three (3) days thereafter unless within such period the key is returned to the Seattle Hyatt House receives notice in writing that it has been lost. Abandoned boxes will be opened at the guest's expense.

4. The Seattle Hyatt House does not take possession of property deposited in safe deposit boxes. Deposits therein shall in no event constitute bailment.

I have this day surrendered my Safe Deposit Box and have removed the contents in good order.

Date _____ 19 ___

Signed _____

Guest

Guest Signature _____
Signature of person (s) authorized to have access to Guest Box.

_____

Approval of Guest (full signature) to above authorization

Courtesy of the Seattle Hyatt House, Seattle, WA.

ROOM CHANGE

If guests for any reason during their stay are moved into another room, all departments concerned must be informed with a change slip similar to that in Figure 3.24. Changes must be made on racks and files, including room rack, information rack, and guest folio.

GUEST MAIL

In recent years, the volume of hotel guest mail handled by the desk has dropped drastically. Most people use the telephone to communicate, and the typical stay in city hotels is down to between one and two nights. Some hotels still maintain a separate "key and mail" station at the desk; more commonly, this function is part of the desk clerk's overall job. The following procedures apply to most situations:

1. Incoming mail is routed to the manager's office, where it is separated into guest mail, hotel mail, personal correspondence, and so forth.

Figure 3.24
Room and rate change slip.

Four Seasons Hotel
NEWPORT BEACH

ROOM & RATE CHANGE

N⁰ 1244

NAME _____

FROM ROOM _____ TO ROOM _____

FROM RATE _____ TO RATE _____

DATE OF CHANGE _____

REASON _____

_____

RECEPTIONIST _____

BELL ATTENDANT _____

Courtesy of Four Seasons Hotel, Newport Beach, CA.

2. Guest mail arriving at the desk is time-stamped and sorted as soon as possible.

3. If the guest is registered, the mail is placed in the mail slot and a message is sent to the guest either by personal contact or through the message light on the guest's telephone. Several up-market establishments, including Four Seasons Hotels and Meridian Hotels, have eliminated the mail and key rack that traditionally served as backdrop decor of the front desk (Fig. 3.25). Messages and letters are not kept in mail slots. Instead, they are delivered directly to the guests' rooms.

4. If the guest has left the hotel, the cancelled registration card or the guest history file is checked to determine the guest's home address. Many hotels keep a list of mail forwarded, in case there is a query about this mail later. If no forwarding address can be found, the letter is stamped ''Not At This Address—Please Return.''

5. If the guest has not arrived but holds a reservation, the item is placed in an alphabetically sectioned holding rack (usually at the bottom row

Figure 3.25
Mail and key rack.

of the regular mail rack). A note is put on the reservation form so that the clerk who checks the person in can locate the mail.

Telegrams, special delivery letters, and similarly urgent matters must be delivered by bell attendant immediately. If the guest is out, a note similar to Figure 3.26 is left in the room. Most guest room telephones have a message light that is controlled from the switchboard. Turned on and flashing, it indicates to the guest that a message is waiting at the desk. A control panel at the message desk indicates the room number by a blinking light. When the guest telephones for the message, it is relayed or delivered, and the message light is turned off.

COMPUTERIZED REGISTRATION

With the help of a computer, registration can begin during the night before the guest arrives, when registration cards, key envelopes for preregistered guests, VIP lists, and arrival lists are prepared at the touch of a few keys. Cashiering functions may be combined with the registration program to permit cross-training of desk clerks and cashiers. Rooming details, such as guest history, reservations data, room status reports, and housekeeping activities, are available on the terminal screen or through printouts. The room rack is eliminated and with it the laborious task of typing and monitoring room and information slips. Communications between housekeeping and the front desk can be automatic: notifications of room completion can be sent to the desk instantly to maintain room inventories.

Figure 3.26
Standard form used to inform a guest to contact the front office.

Room ________ **Date** ______________________________

M ____

Please inquire at Front Office for:

☐ **PACKAGE**
☐ **TELEGRAM**
☐ **REGISTERED LETTER**
☐ **SPECIAL DELIVERY LETTER**

☐ ____

Courtesy of the Sheraton-Landmark Hotel, Vancouver, BC.

Figure 3.27
Registration menu.

```
              HOTEL UNITED STATES COMPUSYSTEM II        (LVL 11B.6)
                    FRONT OFFICE & CASHIER
    ---------------------------------------------------------------
     1.  REGISTRATION OR CHANGE
     2.  ROOM SELECTION
     3.  ROOM TRANSFERS                   PRINTED REPORTS
     4.  MAIL / MESSAGE CALL           13. REGISTERED GUEST LEDGER
     5.  ROOM STATUS OVERRIDE          14. ROOM STATUS REPORT
     6.  CANCEL 6PM ARRIVALS
     7.  GROUP BILLING
                                             C A S H I E R
         VIDEO DISPLAYS
     8.  NAME SEARCH                    15. ENTER OR VOID CHARGES
     9.  GUEST FILE DISPLAY            16. PRINT.DISPLAY.CHECK OUT FOLIO
    10.  ROOM FILE DISPLAY             17. REVERSE A CHECKOUT
    11.  DISPLAY ROOM RATE TABLES      18. TRANSFER A FOLIO
    12.  AVAILABILITY DISPLAYS         19. PRINT (DISPLAY) SHIFT AUDIT
                                      (CR) HOTEL MENU

    ---------------------------------------------------------------
           10-04-85      3:07 AM     TERMINAL 00     SELECT:
```

To start the registration procedure, the clerk calls the appropriate menu to the screen (Fig. 3.27) and selects certain functions. Some are explained in detail here:

Registration

The clerk uses this function to register guests into the hotel or to modify information on those already in. Options include:

- Checking in a guest with a reservation.
- Walking in a guest.
- Preregistering groups.
- Multiple rooms check-ins.
- Room assignment, either automatically or as chosen by the clerk.
- Fixed, recurring guest charges (such as parking or use of a rollaway bed) may be indicated during check-in.

Room Selection

This function replaces the room rack. Computerized Lodging Systems' search mode, called *Fastcheck*, prepares a file during the preceding night, listing only those rooms expected to become available during the next day, sorted in order of room type and highest room rate. Room selection options include:

- Selection of room type, clean or dirty rooms, special features, and floors.
- Temporary blocking of single rooms or groups of rooms.

Room Transfers

If a guest asks to be moved, or if in-house circumstance requires a transfer, all folio information and charges can be moved from one room to another. Room selection is done either automatically or as specified by the clerk, and a request can be sent to housekeeping for an inspection of the original room.

Cancel 6:00 P.M. arrivals

The clerk can review all 6:00 P.M. or nonguaranteed arrivals for today and either automatically cancel them or review them for individual cancellation. The cancelled reservations remain on file for possible check-in later, if vacancies still exist. The released rooms are returned to the computer's inventory of available rooms.

Name Search

This program searches guests by name, going through current registrations and future reservations. The screen will show all names fitting the name limitations entered.

File Displays

One display allows any guest folio, in-house or checked out, to be accessed by name, room, or folio number. Another shows the front-office and housekeeping status of a room, room rates, and names and folio balances of guests who are presently checked in and those who have checked out of that room.

KEY TERMS

Room assignment	Folio
Space available sheet	Bucket
Room rack	Corporate rate

Commercial rate	Overbooking
Airline rate	DNS
Day rate	DNA
Government rate	RNA
Complimentary rate	Walking a guest
European plan (E.P.)	Walk-in
American plan (A.P.)	Preregistration
Modified American plan (M.A.P.)	Housekeeper's report
Salesmanship	Maid's report
Selling the whole hotel	Discrepancy report
Upselling	Double locked
Registration	DND
Credit check	OOO
Rooming	"No information"
Hall porter	VIP
Bell attendant	SPATT
Room attendant	DG
Bellman call sheet	Skip
Room slip	Sleeper
Information slip	*Fastcheck*

ACTIVITIES

1. Chart the steps in the rooming process of a hotel you visit, and explain the clerk's function at each step. How do they differ from those described in this chapter? How are they similar?

2. "Desk clerks are the number one salespersons of a hotel." Explain this to a novice desk clerk. Illustrate your answer with examples.

3. Design a registration form that conforms with the legal requirements of your state or province.

4. What problems might you encounter when establishing a guest's credit during check-in? How would you handle such problems?

5. Convince a bellman that his job involves more than carrying luggage. Demonstrate that he is an integral part of the front-office team.

6. Survey local hotels (by telephone or personal visit) and find out whether they offer plans other than the European plan.

ASSIGNMENTS

A. Contact the person in charge of a hotel front desk. Select an establishment that is most like the one you would like to work for. Explain that you are studying front-office procedures and wish to come and visit behind the scenes at a time most convenient to the operation. You will find that hospitality people tend to be receptive to such requests. Once there, ask to be shown how the guest services cycle works, from reservation to rooming. Prepare specific questions to ask, perhaps by using the headings in this chapter as your guide. Listen, observe, and ask questions. If there are forms that you would like to see, ask for them.

Immediately after the visit, review your prepared questions and record the answers. Write down additional information which your instructor may have asked you to look for. Your findings could be shared with the class in one of the following ways: Prepare a written report of your visit and describe the step-by-step procedures followed at your chosen operation. Support the details with diagrams and forms if appropriate. Discuss anything different from the description in this book or mentioned by your instructor. Why were there differences? Did they make sense to you? What are the advantages or disadvantages of their procedures?

You will be asked to make a ten-minute presentation during the next class, explaining the main features of the procedures you observed. Expect to answer your classmates' questions during the presentation.

B. A brief case study: Assume that a reservation was pulled at 6:30 P.M. because it had passed the 6:00 P.M. time limit. The guest arrives at 6:45 P.M., explaining that a customs check delayed her at the airport. She demands to check in. You have no vacancies; in fact, you are two rooms short. Describe in detail your approach to this situation. Anticipate possible snags and objections.

Roleplay your solution with others in the training group and discuss the differing approaches you observe.

CHAPTER FOUR

GUEST ACCOUNTING

OBJECTIVES

The purpose of this chapter is to:

- Explain the basic front-office accounting functions.
- Illustrate computerized guest accounting.
- List the duties of a cashier.
- Describe methods of account settlement.
- Show how to process credit cards.
- Summarize end-of-shift procedures for cashiers.

INTRODUCTION

As soon as possible after the guest has completed the check-in process, the accounting machinery is set into motion. If a computer is at work, an electronic folio will be generated. Otherwise, a guest account is typewritten on a pre-printed form. As the guest settles in and begins to use the hotel's services, charges and credits are *posted* to the folio, either electronically from points of sale into the computer or manually by way of *vouchers* and a *posting machine*. Later, at the "end" of the business day, a *night audit* is performed to verify the day's transactions and to generate *management reports*. Just before the guest departs, the folio is updated and presented for *settlement*. Accounts may be settled in a variety of ways, from cash to credit card to personal check to third-party billing.

Certain components are part of *any* front-office accounting system, whether it is based on hand-written entries, an electronic posting machine, or a computerized system. In this chapter, basic elements are first explained in the context of an electronic posting machine, later illustrated with a computer application.

BASIC ELEMENTS

Front-office accounting systems must do three things:

1. Provide effective internal controls.
2. Maintain accurate accounts of guest charges and credits.
3. Produce analytical reports of the operations.

The concept of internal control means protecting the hotel against dishonest employees, omissions in certain input data, and inaccuracies during the accounting process. Should an employee be suspected of the theft of cash, or a charge be posted to the wrong guest account, the front office accounting system should be capable of identifying such an event. A hotel's cash flow is influenced by the amount of time that passes between when a guest incurs a charge and when the hotel receives payment for it. Management needs accurate statistics and financial reports to make effective operating decisions. The night audit produces the bulk of such statistics, along with the daily transcript of front-office debits and credits.

Figure 4.1 illustrates the accounting cycle. As guests use the services of the hotel, they incur charges for which the hotel is extending credit. Such credit is given based on the guest's credit rating, as established earlier; and the assumption that payment will be made within a reasonable length of time. Examples of such guest charges are:

Room: the rate charged for the use of a guest room, either overnight or for a portion of the day.

Tax: where applicable, a room or sales tax.

Restaurant: for food and beverages consumed in the dining room, banquet rooms, coffee shop, and from room service.

Beverages: for drinks consumed in the cocktail lounge, cabaret, or room service.

Laundry: for personal laundry being handled by the hotel on behalf of the guest, either done on the premises or sent out.

Valet: usually for dry cleaning, but also for mending, ironing, and so forth done by the housekeeping department.

Telephone: for local telephone calls made from the guest's room, usually plus a service charge.

Figure 4.1
Guest accounting cycle.

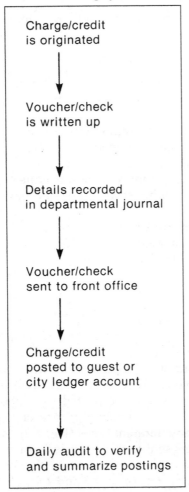

Charge/credit
is originated

↓

Voucher/check
is written up

↓

Details recorded
in departmental journal

↓

Voucher/check
sent to front office

↓

Charge/credit
posted to guest or
city ledger account

↓

Daily audit to verify
and summarize postings

Paid Out: money paid out by the desk on behalf of the guest for services rendered to him, such as gratuities (tips), payment to in-house shops, and delivery charge for parcels.

Miscellaneous: for recreational facilities used, telegrams sent, service charges, or any other charges for which there is no more specific classification.

Hotels customarily set a *floor limit* for the amount of charges that can be accumulated by a guest. As this limit is approached, the person is asked for part or full payment.

Accounts maintained at the front office fall into two categories of *accounts receivable:*

1. *Transient guest* accounts, for persons currently registered and staying at the hotel.

2. *City ledger* accounts, for the following nonguest customers:

    a. Accounts of guests who have left the hotel and have charged their account balance to their company or employer or to a nonbank credit card.
    b. Accounts of businesses who use the hotel's services and to whom billing privileges have been extended.
    c. Accounts of individuals or companies that have used the hotel's facilities for renting meeting rooms or for a banquet.
    d. Accounts of skips (those who left the hotel and have not paid their bills).
    e. Credit balance accounts (reservation deposits).
    f. Hold accounts (accounts of guests who left the hotel for a few days and plan to return to complete their stay).

SOURCE DOCUMENTS

To keep the front-office accounts up to date, all charges and credits must be posted to guest and house accounts quickly and accurately. Hotels use a variety of *source documents* to inform the desk personnel of charges and credits.

The *voucher* is a written record of a charge or a credit, occasionally with a guest's signature (in food and beverage service, for instances), used to inform the front desk that credits and debits must be posted to a folio. As historical documents, vouchers serve as backup documents in case of a guest query or accounting foul-up. Hotels use many different types (Fig. 4.2). A record is kept (*a department journal*) of all vouchers sent to the front desk for posting.

Guest accounts, commonly referred to as *folios,* are either custom designed for a hotel or purchased as standard forms (Figs. 4.3 and 4.4). They are prenumbered for control purposes and have a space at the top where desk clerks type certain information once the guest has registered.

POSTING MACHINES

Since the 1920s, motor-driven posting machines made by the NCR company had been the dominant front-office machines. Initially, the NCR 2000 model set the norm for the industry; 50 years later its successor, the 4200, continued that tradition. In the early 1970s, NCR ceased production of the NCR 4200 (Fig. 4.5), which had become a trusty companion to generations of desk clerks around the world. It is hard to imagine any of today's gadgets experiencing such a long life. With the NCR 4200 machine, each voucher was delivered by hand or pneumatic

Figure 4.2
Sample hotel vouchers.

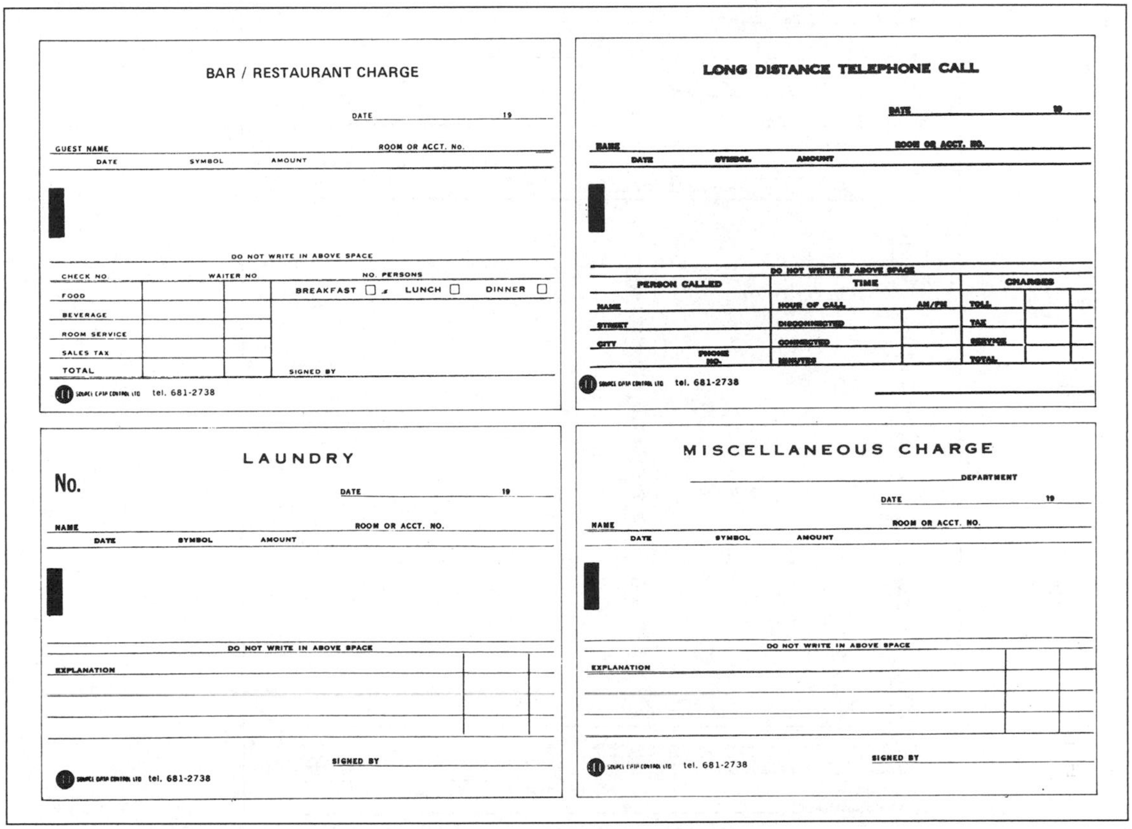
BAR / RESTAURANT CHARGE

DATE ______ 19__

GUEST NAME ______ ROOM OR ACCT. No. ______

DATE | SYMBOL | AMOUNT

DO NOT WRITE IN ABOVE SPACE

CHECK NO. ______ WAITER NO. ______ NO. PERSONS ______

FOOD

BEVERAGE

ROOM SERVICE

SALES TAX

TOTAL

BREAKFAST ☐ LUNCH ☐ DINNER ☐

SIGNED BY ______

tel. 681-2738

LONG DISTANCE TELEPHONE CALL

DATE ______ 19__

NAME ______ ROOM OR ACCT. NO. ______

DATE | SYMBOL | AMOUNT

DO NOT WRITE IN ABOVE SPACE

PERSON CALLED	TIME		CHARGES	
NAME	HOUR OF CALL	AM/PM	TOLL	
STREET	DISCONNECTED		TAX	
CITY	CONNECTED		SERVICE	
PHONE NO.	MINUTES		TOTAL	

tel. 681-2738

LAUNDRY

No.

DATE ______ 19__

NAME ______ ROOM OR ACCT. NO. ______

DATE | SYMBOL | AMOUNT

DO NOT WRITE IN ABOVE SPACE

EXPLANATION

SIGNED BY ______

tel. 681-2738

MISCELLANEOUS CHARGE

______ DEPARTMENT

DATE ______ 19__

NAME ______ ROOM OR ACCT. NO. ______

DATE | SYMBOL | AMOUNT

DO NOT WRITE IN ABOVE SPACE

EXPLANATION

SIGNED BY ______

tel. 681-2738

tube to the desk, there to be posted. A clerk (large hotels had specialized posting clerks or machine operators) took a folio, punched the previous account balance into the machine, then posted debit and credit transactions, one at a time. The machine printed the details on the voucher and the folio and kept an ongoing record on the audit tape (Figs. 4.6, 4.7, 4.8).

At the end of a posting, the machine added the account total and printed it on the folio. The machine, in the process, did not keep track of individual guests' balances, but accumulated totals for each department. If a posting error was made, the folio was inserted, the last balance picked up, and the erroneous amount taken off by way of a compensating posting (a credit for a false charge and a debit for an incorrect credit) (Figs. 4.9 and 4.10). The machine was incapable of adjusting the running departmental total (the laundry department, in this case). A correction sheet was used to record each such incident (Fig. 4.11) and required a manual deduction at the end of the day's business.

Figure 4.3
Guest folio with registration card attached.

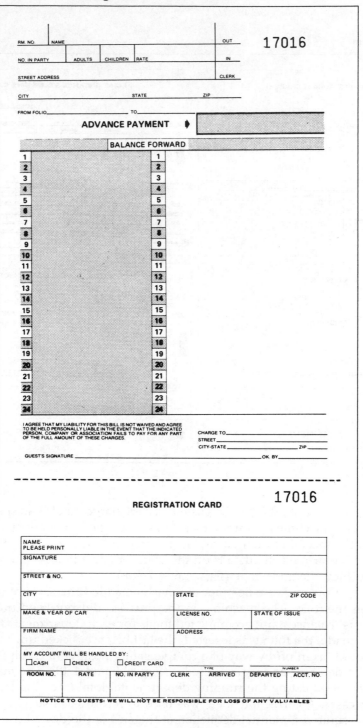

Figure 4.4
Guest folio for use with computerized guest accounting system.

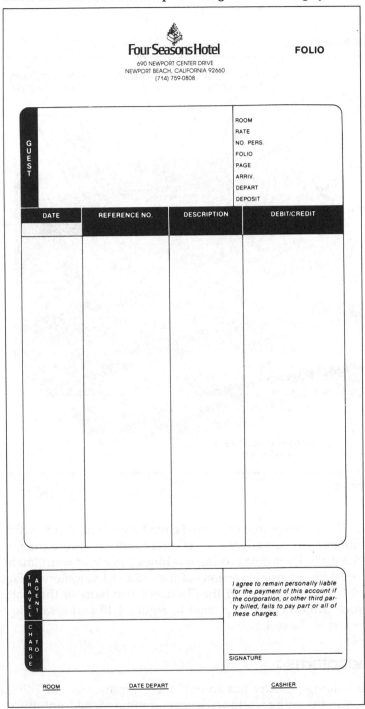

Courtesy of Four Seasons Hotels, Newport Beach, CA.

Figure 4.5
NCR 4200 posting machine.

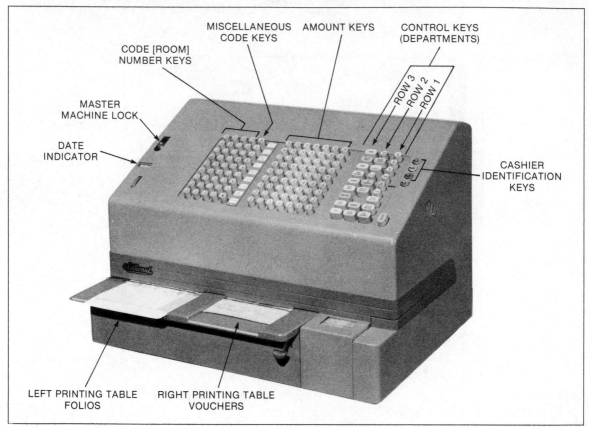

Courtesy of NCR Corporation.

The development of printed circuit boards made the 4200 obsolete. Several manufacturers rushed into the market to try to capture the position abandoned by the 4200. Electronic posting machines came and went, many little more than spruced-up electronic versions of the old mechanical ones. Figure 4.12 shows a machine typical of one of the electronic survivors of that battle. The *audit trail* of such a machine is illustrated in Figure 4.13 and a sample report of a day's business in Table 4.1.

COMPUTERIZED ACCOUNTING

The lodging industry has entered the computer age. In 1979, an estimated 175 hotels in the entire world were using computerized front-office systems. A mere seven years later, two out of every three hotels had installed them. Hoteliers

Figure 4.6
Guest folio imprinted by a posting machine.

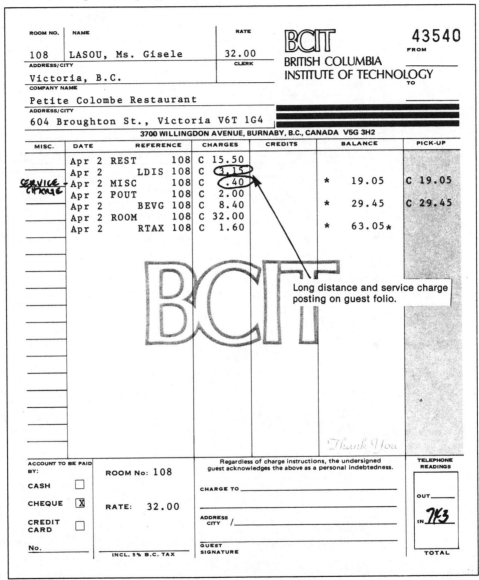

Long distance and service charge posting on guest folio.

Figure 4.7
Voucher imprinted by a posting machine, showing long distance telephone charge.

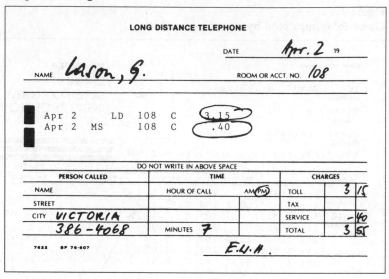

Figure 4.8
Audit tape showing long distance telephone charge.

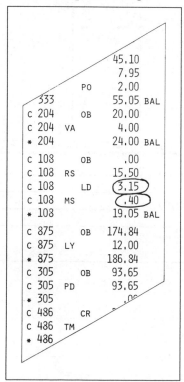

Figure 4.9
Folio showing correction posting.

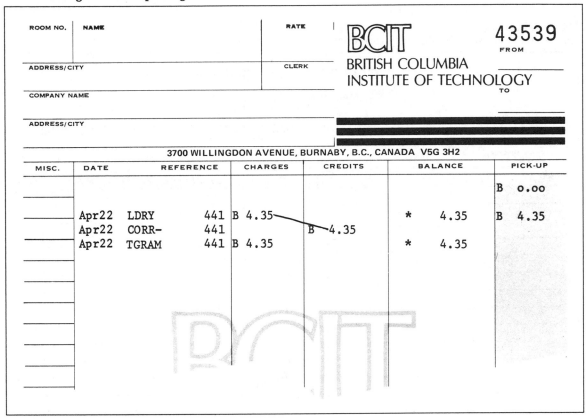

Figure 4.10
Voucher showing correction posting.

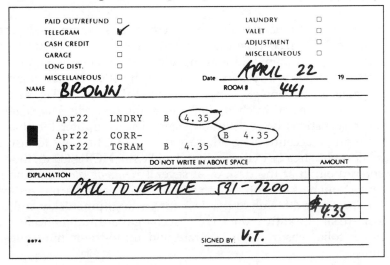

Figure 4.11
Correction sheet showing laundry correction.

CORRECTION SHEET

MACHINE NO._____
(WRITE SMALL AND NEAT)

CASHIER:—ENTER BELOW MEMORANDA ON OVERCREDITS, OVERCHARGES AND WRONG DEPARTMENT
KEY REGISTRATIONS. TO BE USED IN CONNECTION WITH DR. AND CR. CORRECTION
SLIPS. ONE SHEET DAILY FOR EACH MACHINE.

ROOM NO.	VOUCHER NO.	NAME	AMOUNT POSTED	CORRECT AMOUNT	AMOUNT OF ERROR	DEPT. KEY DEDUCTION	EXPLANATION OF ERROR	OPER- ATOR
441		BROWN	4 35	—	4 35	LDRY	should be TGRAM	Re.

replaced electronic machines with computers; some made the jump directly from an NCR 4200–type to a computer system. The number of manufacturers has multiplied manyfold and includes such names as ECCO, HIS, and CLS.[1] With computerized systems, the flow of the guest accounting process (Fig. 4.14) is similar to the one explained earlier in this chapter (Fig. 4.1).

As explained in chapters 2 and 3, the *electronic folio* is generated at either the reservations or registration stage. The computer terminal leads the clerk through an account-generating routine, prompting her to insert relevant information not already in the system. Unlike the NCR 4200 method, charges can be entered either at the desk or at several *points-of-sale* throughout the hotel. Because vouchers do not have to be physically carried from restaurant, bar, room service, or health club to the desk for posting, time delay and possible revenue loss are significantly reduced. Guest charges are automatically added to the electronic folio, ensuring an accurate and up-to-the-minute guest account at all times.

Figure 4.12
NCR 250 posting machine.

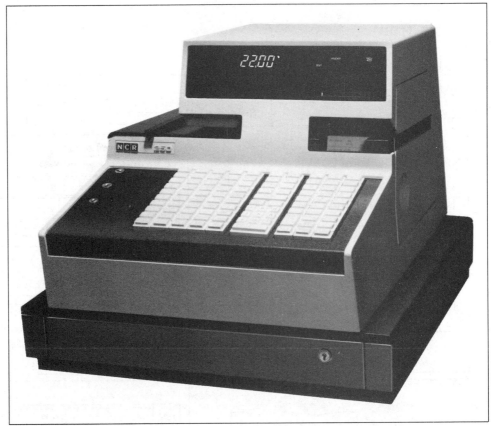

Courtesy of NCR Corporation.

Another drastic change has occurred in the auditing of daily accounts. In a 300-room hotel, for instance, a team of two night auditors used to spend four to eight hours each night posting all late charges, local phone calls, and room and tax charges to each folio, one at a time. The chance of omissions, accidental or deliberate, was considerable. Posting errors made during the preceding 16 hours, whether they had been recorded on the correction sheet or were imbedded in the thousands of transactions that had occurred, had to be ferreted out and corrected. Departmental totals of vouchers had to be balanced against the totals the machines had accumulated. The auditors' shift was not over until all this had been accomplished; often, the night crew stayed into the next morning, checking and rechecking the large volume of individual postings.

Compare that with the amazingly simple night-audit package that is part of the CLS system. To perform an adequate audit, the auditor need only print

Figure 4.13
NCR 250 audit trail.

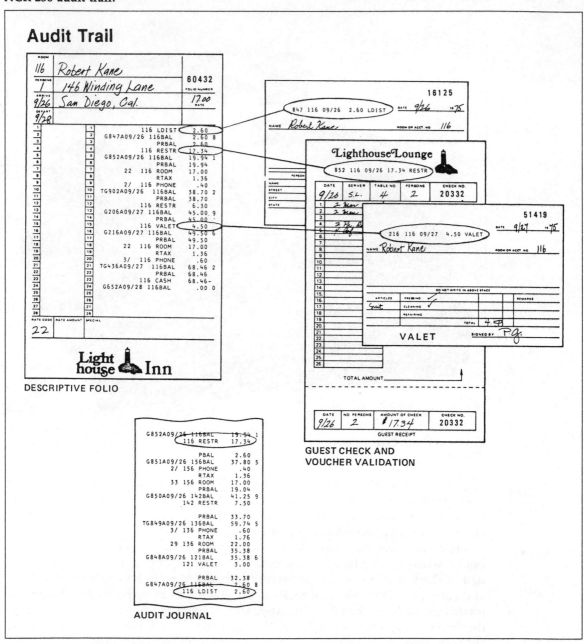

Courtesy of NCR Corporation.

Table 4.1
Report of a day's business.

REVENUE REPORT REPORT = 52				
Rest Ct./Prog. Change/Offline Ct.	Z		206 121	C
Trans. Ct./Term. No Sale/Cashier No Sale	Z		534 52 26	C
1C. Exempt Room Charge	Z	1	23.50	1C
2C. TXBL. Room Charge	Z	198	3390.00	2C
3C. TOTAL ROOM CHARGES	Z		3413.50	3C
4C. Room Tax (10%)	Z		339.00	4C
5C. Special Room Tax (5%)	Z	1	1.18	5C
6C. Local Phone	Z	180	36.00	6C
7C. Long Distance	Z	12	53.55	7C
8C. Restaurant & Bar	Z	20	568.65	8C
9C. Valet/Laundry	Z	24	13.00	9C
10C. Misc. Charges	Z	1	9.30	10C
11C. Banquet	Z	2	2667.43	11C
12C. CASH MDSE SALES	Z	3	42.09	12C
13C. Cigars/Cigarettes	Z		7.85	13C
14C. Photocopies	Z		2.64	14C
15C. Newspapers	Z		1.84	15C
16C. Candy	Z		.59	16C
17C. Toiletries	Z		.69	17C
18C. Magazines	Z		1.00	18C
19C. Jewelry	Z		.59	19C
20C. Novelties	Z		.89	20C
21C. Gift Certificates	Z		.00	21C
22C. Books	Z		26.00	22C
Terminal No./Cashier No./Data/Consect. No.	10001		1A 9/09/89	1065

a report of deposits transferred (taking no more than two minutes), enter credit-card charge codes, and then push one button, causing the computer to generate the entire audit automatically. Figures 4.15, 4.16, and 4.17 are just three of the many reports available. At the completion of the audit, the auditor need only change the date to establish the next day's starting routine, including printing the next day's registration cards. Figure 4.18 shows a menu screen available to the auditor.

CHECKING OUT

This section describes the ways a guest account can be settled during the check-out process. In the days of the posting machine, the clerk asked, ''Are there any late charges?'' before presenting the account to the guest. It could have been,

Figure 4.14
Flow chart of computerized guest accounting cycle.

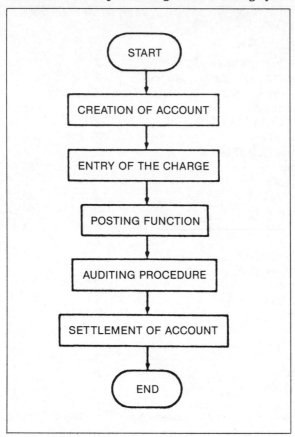

Reprinted with permission of M. Kasavana, *Hotel Information Systems*, p. 195.

for instance, that the guest had just finished breakfast and the coffee shop check had not reached the desk for posting. Similarly, local and long distance telephone, room service, and laundry charges might have been outstanding. After some delay, these were posted to the folio and the statement ready for settlement.

With a computer check-out, the guest is kept waiting a much shorter time and the chances of missing charges are drastically reduced. Folios are preprinted for guests expected to depart on a given day, and as the guests arrive at the cashier's window for departure, the clerk quickly scans the folio on the screen for late charges (Fig. 4.19), prints a new folio only for those that need updating, and presents the printout (Fig. 4.20). In some properties, the guest has access

Figure 4.15
Room revenue report, room by room.

INA = ONE-BUTTON / #1

ROOM NO	NAME	FOLIO	CHECK IN	CHECK OUT	GUEST TYPE	GROUP CODE	SHARE/WITH	RACK RATE	ROOM RATE	VARIANCE	ROOM TAX	NUMBER RMS	GSTS
00AX	F & B AMERICAN EXP	DB 10079	11-29	11-29	TX			.00	.00	.00	.00		1
00AX	*AMERICAN EXP. ADV , DEPO	DB 10127	12-03	12-03	TX			.00	.00	.00	.00		1
00CA	CASH	DB 10094	11-29	11-29	TX			.00	.00	.00	.00		1
00DC	F & B DINER/CARTE	DB 10093	11-29	11-29	TX			.00	.00	.00	.00		1
0101	RABBIT, JACK	AX 10241	12-06	12-13	TX	G1029		100.00	35.00	55.00-	3.94	1	1
0105	MCCARTHY, ANDREW	DB 50178	12-01	12-03	GR			100.00	55.00	45.00-	6.19	1	1
0201	SAMSTAG, CHERYL	CA 10211	12-01	12-03	TX		10217	100.00	100.00		11.25	1	1
0201	MALONEY, CAL	CA 10217	12-01	12-03	TX		10211	100.00	100.00	100.00	11.25		1
0202	HAMILTON, BOB	AX 10237	10-17	12-15	TX	ESG		100.00	40.00	50.00-	4.50		1
0203	RAMADA, HOTEL	AX 10240	12-02	12-15	TX	ESG		80.00	150.00	70.00	16.88		1
0204	DICK, TRACEY	AX 10102	12-01	12-13	TX			140.00	115.00	25.00-	12.94		3
0207	VALENTINO, RUDOLPH	VI 50538	12-03	12-05	SF			90.00	60.00	30.00-	6.75		1
0301	YANKEE , DOODLE	CA 10222	12-01	12-04	TX			160.00	100.00	60.00-	19.25		3
0303	MOORE, MICHAEL	VI 10004	11-28	12-04	TX			90.00	90.00		18.13		1
0304	BILLARD, GUS	MC 10005	11-28	12-03	TX			160.00	90.00	70.00	18.13		3
0305	*RUDOLPH , VALENTINO	VI 50537	12-03	12-05	SF			90.00	60.00	30.00-	14.75		1
0307	ACKERMAN,	VI 50528	12-02	12-04	GR			80.00		90.00	.00		1
0312	*TEST, GUEST	AX 10242	12-03	12-05	SH	CLS		100.00	100.00		17.25		1
0315	SPACEMAN, BILL	MC 10235	12-01	12-05	TX	TEST		90.00	90.00		18.13		1
0403	*SMITH, JOHN~	CA 10116	12-03	12-05	TX			115.00	90.00	25.00-	10.13		2
0404	GOLDFARB, PHILIP	CO 50531	12-02	12-04	CO	GOLF		115.00	49.50	55.50-	15.80		2
0409	SPACEMAN, BILL	MC 10226	12-01	12-05	TX	TEST		90.00	90.00		10.13		1
0410	FEDERATED , FRED	CA 10216	12-01	12-04	TX			115.00	70.00	25.00-	10.13		2
0415	YOURSELF, YOU	CO 50529	12-02	12-04	CO	GOLF		115.00	49.50	65.50-	15.80		2
0502	MANNY, LEON	AX 50141	11-29	12-04	TX			80.00	60.00	20.00-	6.75		1
0503	ROLANDS, JOE	AX 50141	11-29	12-04	TX			70.00	60.00		6.75		2
0505	ROBINSON, MARY	CO 50530	12-02	12-04	CO	GOLF		115.00	49.50	65.50-	15.80		2
0507	HOLLYE, M/M MIKE	AX 50137	11-29	12-12	TX			115.00	85.00	30.00-	9.56		2
0515	ACKERMAN, JOLENE	VI 10229	12-01	12-11	TX			70.00	70.00		10.13		2
0606	FRAZIER, DOUG	VI 10047	11-29	12-03	TX			100.00	75.00	25.00-	8.44		1
0510	LACKNER, MELINDA	DC 10057	11-29	12-03	TX			100.00	115.00	15.00	12.94		1
0704	KENNEDY, ED	AX 10056	11-27	12-03	TX			100.00	162.00	62.00	18.23		1
0705	MANCILLA, MARVIN	MC 10058	11-29	12-04	TX			90.00	60.00	30.00-	6.75		1
0706	PORCELLO, LUCY	VI 10060	11-29	12-03	TX			100.00	80.00	20.00-	9.00		1
0707	TURNER, ANNE	AX 10065	11-29	12-03	TX			90.00	60.00	30.00-	6.75		1
0708	PEEK , JERRY	VI 10009	11-28	12-03	TX			115.00	100.00	15.00-	11.25		2
0803	*JONES, BOB	VI 50527	12-03	12-04	C1			90.00		90.00	.00		1
0805	*WILLIAMS , HANK	AX 50535	12-03	12-04	TX			90.00	60.00	30.00-	6.75		1
0901	TWEDT, KIRSTON	AX 10069	11-27	12-07	TX			100.00	162.00	62.00	18.23		1
0904	HOFFA, JIMMY	VI 10230	12-01	12-03	TX	TEST		150.00	100.00	50.00-	11.25		2
0907	WILLIAMSON, BILL	AX 10086	11-29	12-06	TX			115.00	60.00	55.00-	6.75		2
0910	WILLIAMS, BOBBY	DC 10070	11-29	12-04	TX	HONEY		125.00	180.00	55.00	20.25		2
1001	HO, MITCHI	DC 10088	11-29	12-05	TX	HONEY		150.00	180.00	30.00	20.25	1	2
1003	MELTON, OSWELL	DB 10013	11-28	12-29	TX			140.00	100.00	40.00-	11.25	1	3

| T O T A L S : | | | | | | | | 4,175.00 | 3,392.50 | 782.50- | 460.41 | 39 | 58 |

(UNADJUSTED)

Figure 4.16
Room revenue report, statistical summary.

ED SVCS TRAINING HOTEL — PAGE 8 — [ONE-BUTTON] — DECEMBER 3, 1986

ROOM REVENUE REPORT — #4 — 5:20 PM

STATISTICAL SUMMARY

	TODAY	PERCENT	MONTH-T-D	PERCENT	YEAR-T-D	PERCENT
SINGLE OCCUPANCY	22	25.6 %				
MULTIPLE OCCUPANCY	17	19.8 %				
TOTAL OCCUPIED ROOMS	39	45.4 %	948	50.2 %	948	50.2 %
VACANT ROOMS	47	54.7 %	942	49.8 %	942	49.8 %
TOTAL ROOMS	86	100.0 %	1,890	100.0 %	1,890	100.0 %
TOTAL ROOM REVENUE	3,392.50		93,904.88		93,904.88	
AVG RATE/ROOM: (ADR) :	86.99		88.51		88.51	
TOTAL GUESTS	58		1,520		1,520	
AVG RATE / GUEST	58.49		55.20		55.20	
AVG GUEST STAY	6.7 NIGHTS					

OCCUPANCY ANALYSIS		VACANCY ANALYSIS	
REVENUE PRODUCING ROOMS	38	UNSOLD ROOMS	46
COMPLIMENTARY ROOMS	1	OUT OF ORDER ROOMS	1
TOTAL OCCUPIED ROOMS	39	TOTAL VACANT ROOMS	47

Figure 4.17
Daily closing report.

DAILY CLOSING REPORT

5:25 PM

(UPDATING FILES)

SEQ CD	ACCOUNT DESCRIPTION	TODAY			MONTH TO DATE 12-03-85			YEAR TO DATE 12-03-85		
		#CCS	DEBIT	CREDIT	#CCS	DEBIT	CREDIT	#CCS	DEBIT	CREDIT
350 HS	HAIR SALON		.00	.00	5	357.94	.00	6	357.94	.00
355 BS	BARBER SHOP	1	45.75	.00	5	139.76	.00	6	139.76	.00
360 NS	NAIL SALON	1	12.50	.00	5	4,536.50	.00	6	4,536.50	.00
365 CH	DAY CARE		.00	.00	5	127.00	.00	5	127.00	.00
370 HH	HEAT WAVE ADMISSION		.00	.00	3	25,750.00	.00	3	25,750.00	.00
375 MA	MASSAGE	2	65.00	.00	9	225.00	.00	8	225.00	.00
	CLUB ACTIVITIES	4	123.25	.00	34	31,146.20	.00	34	31,146.20	.00
400 RT	ROOM TAX	15	142.34	.00	985	7,945.61	.00	996	7,945.61	.00
405 TX	SALES TAX	4	29.70	.00	29	515.02	.00	29	515.02	.00
420 GR	GRATUITY		.00	.00	7	492.25	.00	7	492.25	.00
430 DE	ADVANCE DEPOSIT	2	115.00	.00	110	23,252.00	.00	110	23,252.00	.00
440 CM	COMMISSIONS		.00	.00	12	.00	1,178.00	12	.00	1,178.00
	RETAIL OUTLETS	21	297.04	.00	1144	32,204.98	1,178.00	1144	32,204.98	1,178.00
TOTAL	RECEIPTS:	65	3,995.07	.00	2542	192,146.16	19,392.00	2542	192,146.16	19,392.00
450 CA	CASH	3		340.00	105	.00	29,992.70	105	.00	28,992.70
452 CK	CHECK			.00	19	.00	2,480.00	19	.00	2,480.00
455 CB	CARTE BLANCHE	1		100.00	5	.00	2,205.94	5	.00	2,205.94
460 DC	DINERS CLUB			.00	25	.00	1,732.24	25	.00	1,732.24
465 VI	VISA	5		50.00	25	.00	5,650.70	25	.00	5,560.70
475 AX	AMERICAN EXPRESS	3		.00	134	.00	49,102.14	134	.00	49,102.14
480 CD	CASH DROP			.00	3	.00	.00	3	.00	.00
485 MC	MASTER CHARGE			.00	22	9,900.00	6,062.25	22	9,900.00	6,062.25
495 TP	TIPS PAID OUT			.00	5	68.10	.00	5	68.10	.00
497 PO	PAID OUT: MISCELLANEO			.00	2	50.00	.00	2	50.00	.00
499 RE	PAID OUT: REFUND			.00	11	.00	329.87	11	.00	329.87
	TAXES & GRATUITY	13		500.00	356	10,018.10	96,565.84	356	10,018.10	96,565.84
800 DB	DIRECT BILL			.00		.00	.00		.00	.00
805 TF	TRANSFER FOLIO	4		.00	6	.00	.00	6	.00	.00
810 IL	TRANSFER TO LEDGER	2		414.40	62	.00	59,712.47	62	.00	59,712.47
	AUTO-POSTS TO C/L			95.33		.00	69,033.72		.00	69,033.72
820 TC	TRANSFER CREDIT	1		786.00	2	.00	1,349.00	2	.00	1,349.00
820 TD	TRANSFER DEBIT	2		.00	6	1,349.00	.00	6	1,349.00	.00
825 BF	BALANCE FORWARD			.00		.00	.00		.00	.00
830 AD	ADVANCE DEP TRAN TO L			.00	10	.00	1,090.00	10	.00	1,090.00
	SETTLEMENTS	9		1,495.93	86	1,349.00	131,089.86	86	1,349.00	131,089.86
	NET ADDITION TO GUEST LEDGER			1,989.14		43,629.77-			43,629.77-	
GRAND	TOTALS:	87	1,925.93	1,995.93	2904	203,513.26	203,513.26	2984	203,513.26	203,513.26

Figure 4.18
Computer audit menu.

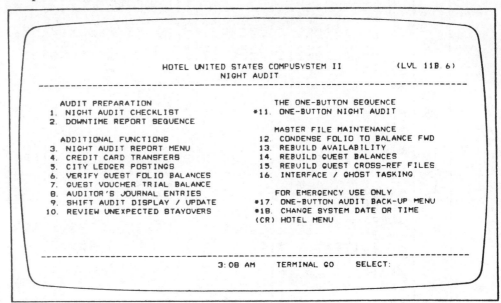

Figure 4.19
Terminal and keyboard located at the front desk.

Courtesy of New World Harbourside Hotel, Vancouver, BC.

Figure 4.20
Computer-generated guest folio.

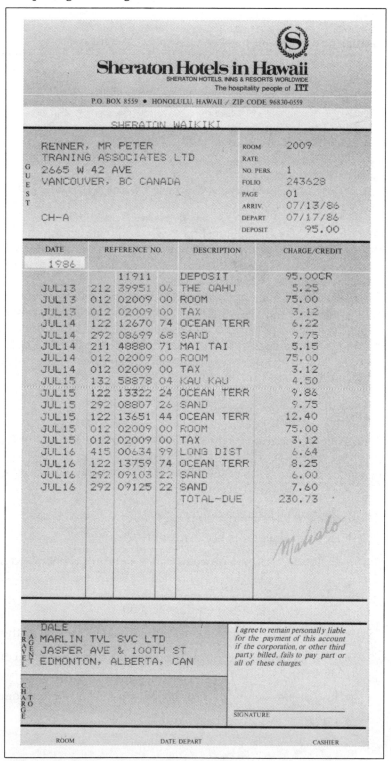

Courtesy of Sheraton Waikiki Hotel, Waikiki, HI.

Table 4.2
Methods of payment for hotel services (North America).*

	Total Region	Canada	United States	Caribbean
Cash	28.8%	30.1%	29.7%	22.0%
Credit Card	49.6	49.7	53.7	25.2
All Other Credit	21.6	20.2	16.6	52.8

*Based on arithmetic mean.
Source: 1986 Worldwide Hotel Industry (New York: Horwath & Horwath), p. 71.

to her folio details on the guest room TV, and by touching the screen or pressing buttons on her telephone can initiate charges to her credit card. In another setting, the guest bypasses the busy desk and goes to an automatic check-out booth, similar to a banking machine.

Guest accounts may be settled in two basic methods: by some form of cash or by credit card (Table 4.2). On the computer, settlement is handled with a few keystrokes. News of the checkout is automatically communicated to housekeeping and points of sale so that no further charges will be accepted for this guest. Folios of departed guests with nonzero balances are transferred to a nonguest ledger and prepared for mailing of invoices.

THE CASHIER'S DUTIES

The cashier, a member of the front-desk team, performs the following duties:

- Posts the charges and cash accounts.
- Keeps the guest accounts current.
- Ascertains charges on check-out.
- Records payments on check-out.
- Follows check-out procedures for different types of payment.
- Handles cash transactions.
- Balances cash at the end of the shift.
- Checks credit cards against bulletins, and obtains authorizations.
- Follows hotel procedures for detection of forged and counterfeit money and checks.
- Looks after safety deposit boxes, keys, and related items.
- Obtains keys upon check-out.

- Obtains forwarding addresses of guests for mail.

- Notifies housekeeping of guests checked out.

- Handles complaints.

Front-office managers prefer to *cross-train* desk employees, requiring each clerk to be proficient in all front-desk functions, from reservations to checkout. This makes staffing schedules more flexible, adds variety to clerks' work routines, and, most importantly, allows for the shifting of personnel as the demands of the front desk change throughout a day.

Miscellaneous Cashier Duties

This section describes an assortment of cashiering tasks that must be performed, both during check-out and as part of daily routines. In computerized systems, transactions are performed based on the clerk's keyboard input. For the purpose of illustration, this section uses examples involving posting machines.

Gratuities or tips. A guest may write "add 15% tip" or "plus $2.00 gratuity" to a check presented by a food and beverage server. The hotel, as a service to guest and staff, pays this money out to the employee. A paid-out voucher (Fig. 4.21) is made out and signed by the waiter. If there are only a few staff paid-out vouchers per day, payment will be made at the front office. If there are many, the cashier in, say, the restaurant, pays out the tips and keeps a record in a departmental journal.

Other paid outs. The hotel may also pay out funds for guests using facilities and shops in the hotel that are not operating departments of the organization. Some properties, for instance, rent out space to a florist, clothing store, hairstylist, travel agent, or newsstand. Registered guests can charge purchases and services to their hotel accounts. A paid-out or petty cash voucher (Fig. 4.22) is issued by the shop, signed by the guest, and sent to the front desk for payment.

A similar situation may arise when a guest requests that the hotel accept a COD delivery in his absence. Examples are courier charges or special deliveries from merchants. Unless the guest is well known to the front desk staff, a prior authorization of the COD by a duty manager is required.

Refund of advance payments. If, upon check-out, a guest's account has a credit balance, the amount must be refunded to the guest. This is done with a paid-out posting for that amount, effectively reducing the account balance to zero.

House paid outs. In some instances, the cashier may be asked to pay out funds on behalf of the hotel. These are called *house paid outs*. They might include emergency payroll disbursements for employees, out-of-pocket expense refunds for management staff, freight bills, or urgently needed purchases for a department,

Figure 4.21
A paid-out voucher.

PAID OUT

No. DATE 19

NAME ROOM OR ACCT. NO.

DATE SYMBOL AMOUNT

DO NOT WRITE IN ABOVE SPACE

EXPLANATION

SIGNED BY

SDC SOURCE DATA CONTROL LTD tel. 681-2738

such as fresh fruit for the kitchen, extra ice cubes for the cocktail lounge, or COD charges for deliveries to the general office.

Cash Receipts

During a typical shift, a cashier takes in more money than is paid out. Receipts fall into several categories.

Deposit payments. Deposit payments are sent by people who have made a reservation. A city ledger account headed "reservation deposits" (Fig. 4.23) is maintained at the desk, and all payments are posted to it. A voucher is made out in multiple copies (Fig. 4.24), one sent to the guest for confirmation, one retained at the cashier's desk, and the other attached to the reservation record. On the day of the guest's arrival, the amount is transferred to a guest folio. Some hotels post reservation deposits immediately to guest folios, which are then kept in a separate section of the bucket awaiting the guest's arrival.

Figure 4.22
A petty cash voucher.

FOUR SEASONS HOTEL NEWPORT BEACH

PETTY CASH VOUCHER

DATE _____ AMOUNT $_____

PAY TO _____
           NAME   DEPT

_____ DOLLARS

FOR _____

_____

CHARGE TO _____ ACCT.

RECEIVED PAYMENT

_____
         HEAD OF DEPT

_____   _____
          MANAGER

Courtesy of Four Seasons Hotel, Newport Beach, CA.

Paid in advance. Guests may be asked to pay in advance for their night's room charge if they are unable to present a credit card or similar credit evidence. The guest is given a receipt (Fig. 4.25). Later in the day, the night clerk posts the room rate and tax, reducing the balance to zero. To avoid being left with unpaid extra amounts, hotels usually issue a "No charge allowed" or "Cash on delivery—COD" notice to departments such as switchboard, restaurants, and cocktail lounge. A guest paying in advance may not bother to formally check out at the desk; as far as he is concerned, his account has been settled. This could present an internal problem, since the removal of the folio and accompanying registration card usually triggers a change on the room rack and a check-out notification to the switchboard and the housekeeping department. The cashier should, therefore, go through the bucket around noon each day and *pull* all advance payment folios. If guests have checked out (which would show on the morning's housekeeping report), the folio is treated as a check-out, time-

Figure 4.23
City ledger account for advance deposits.

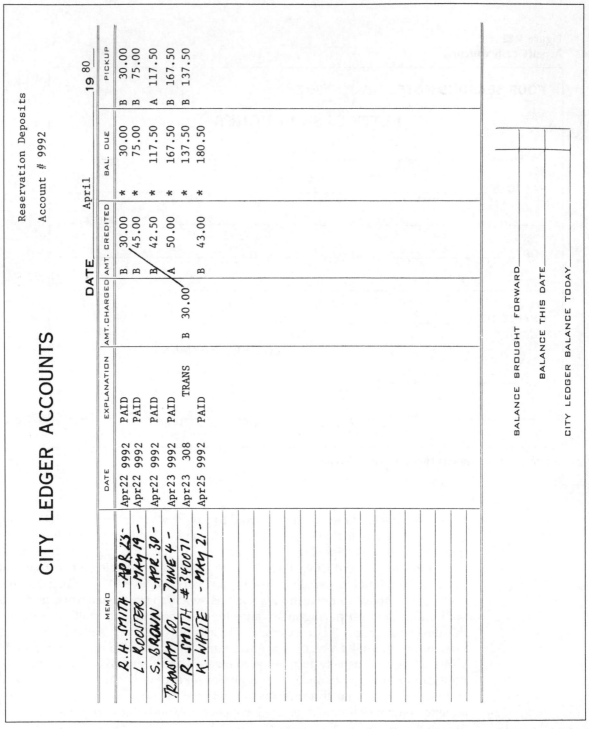

Figure 4.24
Advance-deposit voucher.

TRANSACTION DATE	ARRIVAL DATE	№ 00294	
GUEST NAME		NET REMITTANCE	
		COMMISSION	
		TOTAL	

NAME _____

TA. OR FIRM_____

STREET_____

CITY/STATE_____ ZIP_____

☐ NEW DEPOSIT   ☐ RE-ENTRY   ☐ CASH   BY_____

HYATT HOTELS

NOTES

Advance Deposit

10-19-78 SG

Courtesy of Seattle Hyatt House, Seattle, WA.

stamped, and placed with other zero folios. If the guest is still in the room past the check-out time, a room clerk or supervisor must contact the guest and make arrangements for either departure or an additional night's payment.

CREDIT CARDS

Types

Banks, trust companies and credit unions participate in the offering of such cards as VISA, MasterCard, Barclaycard, Eurocard, and Access. Certain commercial organizations also offer cards, including Diners Club, American Express, Carte Blanche, EnRoute, and JCB International. American Express's Optima

Figure 4.25
Cash receipt voucher.

CASH CREDIT

ACKNOWLEDGMENT IS MADE OF RECEIPT OF AMOUNT PRINTED BELOW.   THIS HAS
BEEN CREDITED TO YOUR ACCOUNT. THANK YOU.

DATE _____ 19 ___

NAME _____   ROOM OR ACCT. NO. _____

DATE	SYMBOL	AMOUNT

DO NOT WRITE IN ABOVE SPACE

☐ BILL NOT PRESENTED WITH PAYMENT

☐ PAYMENT TO APPLY ON ACCOUNT

☐ ADVANCE PAYMENT

SDC SOURCE DATA CONTROL LTD   tel. 681-2738   SIGNED BY _____

card lies halfway between a bank card and a travel card in terms of cardholder
and merchant benefits. Hotels prefer credit cards over personal checks, since
their acceptance is safer and their collection speedier. Table 4.3 shows how credit
card use is distributed in North American hotels.

Credit card companies earn their money in three ways: (1) by charging an
initial membership fee; (2) by charging high interest rates for customer bills paid
after a certain date; and (3) by assessing a fee, which is deducted from the daily
card deposits. Such fees, called *commissions,* are set according to overall sales
volume and range from 2 percent upwards. Some card companies create a delay
between card acceptance and the receipt of the funds. Bank cards are fastest,
debiting the hotel's account the moment the card receipts are deposited. The
American Express Company claims to make payment by mail within three days
of receiving the charge records.

Table 4.3
Distribution of hotel sales and percentage
of credit card use.

Sales Distribution	
Cash Sales	31.9%
Credit Card Sales	51.5
All Other Credit Sales	16.6
Total	100.0%
Percentage of Credit Card Sales by Card	
American Express	47.9%
Visa	26.7
MasterCard	17.3
Diner's Club	6.0
Other	2.1
Total	100.0%

Source: 1986 U.S. Lodging Industry (Philadelphia: Laventhol & Horwath), p. 17.

PREPARING A CHARGE RECORD

The following are a composite of the procedures dictated by most credit card issuers. Guidelines may differ from card to card and clerks must follow the "operating guides" provided for each.

Checking a Card's Validity

Cards may be lost, stolen, expired, or presented by someone other than the legitimate cardholder. Clerks must be vigilant; cards accepted in error will not be honored by the issuing company, while stolen cards recovered may result in a monetary reward to the clerk.

Follow these procedures before accepting a credit card:

1. Determine if the hotel accepts a particular card. Check the genuineness of the card: color symbols, holograms and wording.

2. Check the *bulletin*. Hundreds of cards are listed in bulletins, published weekly by the credit card companies. Fig. 4.26 is a sample page from American Express' cancellation bulletin. If a card is listed, clerks are instructed to hold on to it and telephone the card company's authorization number. Anyone who turns in a listed card is promised a cash reward, typically $25.

Figure 4.26
Cancellation bulletin.

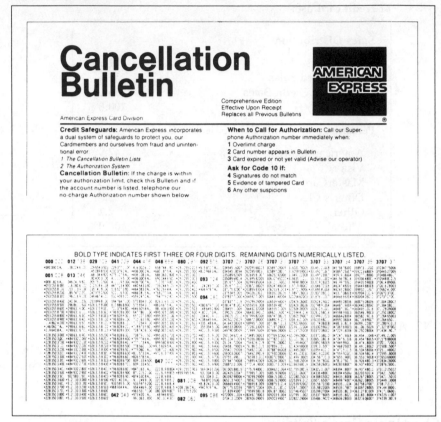

Courtesy of American Express Company.

3. Check the expiration date. Expired cards may be accepted, but must be phoned in for an authorization.

Completing Sales Drafts

Now that the card appears to be acceptable, follow these steps to complete the triplicate set of credit card slips (*sales drafts*).

1. Use the correct forms. (Fig. 4.27 is the one used for The American Express Card). In many instances, generic forms are used for several different cards.

Figure 4.27
Sales draft with delayed charges* added.

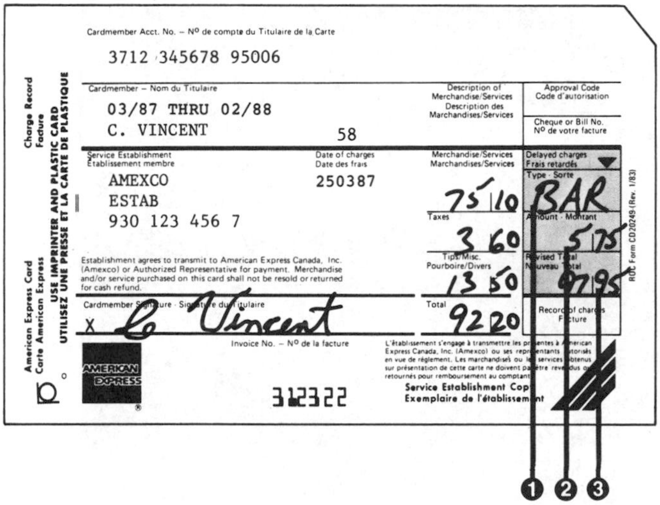

Courtesy of American Express Company.
*See p. 154 for 3-step procedure

2. Write the description of the charge, include the folio number, showing the total charge and sales tax separately.

3. Have the guest sign, and check the signature against the one on the back of the card. A spouse using an extra card in the cardholder's name may sign that person's name, but the signature on the card must match that on the sales draft.

4. Process the sales draft in the *imprinter* (Fig. 4.28). Retain the card for the next few steps.

5. Make sure that all duplicate copies are legible. If any copy cannot be read, destroy the entire set before the guest's eyes, and prepare a new sales draft.

6. If the sale is over the *floor limit*, obtain authorization. The floor limit is the amount the hotel may accept without authorization and which, if the card is valid and not listed in the warning bulletin, will be paid by the issuer. The procedure for authorization is described in the next section.

7. Return the card and the customer copy of the sales draft to the guest. Offer to tear up the carbons while the guest watches.

Figure 4.28
Credit card imprinter.

Courtesy of New World Harbourside Hotel, Vancouver, BC.

Obtaining Authorization

Clerks must obtain an authorization before accepting a card in these cases:

1. The total charge, including tax, exceeds the hotel's floor limit.

2. The cardholder does not have his or her card.

3. A dependent is using his or her guardian's card.

4. The card is not valid or is expired.

5. The imprinter is broken and the sales draft is prepared by hand.

6. A charge is made based on a telephone (TO) or mail order (MO). This applies especially to advance deposits and billings from no-show guaranteed reservations.

7. The clerk has any doubt about the cardholder's identity. In these cases, an authorization call and insistence on a second picture ID is strongly recommended.

Processing Delayed Charges

Occasionally, a charge arrives at the desk after the guest has settled the account. The original sales draft must not be altered. Instead, these procedures are followed:

1. Type or print the cardholder's name, address, and account number in the appropriate space on a second sales draft.

2. Obtain and record an authorization number.

For The American Express Card, a special section on the original *charge record* (Fig. 4.27) requires the cashier to indicate the type of delayed charge (1), enter the amount of delayed charge (2), and write in the revised total (3).

Calling for an Authorization

The authorization is obtained by calling a special 24-hour telephone number. In most cases, approval is readily granted, but it may be refused when a card has been reported lost or stolen or shows ''cancelled'' on the card company's computer. In the upper right-hand corner of the charge record, the clerk enters the approval code given by the operator.

Updating an Authorization During a Guest's Stay

If a guest's card has been imprinted upon check-in, regular checks must be made on the charges that accumulate on the folio. If they are about to exceed the floor limit, a new authorization for an amount suitable to the guest's spending pattern must be obtained. Such approvals are noted on the reverse of the guest folio (see Fig. 3.12).

Electronic Authorization

In most locations, electronic devices with a telephone link-up to a central computer do away with the fallible checking of cancellation bulletins or waiting for authorization calls. These on-line credit authorization terminals (Fig. 4.29), located at the front desk and other points of sale throughout the hotel, offer direct access to the card company's files. The clerk slides the card, with its magnetized strip on one side, through the terminal. The information carried on the strip is transmitted, along with the amount of the charge, to the card company's computer. After verification of the card, an authorization of the credit amount is flashed on the digital display board. For problem cards, an indicator prompts the clerk either to wait, re-enter the card, or telephone the authorization center for further instructions.

ACCEPTING TRAVELER'S CHECKS

Traveler's checks are documents issued and guaranteed for payment by banks, such as Barclay's and VISA-affiliates, and credit institutions, such as American Express and Cooks. They are issued in internationally accepted currencies, including U.S. and Canadian dollars (Fig. 4.30) German marks, Swiss francs, Brit-

Figure 4.29
Credit card authorization terminal.

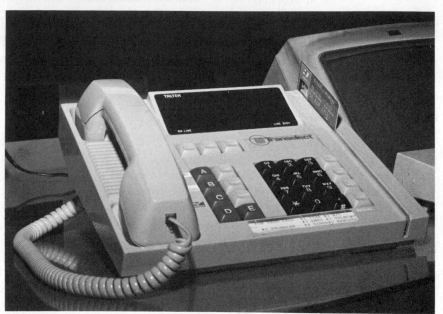

Courtesy of New World Harbourside Hotel, Vancouver, BC.

ish pounds sterling, and Japanese yen. In the case of the dollar checks, they are available in denominations of $10, $20, $50, $100, and $500. There is no time limit for their validity. To accept an American Express traveler's check, for example, the two-step procedure outlined in Figure 4.31 must be followed. If a check has already been countersigned by the customer or if the clerk doubts that the signatures are the same, the guest is asked to sign again on the reverse side. If a countersigned check is presented by anyone other than the person whose signature already appears in the upper left corner, the clerk should ask the presenter to endorse it on the reverse side. Once endorsed, traveler's checks are treated as cash.

ACCEPTING PERSONAL CHECKS

Hotels would rather not accept personal checks for the payment of accounts. The fact that a person can produce a piece of identification does not guarantee her credit standing. Should a guest insist on paying by check, the BAD PIES method of check acceptance can guide the process:

> B—Bank: is the check written on a legitimate bank, with branch and address given?

Figure 4.30
Traveler's checks in Canadian dollars (top) and in US dollars (bottom).

Courtesy of American Express Company.

A—Amount: are the written amount and the figure amount the same? Are they the same as the total bill?

D—Date: is the check dated the date of check-out?

P—Payee: is the hotel name written correctly? Is the check made out to the chain instead of the particular hotel?

I—Identification: does the guest have the particular ID the hotel stipulates?

E—Endorsement: is the endorsement acceptable? Stamp the check ''For deposit only.''

S—Signature: does it check against the guest's identification?

Figure 4.31
Traveler's check acceptance procedure.

Courtesy of American Express Company.

The clerk should always follow these rules:

- Do not accept post-dated or stale-dated checks.
- Refuse double-endorsed or third-party checks.
- Observe the signature while it is being written.
- If the check has been signed out of the clerk's view, ask that the signature be repeated, and initial it as witness.

One way to reduce the risk of accepting personal checks is to take advantage of a check-guarantee service offered by credit card companies. The cardholder's personal checks are guaranteed up to a certain amount as long as prescribed procedures for checking the bulletin and making authorization calls are followed. The service offered by The American Express Company requires the clerk to do the following:

1. Check the valid date on The American Express Card.
2. Check the card number against the cancellation bulletin or other means provided.

3. Make sure that the check has the name, branch, and address of the bank on which it is drawn.

4. Compare the signature on the check with the signature on the card.

5. Imprint the card number on the back of the check.

6. Record, either on the back of the folio or on the registration card, the credit card number and the amount of the check.

OTHER SETTLEMENT METHODS

Transfer to Another Guest

Occasionally, a guest requests that another guest's charges be put on his account. The cashier posts a credit transfer on the check-out folio and a debit transfer for the identical amount on the stay-over folio. Most standard guest folios have a space for the authorization of this and similar charge instructions (Fig. 4.32).

Company Billing

A similar situation occurs when a company or organization has arranged to allow its employees or members to sign for all or part of their charges. The amount is then posted to that company's city ledger account.

Figure 4.32
Charge instructions at the bottom of a folio.

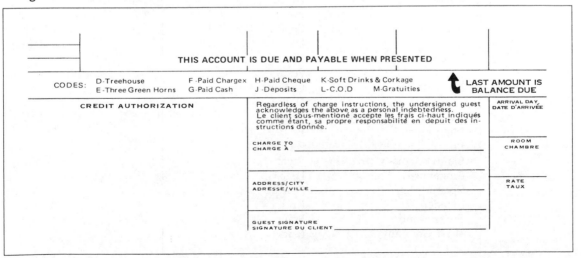

END-OF-SHIFT CASHIERING PROCEDURES

At the conclusion of a shift (or *watch*, as in A.M. watch) the cashier compiles a report, listing all cash receipts, cash disbursements–guests, and cash disbursements–house (Fig. 4.33). Paper and coin money is sorted into domestic and foreign currencies (Table 4.4) and listed on a cashier's deposit form (Fig. 4.34), which is printed on a large envelope. Bank checks, traveler's checks, and disbursement vouchers (paid out and petty cash) are placed in this envelope, together with all cash. The total amount of funds on hand should agree with a "paid" reading obtained from either the posting machine or the computer. Dis-

Table 4.4
Foreign currencies.
This table shows major foreign currencies. Check-out computers usually contain programs that allow for conversions between local and foreign currencies.

Country	Currency
Australia	Dollar
Austria	Schilling
Belgium	Franc
Britain	Pound
Canada	Dollar
China	Yuan
Denmark	Krone
Finland	Markka
France	Franc
Greece	Drachma
Hong Kong	Dollar
Ireland	Punt
Israel	Shekel
Italy	Lira
Japan	Yen
Mexico	Peso
Netherlands	Guilder
New Zealand	Dollar
Norway	Krone
Philippines	Peso
Portugal	Escudo
Saudi Arabia	Riyal
Singapore	Dollar
Spain	Peseta
Sweden	Krona
Switzerland	Franc
West Germany	Mark

Figure 4.33
Cash sheet.

			HOTEL_____		
			DATE_____		
	FRONT OFFICE CASH SHEET				
			6876 HMR-317		

CASH RECEIPTS			**CASH DISBURSEMENTS—GUESTS**		
ROOM NO.	NAME	AMOUNT	ROOM NO.	NAME	ITEM	AMOUNT

CASH DISBURSEMENTS—HOUSE

RECAPITULATION

TOTAL RECEIPTS	
DISBURSEMENTS—GUESTS	
DISBURSEMENTS—HOUSE	
TOTAL DISBURSEMENTS	
DEPOSIT	

Figure 4.34
Cashier's report and deposit envelope.

DEPARTMENT CASHIER'S REPORT			
DAY DATE 19			
CASHIER			
DEPT.			
SHIFT A.M. ☐ TO A.M. ☐ P.M. ☐ P.M. ☐			
	AMOUNT		✓
CURRENCY $1.00			
" $2.00			
" $5.00			
" $10.00			
" $20.00			
" $50.00			
" $100.00			
COIN 1¢			
" 5¢			
" 10¢			
" 25¢			
" 50¢			
" $1.00			
BAR STUBS:			
PAID OUTS:			
VOUCHERS AND CHECKS:			
TOTAL AMOUNT ENCLOSED			
NET RECEIPTS			
DIFFERENCE			

crepancies are listed as *over/under* and cashiers are usually instructed to submit their cashier's envelopes and reports, even if they did not *balance.* The envelope is deposited in a safe or delivered directly to a central office, where it is checked and over/under errors are traced and rectified. Each cashier's station begins and ends the shift with a *float,* an amount of money on hand required to make change.

LAST IMPRESSIONS

In addition to expertise in the procedures outlined in the preceding paragraphs, the cashier must possess good interpersonal skills. He or she must be able to address the sensitive issue of credit, explain billing details, and handle complaints presented by the departing guest. Often, the cashier is the guest's last personal contact with the hotel. This last(ing) impression will reflect on the entire guest service cycle, which began with the initial reservations inquiry, and now comes to a conclusion.

KEY TERMS

Folio	Audit trail
Posting	Electronic folio
Voucher	Point-of-sale
Posting machine	Cross-training
Night audit	Pulling a file
Management report	Cancellation bulletin
Settlement	Delayed charge
Guest history file	Imprinter
Cash flow	Traveler's check
Accounts receivable	BAD PIES
Authorization	Cash sheet
Floor limit	Cashier's envelope
Transient guests	Cash disbursements
City ledger	Petty cash
Paid out	Float
Source documents	Over/under
Departmental journal	Balance
Cash sheet	

NOTE

1. ECCO Computers, Inc., Santa Ana, CA 92702; HIS Hotel Information Systems, Pleasant Hill, CA 94523; CLS Computerized Lodging Systems, Long Beach, CA 90815.

ACTIVITIES

1. Survey five lodging operations in your community and find out what accounting systems they employ. Then find the answers to the following questions and report to your study group:

   a. Do they use manual, mechanical, or electronic systems? How does the number of rooms, chain affiliation, and style of service relate to the accounting system they use?
   b. What is the role of the night auditor in each of the five situations you have surveyed?
   c. How are guest charges communicated to the front desk for posting?
   d. What percentage of accounts are settled by credit card and how does that compare to the average reported in Table 4.3?

2. Your supervisor has asked you to calculate certain operating statistics, based on yesterday's business:

Rooms in the house	230
Rooms occupied	173
Rooms O-O-O	2
Number of guests overnight	277
Total rooms revenue	$6,550

   Calculate the occupancy percentage, the average rate per room occupied, the average rate per guest, and the average number of guests per room occupied.

ASSIGNMENTS

Working alone, fill out a front-office cash sheet (Fig. 4.33) using the data given below. You should arrive at a figure for the daily deposit to be handed to the accounting office in the cashier's envelope.

Check-outs:

Room	Name	Amount
1434	Smith, R. L.	$332.50
3239	Brown, Mr. D.	229.75
2852	Kelly, Mrs. S.	456.60
3310	Hagen, E. W.	1995.85
1245	Timmons, V.	283.20
3318	Turvey, Ms. A.	751.47
1266	Mongrain, Mrs. S.	546.72
2424	Baclava, Mr. G.	235.50

Paid Outs: Cash Refund

3310 Hagen, Mr. E. $14.50 gratuity dining room, Check 100932.

1411 Yearsley, Mrs. E. $11.00 taxi to pick up letter. OK'd by manager on duty.

$23.50 freight COD, per food & beverage manager.

2273 Painter, Mr. R. $9.35 gratuity room service, Check 66381.

$85.00 advance wages for Clare McGivern, OK'd by general manager.

2298 Sawada, Mr. S. $26.10 flowers ordered from Grace Flowers, charged to room.

CHAPTER FIVE

BASIC COMMUNICATION SKILLS

The purpose of this chapter is to

1. Describe the four basic communication skills: paraphrasing, perception checking, making "I" statements, and behavior description.

2. Apply these skills to telephone and switchboard interactions.

3. Describe ways to handle guests' complaints.

INTRODUCTION

This chapter describes four communication skills that can be used whenever it is important that two or more people understand each other. The first two, paraphrasing and perception checking, are best used to help to understand the content and meaning of another's message, while the last two, making "I" statements and behavior description, permit others to understand you better.

PARAPHRASING

Paraphrasing is used to make sure you understand the ideas, information, and questions of others. To paraphrase means to state the other person's idea in your own words or give an example that shows what you think the person is talking about. A good paraphrase is usually more specific than the original statement. For example:

Guest: Can you help me? I need to get in touch with a Mr. Wooster.
Clerk: Of course, sir. Do you wish to leave a message for him?

This paraphrase does not capture the full content of the guest's message. It catches the general meaning only and forces the guest to add further information so that the clerk fully understands the situation. A revised example follows:

Clerk: You wish to reach Mr. Wooster. Is he staying with us?

This paraphrase captures the essence of the inquiry and then moves to the problem-solving phase. Mr. Wooster could be any of the following: a registered guest, someone holding a reservation, a guest in the dining room, someone attending a banquet, or a staff member of the hotel.

These examples are simplistic, but they demonstrate the basic function of a paraphrase: to show the sender what the content of the message is from the receiver's viewpoint. Here is another example:

Guest: I am dissatisfied with my room.
Clerk: Would you like to change to another one, ma'am?

This paraphrase does not reflect what has been said. Instead, the clerk rushes in with a quick solution, called *band-aiding*, without being clear on what the problem really is. Even if the guest agrees to the room change, we still do not know what she did not like about the room. We only have an illusion of understanding. Revised paraphrase:

Clerk: I'm sorry the room does not meet your needs, Mrs. McGivern. How can I help?

This seems an accurate reflection of the guest's complaint. It avoids the negatively charged word "dissatisfied," while at the same time shifting the focus to problem solving.

Paraphrasing is extra work and may at first feel awkward and artificial to use. At first glance, it is much easier to ask the other person for clarification by asking "What do you mean?" or exclaiming, "I don't understand." By paraphrasing, we show what our present level of understanding is and enable the sender to respond to, and clarify, any misunderstanding we have revealed. Since desk clerks are frequently asked for information, it would be to their advantage to make sure that the message to which they are responding is really the message the other person is sending before agreeing, disagreeing, or answering. To paraphrase is one way to test such understanding.

PERCEPTION CHECKING

Most verbal communications carry two messages: one at the *content* and another at the *feeling* level. With some statements, the content is obvious and the feelings are of less or no importance. For example: "At what time does the airport shuttle leave?" With other statements, the feelings are of higher importance than the content. For example: "I've lost my wallet, with all my IDs and my airline ticket." Perception checking is the skill used to ensure that you understand the feelings underlying a person's message. To make a perception check means to state what you perceive the other to be feeling. A good perception check conveys the message, "I want to understand your feelings as well as the facts. Is this the way you feel?"

Some examples:

"Are you disappointed that you have to work tomorrow?"

"You seem upset about something. Is there anything I can do?"

"You seem cheerful this morning. Had some good news?"

A perception check identifies the other's feelings in some way (disappointed, upset, cheerful) and does not express approval or disapproval of the feelings. It merely conveys, "This is how I understand your feeling. How accurate am I?" It also shows your interest and concern for the other person.

Your inference about people's feelings can be, and often is, inaccurate. Thus, if a clerk feels guilty about something he has done, he may perceive others as angry, accusing or disapproving towards him. By using perception checking, he can find out what others are feeling.

BEHAVIOR DESCRIPTION

This skill is aimed at letting the other person know what behavior you are responding to by describing clearly what you observed. The following examples contrast behavior descriptions (statement a) with other possible responses (statement b):

Example 1

   a. Mr. Brown, you moved ahead of others waiting to check in.

   b. Some people seem to be in a hurry around here.

Statement b is not a behavior description but an accusation of unfavorable motives.

Example 2

   a. Marge, I noticed today that you answered guests' questions before they had finished their sentences.

   b. Marge, you were quite rude to guests today.

Statement b labels Marge as rude without giving her specific information about the behavior being discussed. She has no information or evidence about the validity of the criticism.

Example 3

   a. I appreciate your concern, sir, but I'd like to explain to you the reason we had to let your reservation go at 6:00 P.M.

   b. If you are constantly interrupting, I won't be able to explain to you why we haven't got a room for you.

The word ''constantly'' in statement b implies that the other is being intentionally rude and is not interested in an explanation. All that can be observed is that the guest is agitated and upset about the prospect of not having a room for the night.

To develop the skill of behavior description, you must sharpen your observation so that you can pinpoint what actually occurs. As this ability develops, you may find that many of your conclusions are based less on observable evidence than on your own feelings of irritation, insecurity, or fear. By using your objective skills to work for observation and analysis, you are more likely to state a clearly observable behavior than an underlying assumption about the other's motives. Such objective information is likely to be useful to the sender and to help him adjust or evaluate his behavior accordingly.

MAKING ''I'' STATEMENTS

This skill is most useful when it is important that others understand how you are feeling. An ''I'' message makes clear the feelings you are experiencing by naming or identifying them. Such a statement must refer to ''I,'' ''me,'' or ''my,'' and must specify some kind of feeling by name, simile, or other figure of speech. Because *describing* feelings is easily confused with *expressing* feelings, the following contrasting examples serve as clarification:

Expressions of feelings	*Descriptions of feelings*
''Didn't you say you'd be here in twenty minutes?''	''I am glad you got here. I was concerned you wouldn't get here in time, and I'd have had to let your reservation go.''
''Yesterday was a miserable day.''	''I feel I really screwed up on my first day at the desk.''
''This is a nice place.''	''I like working with you. I appreciate the way you pitch in when I'm busy.
''It isn't my fault, you know!''	''I am sorry you had such a difficult time reaching us on the phone.''

In addition to expressing feelings through questions, accusations, and judgmental statements, we can also show them through nonverbal expressions such as sighing, becoming silent, turning away from the speaker, or keeping him waiting unduly. These expressions are likely to be misread. A sigh, for instance, can indicate quite a number of different feelings. The other person is left to guess which is our real message.

Accurate "I" statements are designed to avoid such ambiguity. They should not make the other person feel guilty ("Look what you've done") or attempt to coerce her into changing (". . . so I won't feel bad about what you did"). Instead, by reporting what goes on inside him, an effective communicator can give the recipient of the message additional information to aid him in understanding and appreciating the message more fully.

TELEPHONE SKILLS

Working at the desk involves answering questions, relaying information, and obtaining details from others over the telephone, from inside and outside the operation. The following practical hints are mostly common sense, but are too often ignored. Just remember the last time you were put "on ignore" or given the runaround by some anonymous respondent. Some basic rules for good telephone handling follow.

Speak Distinctly

Speak in a normal tone. Speak directly into the telephone with your lips about half an inch from the mouthpiece.

Be Prepared

The telephone directory, a listing of frequently called numbers, a calendar, message pads, and a pen should be kept within easy reach of the telephone.

Plan Ahead

An old proverb says, "Speaking without thinking is like shooting without aiming." Plan the call before beginning to dial. Forms, figures, charts, or notes should be ready beforehand.

Answer Courteously

The caller judges the clerk's attitude by what she hears when making the first contact. Therefore, it is essential to respond promptly, pleasantly, and efficiently. All telephone calls should be answered before the second ring. Clerks must identify themselves by position and name. Examples: "Front desk, Eva speaking." If the call is meant for someone who is not available, explain briefly and offer assistance. Example: "The front-office manager is away from the desk until 10:00 A.M. May I help you in the meantime?" Or: "Dana is not on duty this morning. He will be here at 3:00 P.M. Do you wish to leave a message, or can I be of assistance?"

Take Accurate Messages

For a complete telephone message, the following information should be recorded:

- Name of person called.
- Name of the caller, and company.
- The caller's telephone number and extension.
- The caller's city.
- The message.
- The action requested and promised.
- The date and time of the call.
- The name of the person recording the call.

Restate the details so that the caller can confirm that all facts are understood.

Put Callers "On Hold" With Courtesy

If it is necessary to leave the line, give the caller the choice of waiting or being called back. If the caller wishes to wait, the telephone should be put down gently, and, if it is equipped with a hold button, this should be depressed. The caller should always be told that he is being put "on hold" and not left there for more than a few moments. Example: "I am sorry to have kept you waiting, Dr. Kluckner. I am still trying to locate the information for you. Do you wish to hold or shall I telephone your room when I find out?"

Transfer Calls Carefully

Transfer a call only when the person to whom you are transferring it can help the caller. Avoid giving even a hint of "passing the buck." The caller must always be told the reason for the transfer. Example: "Mr. Sawada, the person to talk to is Christine, our reservations supervisor. Shall I transfer you?"

End Calls Politely

Finish the conversation by using a suitable closing phrase that expresses appreciation for the call or regret if the caller's wish could not be accommodated. Examples: "Thank you for making this reservation, Mrs. Mongrain. We look forward to having you at the Cromwell Hotel." Or, "I'm sorry I was unable to help you this time, Mr. Einstein; please call us the next time you need a reservation." Let the caller hang up first.

SWITCHBOARDS

Only twenty years ago, automatic switchboards took the place of manually oper-ated *PBX* switchboards. Now manufacturers offer *communication centers* and *in-formation systems.* Some of the features of interest to the staff include:[1]

- Displays number of calls waiting to be answered.

- "Parks" incoming calls next to a busy number until that number is free.

- Displays the calling guest's name on a 15-character digital display drawn from the hotel's registration computer. This allows all calls to be an-swered immediately with the guest's name.

- Displays the room number of a calling party, allowing service depart-ments (such as room service) to verify the source of an order.

- Allows the operator to enter wake-up calls. When the call is placed, a recorded message in a selected language informs the guest of the time. If the guest does not respond, the system redials after a few minutes, then informs the operator.

- Allows for a "Do not disturb" designation: no calls are connected from the switchboard to the room, and direct calls from other extensions are automatically rerouted to the operator.

- Long distance charges are automatically posted to the electronic folio in the hotel's computer system.

- A room phone can be cut off, to prevent unauthorized calling from that room. This can be done after the guest has checked out or while a guest is absent.

- A single-button dial provides direct access to internal and external pag-ing systems to summon the manager on duty, maintenance, housekeep-ing, and other staff needed on short notice and available by beeper.

Guests, too, benefit from state-of-the-art telephone systems through fea-tures such as:

- Special push-botton numbers provide access to information on hotel ac-tivities, schedules, and announcements.

- Wake-up calls can be requested from the switchboard (and programmed there) or entered by the guest from a room or house phone. After calling a special number, the guest is prompted to press other numbers to pro-gram the exact time when the call is desired.

- For waiting messages, a light on the guest phone advises the guest to call the message center.

- For long distance calls, time and charges can be displayed on the guest's phone set.

- Guests traveling with portable computers can plug these into special built-in data adapters and connect with data bases and their back-home office computer.

- In an emergency, a guest simply takes the phone off the hook; no dialing is required. After a brief delay, the call is routed to the emergency key on the operator's console.

- Conference calls with other parties in the hotel or outside can be arranged easily.

HANDLING GUESTS' COMPLAINTS

This section explains how communication skills can be applied in dealing with guest complaints.

Front-office work frequently involves responding to guests' complaints. Every time this occurs, the staff's communication skills are put to the test. To the guest, clerks represent the entire hotel. Therefore, you must accept the responsibility of being the hotel's representative: you simply cannot hide behind an "it's not my job" attitude. Even for matters clearly outside the desk's influence, guests frequently come to the desk to seek satisfaction. Clerks must be familiar with company policies on contentious matters and know how much leeway they have to accommodate guests with special demands. They must also be able to listen and respond with objectivity, know what to do and to promise, and be able to decide when a supervisor needs to be called. Some basic guidelines for complaint handling follow.

Listen Objectively

The desk clerk must be objective. A guest who is upset about hotel service may quickly arouse a defensive attitude. The key is to remain objective while at the same time showing a genuine concern. Listen to the whole message the guest is sending. Paraphrasing is especially useful at this stage, as you attempt to filter through the story and guest's emotions to get at the facts.

Show Empathy

Listen for the *feelings* as well as the *content*. The use of empathetic statements, such as, "I can understand how upset you must be, Mrs. St. Louis, having to wait for your breakfast," acknowledges and legitimizes the complainant's feelings, without accepting responsibility for the cause. Even if you have heard the same complaint before and already know whose fault it is, this guest's situation is unique and must be attended to fully. A guest complaining about a service just wants to talk to someone belonging to the hotel: she has, in this instance, no personal complaint about the listener.

Refer to Your Supervisor

Refer problems to others if that is appropriate. If the guest creates a disturbance or is holding up traffic at the desk, you can politely say, ''If you'd be good enough to step into the office to your right, Mr. Keen, our credit manager will be able to take care of your concern.'' Better yet, ''This is Barbara Roman, our credit manager. She'll be glad to sort this matter out with you, Mr. Keen.'' Avoid antagonizing the guest further by saying, ''Please don't upset the other customers in the line. The front-office manager's office is over there if you wish to make a complaint.''

Identify the Problem

Once the guest's feelings have been attended to, the complainant will find it easy to respond to, ''What is it you wish me to do, Mr. Boles?'' or a similar request for specifics. The guest might only want someone to know about the problem, or she might expect a specific remedy.

Acknowledge the Problem

Offer some assurance that the complaint has been heard and will be attended to. If the complaint is a result of the clerk's own action, an apology is appropriate, along with an offer to provide a consolation service. If the situation clearly involves people elsewhere in the hotel, but within the clerk's realm of influence, then action should be specified. For example, ''I'll call the housekeeping department immediately and have them replace the missing blanket in your room, Mr. Pallett''; or, ''I'm glad you are bringing this to our attention, Ms. Klein. I'll page the maintenance department and ask them to have a look at your TV. Would that be acceptable to you?''

Note the frequent use of the guest's name and the outline of what the clerk proposes to do. If the situation is beyond your authority to handle adequately, it may be prudent to refer the guest to someone else. If, for instance, the guest demands a drastic rate reduction because his room was unsatisfactory, the clerk may have to refer the matter to the manager on duty. In such a case, you might say, ''Mr. Green, I appreciate your dissatisfaction with room 343 last night. I am not authorized to reduce your room rate. I'll ask Miss Simpson, the duty manager, to take care of your request.''

Be Prepared to Deny Certain Requests

At times, clerks have to say "no" to a guest's demand. Most people find it difficult to send or receive a negative message. Take the case of the guest who wishes to take a large dog to her room, only to be told that the "pets allowed" rule applies only to small pets. Saying no and giving a brief explanation, while maintaining eye contact and speaking with a sympathetic tone of voice, is the best approach. For example: "This must be an unpleasant surprise to you, Miss Raider. I can recommend a kennel nearby that has given our guests very good service on previous occasions. Do you wish me to telephone and reserve a place for your dog?" Naturally, should the guest refuse to leave and challenge the rule, a referral to senior desk staff is necessary.

Always Follow Up

The desk clerk is responsible for the follow-up, the final step in responding to a complaint. For instance, if a call to the housekeeper was promised, do it as soon as possible. Keeping brief notes or a complaint log assists in follow-up, even in the midst of a busy day.

KEY TERMS

Paraphrasing	Expressing feelings
Band-aiding	Perception checking
Content level	Describing behavior
Feeling level	Making "I" statements
Describing feelings	

NOTE

1. Technical details provided by NEC Telephones, Inc., Melville, NY.

ACTIVITIES

1. Alone, or in groups of four, take five minutes to make a list of the kind of communications behaviors that you consider helpful and those you find hindering.

2. Explain what a paraphrase is. How can you improve your understanding of another's message by using this skill?

3. Write down three different situations in which a perception check would aid in making communication more effective.

4. List the steps of good complaint handling in customer service. How would you impress upon your staff the importance of following these steps whenever possible?

ASSIGNMENTS

A. Form groups of four people. Seat yourself in a cluster, somewhat away from the other groups in the room. Your task is to share with each other the list of helpful and hindering communications behaviors you made in Activity 1. You might each start out with, ''It really bugs me when people . . .'' and then ''I find it really helpful when I communicate with others to . . . .'' After about five minutes of sharing, write your answers on a sheet of paper or on the chalkboard. Under the guidance of your instructor, the groups can then share the total list of the entire group.

B. Within a group of four, divide into pairs. Designate one person in each pair A, the other B. Then do the following:

1. A makes a statement to B either about himself, about B, or about the relationship between them. He should try to make a statement that says something personal and that has some meaning to both.

2. B now paraphrases A's statement, stating in her own words what she has just heard A say. No discussion of the statement's content is permitted at this stage, just a statement and a paraphrase. When A is satisfied that B has really understood his original statement, A makes a second statement. B paraphrases it.

3. Now reverse the process. B makes a statement, A paraphrases it to B's satisfaction. B makes a further statement, A paraphrases it to show his understanding.

4. Individually, write down your responses to these questions: How easy or difficult was it for you to paraphrase the other's statements? What was it like for you to be listened to intently by the other person?

5. Join in your group of four and share the responses to the questions above and to the experience in general. This should take about four minutes.

6. Take another two minutes to look back and discuss in your group of four the way in which you have just communicated with each other. Did anyone paraphrase?

C. Make three telephone calls to hotels, motels, restaurants, or similar service companies in your area. Your task is to obtain answers to prepared questions relating to the products and services offered by that firm. You might ask a hotel for details on their banquet policies; a motel about their special weekly rates and pet policy; a restaurant on their menu prices and special meals for vegetarians. Keep notes on your questions, the answers you obtain, and the quality of communication skills displayed by the person at the other end of the phone. Be prepared to relate your experience to the material in Chapter 5 and present your observations to the group.

D. In teams of two, design a 10-minute training session you could give to a small group of desk clerk trainees. The topic: handling complaints. The objectives: At the end of the training session, the trainees should be able to:

1. List the steps in handling guest complaints.

2. List the "don'ts" in complaint handling.

3. Display their understanding of the above by taking part in a brief role-playing exercise involving a complaining guest and a clerk. One or more teams will be called upon to present their training session during the next class meeting. The other participants will be your trainees. They and your instructor will comment on the effectiveness of your training session. Such effectiveness will be measured by the degree to which your trainees have accomplished the objectives stated above.

CHAPTER SIX

TRANSACTIONAL ANALYSIS AT THE FRONT DESK

OBJECTIVES

The purpose of this chapter is to:

- Present an overview of the theory of transactional analysis.
- Describe ways to apply transactional analysis in customer relations.

INTRODUCTION

Transactional analysis, or TA, is a theory of personality and social action based on the analysis of transactions between two or more people. Exchanges between people, expressed verbally or nonverbally, are called *transactions* because each party gains something from them. Anything that happens between two or more people can be broken down into a series of single transactions. TA training, according to the authors of *Games Nobody Wins,* is intended to develop better and more honest relationships between all parties in hospitality transactions.[1]

TA is easy to learn and provides communication tools ideally suited to customer service. It helps increase a person's on-the-job effectiveness because of better self-understanding and greater insight into transactions. It gives a common language for people working together to solve their communications problems. It is a nonthreatening approach to the evaluation of one's communication philosophy and practices.[2]

A BRIEF OVERVIEW OF TA

Dr. Eric Berne developed the original theory of TA from the observation that there seemed to be several different people inside each individual and that these various selves transacted with other people in different ways.[3] Imagine a clerk talking rather loudly with a fellow worker in the back office, his body tense, his voice raised and edgy, his face unsmiling, as he reprimands the other person for having accepted five reservations in spite of the full-house situation. Suddenly the telephone rings, and, as he speaks to a customer, his posture, tone of voice, and facial expressions change as he attends to the caller's needs. His voice becomes attentive and friendly, his choice of words becomes accommodating and helpful. In TA terms, he has just changed *ego states*; he has switched into one of his other selves.

Ego States

Each person has three ego states, called *Parent*, *Adult*, and *Child*. These words have specific meanings in TA usage that are different from their usual meanings.

The parent.   The Parent ego state contains the attitudes and behavior incorporated by an individual from the people who had an influence over her life experience, primarily parents, but also siblings, neighbors, teachers, aunts, uncles. For example, a man may squint his eyes when angry, as his father did. Parent behavior may be critical, judgmental, or nurturing. A clerk saying to a tired-looking guest, "You must have had an exhausting day," is speaking from her *nurturing* Parent. Another, greeting a guest who has no reservation with, "You should have made an advance reservation—most people do," speaks from his *critical* Parent. Being in customer-service work often requires a clerk to act in a helping role, giving ample opportunity to use this Parent behavior. By becoming aware of the nurturing and critical options, a clerk can become increasingly more helpful.

The adult.   The Adult ego state has little to do with actual age. It is the name given to the data processing side that every person possesses: the ability to gather, organize, store, combine, analyze, and give information. Such information is gathered throughout life, and includes thoughts developed since birth as well as information presented at the time when a response is expected. The following statement reflects the ability of the Adult ego state to estimate, compute, and present information dispassionately: "If you leave right away, you can still make the airport bus. It will get you there in 10 minutes, with enough time to clear customs."

The child.   The Child ego state contains feelings about life, the responses of a small person to what he sees and hears. It also contains the recordings of the child's early experiences, how he responded to them, and the positions he took with respect to others. The Child ego state is present at any age; a person merely responds as if he were a child. The exhausted traveler arriving at the hotel may feel intimidated and overwhelmed by the surroundings, just as she felt as a child. She uses the responses that worked well for her as a child: demanding attention for herself and resenting being "pushed around."

There are three parts to the Child: the *Natural* Child, the *Adapted* Child, and the *Little Professor*. The Natural Child (NC) is affectionate, sensuous, and impulsive and does what comes naturally. A person clapping his hands in delight when confronted with some good news is one example. The NC is also fearful, self-indulgent, self-centered, rebellious, and aggressive. A group of employees standing at the notice board discussing a new company rule regarding dress regulations may respond: "Boy, next they're going to dictate what color hair we're allowed to have." The NC can emerge in unpleasant roles (a guest demanding to have things done immediately) or pleasant roles (a guest commenting on the efficient and courteous service).

The Adapted Child (AC) is the trained child who has learned to say "please," "may I," and "thank you" and is likely to do and say what parents (or the boss, or guests, or friends) insist on, and sometimes this brings about a feeling of being "not-OK." A guest making an unreasonable request to the desk clerk may be given a polite, but forced, "Yes, sir!" because that is the behavior expected from a clerk under the rule that the guest is always right.

The Little Professor (LP) is the third part of the Child. It is the part of the Child that is intuitive, manipulative, and creative. Two examples are (1) guest, after being told there are no vacancies, responds with a wistful smile and the request, "Have another look—you people always have a little room tucked away somewhere," and clerk, when confronted with an overbooking situation, engages his LP and suggests that "Perhaps we could have the bellman go upstairs and make up the late check-outs. That would give us two extra rooms."

A person who is being creative combines her Adult and Little Professor to solve problems, settle disputes, create better relationships, develop improved systems, and take similar positive actions.

The structure of the ego states can be represented with three circles, as shown in Figure 6.1. Each person has the capability and choice of responding to a given situation with data from each of the ego states. The following are examples which illustrate this point.

Figure 6.1
Structure of ego states.

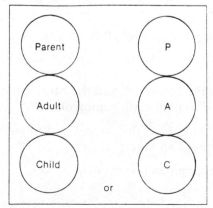

Situation 1

A reservation clerk cannot locate a letter. The supervisor responds:

Parent: How many times do I have to tell you that all correspondence has to be filed according to date of arrival?

Adult: Check in the alphabetical file for two or three days prior to and after the expected arrival day. It's likely that you misfiled the letter. If you still can't find it, check with me and we can look together.

Child: Gee, you've lost the only information we had on that reservation. Now what are we going to do?

Situation 2

A clerk has been fired because of repeated complaints by a guest about her conduct. Her colleagues discuss the event:

Parent: She had it coming. She never really fitted in with this team.

Adult: That's the second firing in one week. We're going to be short-handed in the mornings.

Child: Nobody really cares about you here. One guest complains and out you go. I'd better start looking for a job somewhere else.

Situation 3

A guest appears at the desk and, in a loud voice, demands to speak to someone about the "lousy service in the dining room." The clerk responds:

Parent: Please lower your voice. You are causing a scene.

Adult: You are unhappy with the dining room service? Would you please step over to the desk? I will page the assistant manager on duty. I'm sure he'll be able to assist you.

Child: It must be upsetting not getting good service. What happened?

Situation 4

The electricity is temporarily turned off and the cashier has to operate the cash register manually. The other clerk comments:

Parent: You're really working hard this morning. I'm sure the electricity will be back in a short time. Can you manage?

Adult: This power interruption will be over by 10:00 A.M. The repair crew just called.

Child: Why don't you just write ''paid'' on the accounts now and then ring them up when the electricity is back? This is fun, just like in the good old days.

In all of these situations, the vital clue to the source of each response will often be provided by the gestures, body stances, and tones of voice that accompany the words. Even a simple phrase, such as ''good morning,'' can be said so that it conveys different meanings. It can be stated as a caring Parent message (implying ''How are you after that heavy day yesterday?''), as a matter-of-fact Adult message (''What can I do for you, Madam?''), or as a playful Child acknowledgment (''Hi! Am I ever glad to see you!'').

Ego states can often be recognized by typical gestures and facial expressions. Examples are the following:

Parent

Pursed lips

Pointed index finger

Head wagging

Foot tapping

Hands on hips

Arms folded across chest

Sighs

Adult

Straightforward expression

Attentive expression with face, eyes and body

Child

Pouts

Laughter

Giggling

Exaggerated gestures of confusion, delight or anger

Downcast eyes

Whining voice

Quivering mouth.

Key words also help in the recognition of typical statements originating with certain ego states. Examples include the following:

Parent

Always

Never

Should

Ought

Had better

Must

How many times do I have to tell you?

Once and for all

These words and phrases are almost always included in a Parent statement. The following evaluative words may indicate a Parental message, as they are judgmental about another person or events:

Stupid

Naughty

Poor dear

Lazy

Disgusting

Adult

What

Why

Where

How many

When

How much

True

False

Objective

Unknown

Most likely

I think

I see

In my estimation

Child

Gosh

Gee

Wow

Boy, oh boy

Golly

I wish

I hope

I'm gonna

I don't know

I don't care.

SCRIPTS

A second key TA concept has to do with the script we develop as children. It reflects our view of our own worth during our first years on earth. A script is like a blueprint for a life plan, and it develops while the child interacts with persons who are emotionally significant and while he is involved in dramatic life situations. For instance, a young girl who learns to think of herself as awkward and not mechanically minded will act awkward and helpless when confronted with anything to do with machines. Similarly, a boy who learns to think of himself as weak when showing emotions grows up not showing feelings, and he may find it difficult to deal with anything emotional, either within himself or with others. He may consider the display of emotions as ''not-OK'' and unmanly.

TRANSACTION

The third concept of TA is the application of basic theory to what happens when two people begin to communicate: the analysis of transactions. These are big words, but their meaning is simple and straightforward:

Transaction consists of a stimulus by one person and a response by another, which response, in turn, becomes a new stimulus for the other person to respond to. The purpose of the analysis is to discover which part of each person—Parent, Adult, or Child—is originating each stimulus and response.[4]

Transactions may occur between one or more ego states of one person and result in a response from one or more ego states of another. Depending on how the response occurs, the resulting transaction can then be classified as either *complementary* or *crossed*. A third type, *ulterior* transactions, is explained below in the section on games.

A complementary transaction occurs when a message gets the predicted response from the other person. The examples in Figure 6.2 illustrate such situations. To understand these interactions, both communicators must consider the nonverbal clues that accompany each message. Words alone do not convey the complete message. They must be evaluated in the context of the body movement, facial expressions, and tones of voice, as well as of previous relationships and the relative intimacy of the communicators.

Crossed Transactions

Some transactions are crossed. The sender intends the message to be received and responded to by a certain ego state, only to get an unexpected or inappro-

Figure 6.2
Three complementary transactions.

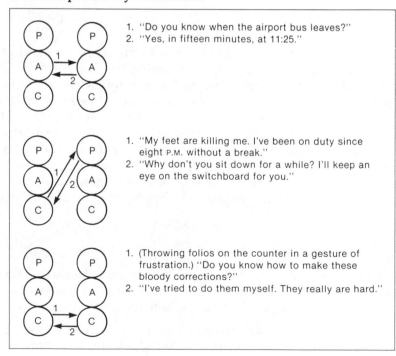

1. "Do you know when the airport bus leaves?"
2. "Yes, in fifteen minutes, at 11:25."

1. "My feet are killing me. I've been on duty since eight P.M. without a break."
2. "Why don't you sit down for a while? I'll keep an eye on the switchboard for you."

1. (Throwing folios on the counter in a gesture of frustration.) "Do you know how to make these bloody corrections?"
2. "I've tried to do them myself. They really are hard."

Figure 6.3
Three crossed transactions.

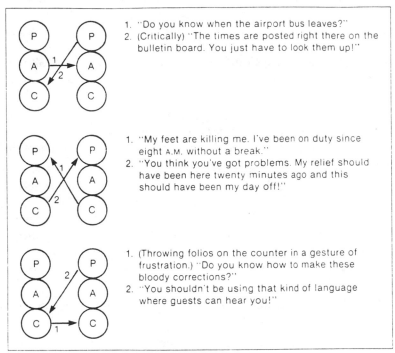

1. "Do you know when the airport bus leaves?"
2. (Critically) "The times are posted right there on the bulletin board. You just have to look them up!"

1. "My feet are killing me. I've been on duty since eight A.M. without a break."
2. "You think you've got problems. My relief should have been here twenty minutes ago and this should have been my day off!"

1. (Throwing folios on the counter in a gesture of frustration.) "Do you know how to make these bloody corrections?"
2. "You shouldn't be using that kind of language where guests can hear you!"

priate response. This common experience is illustrated in Figure 6.3. These crossed transactions demonstrate situations in which real communication stops. Instead of telling the guest the exact time the bus departs, the clerk lectures the guest with a "you dummy" message. The guest still does not know when the bus leaves. Instead of giving the clerk with the hurting feet a bit of sympathy, the respondent takes the opportunity to complain about his own problems. In the third example, the frustrated clerk could benefit from a bit of understanding and advice on how to fix the errors on the folios. Instead, the response cuts off such interaction; the clerks must first settle the issue of inappropriate language in front of guests.

These crossed transactions are likely to set off an exchange of similarly unproductive interactions. In situation 1, the guest might respond with "No need to be rude, young man," which would leave the clerk with a reprimand and the impression that guests are "not-OK," while the guest would depart with a similar feeling about the hotel and its entire staff. A crossed transaction can also cause people to withdraw or turn away from each other. The clerk with the hurting feet is not likely to bring another personal issue to the other clerk's attention. Likewise, the person with the correction problem will think twice about asking for assistance again.

There is a technique that can be used to avoid being drawn into the inappropriate and sometimes hurtful net of a crossed transaction. One of the functions of the Adult ego state is *probability estimating*.[5] (Note 6). Like a muscle in the body, the Adult grows in efficiency through training and use. If the Adult is alert to the possibility of trouble through probability estimating, it can devise solutions to meet the trouble if and when it occurs. The following exchange, in which a guest is annoyed because he waits in line for check-in behind a large group, illustrates the use of this technique:

Mr. Robertson: If you wouldn't spend so much time talking with your colleagues, I'd get some service. I've been waiting for five minutes.
Clerk: I'm sorry if I kept you waiting. Do you wish to check in?

This response to Mr. Robertson's comments demonstrates that the clerk was able to sort out the double message. The guest communicated his annoyance at being kept waiting and also implied that others ahead of him were treated with excessive attention. By computing the total information received, the clerk responded with a message of understanding for the annoyance—without taking blame—and a businesslike statement of willingness to be of service. She could have responded from her Parent. In that case, the situations might have developed like this:

Clerk: You should have gone to the next counter instead of waiting for this group to check in.

This statement does nothing to acknowledge the guest's feelings, nor does it offer any hint of a solution. It cuts the communication off at a point where it should begin. This guest's stay is off to a bad start. Similarly, the real communication would have been stopped had the clerk responded from her Child. In that case, she might have made some exaggerated gesture of cleaning up the counter after the group's check-in, expressed her annoyance at being put in her place by means of facial expressions, and acted in an arrogant manner.

Even the most experienced clerk may at times succumb to the temptation of acting like a rebellious Child. This is particularly true during busy periods when there is a constant flow of guests arriving at the desk and making demands of the staff. A good rule to practice is: If in danger of being hooked into a crossed transaction, analyze the situation from the Adult ego state and respond appropriately. This is what the clerk did in the initial response. Some examples of this rule in practice are:

"Waiting in line can be annoying."

This means, "While I don't think I have spent too much time checking in the group before you, I accept your feeling of being treated with less courtesy."

"Do you wish to check in?"

This means, "Now that I have reassured you of my concern, I need to address your Adult and find out what the nature of your business is."

STROKES

Every person has a basic need to be touched and recognized by others. This need can be satisfied with *strokes*, which can be given in the form of actual physical touch or in some symbolic form—a look, a word, or any act (negative or positive) that says, "I know you are there."[6] The desk clerk has many opportunities for giving positive strokes. A warm, smiling greeting to a person who steps up to the desk, and the friendly use of a guest's name as soon as it is known, both have rich stroking value. They also add to the impression that "We care, we like having you as our guest, we think you are OK." The clerk who does not look up when greeting a guest, does not smile when talking to others, or is busy counting keys while talking to someone on the telephone is likely to start a relationship poorly. The message being sent to the receiver's Child is, "You don't count, I haven't got time to deal with you, you aren't important, you are a nobody."

People who do not get enough positive strokes will look for negative ones: these hurt, but they are better than none at all. Early in our lives, we learned how to handle these painful feelings; all we had to do was watch how those around us dealt with their negative strokes. The result is a technique that in TA is called trading stamps.

TRADING STAMPS

Most of us learned during our childhood that free expression of our feelings (hurt, anger, joy, pain) was not encouraged by those around us. Messages such as: "Boys don't cry," "Mind your temper," "Don't be a sissy," "Chin up," and "Now, now," denied us the positive strokes we looked for, and we began to save up our feelings for later use. This collection is akin to the collection of trading stamps that can be cashed in for free prizes. We can collect two kinds of stamps: dirty stamps, which represent not-OK feelings such as anger, depression, guilt, and frustration; and Gold Stamps, which represent OK feelings such as joy, affection, pleasure, delight, and enthusiasm.

A fictitious case may help explain this concept. Early in life, Mike learned that he was inadequate; he was told it often and adopted it as part of his script. This favorite feeling-response stayed with him when he left school and began working. He now collects what are sometimes called gray or brown stamps; he usually has an "I'm not-OK" position and manipulates people and situations from a victim role. After saving enough stamps to fill one book (for instance, by making a series of little mistakes on the job), he may cash that book in for a "free sulk." By saving up four books full of inadequacy stamps, he feels entitled to a "free" minor blow up—for instance, telling a guest not to treat him like a servant. With twenty books, he could obtain a big prize, a "free quit" at work or a split with his girl friend. "Free" in each case means free of guilt, since Mike feels entitled to do all these things.

The important thing to keep in mind about dirty-stamp collectors is that they will frequently seek out others with whom to cash their stamps. A guest might collect angry stamps all day. First, his breakfast comes late from room service, and he has to miss it in order to catch a flight; then his luggage gets mixed up, and he arrives at the hotel without it; then his reservation has been misfiled, and the delay causes him to miss an important phone call. This person might be ready to cash in his book of stamps when he is told that the hotel will not honor his personal check. He may feel entitled to blow up at the clerk and leave her at the receiving end of the free anger and insult, perhaps even addressing a free letter of complaint to the head office of the company. Unless the desk clerk can recognize what is happening, by using her Adult to compute the situation analytically, she can easily start her own collection of dirty stamps from the person who is cashing in his. In this way, collecting trading stamps can become a continuous, dysfunctional process between people.

In the discussion of games which follows a technique to stop this vicious cycle is explained. The person who is operating primarily from a life position of ''I'm OK, you're OK'' often decides to give up collecting negative stamps and start a positive gold-stamp collection instead. The collection rules are similar to those for negative stamps. Diane, a reservations clerk, after learning about TA decided to collect gold stamps for a feeling of self-appreciation. Rather than rejecting positive strokes, she went out of her way to accept and acknowledge them. Every time someone said something complimentary to her, she accepted the comment and added a gold stamp to her collection. She smiled at work, was cheerful even when the work was getting the better of her, had a kind word for her colleagues and guests, and tried to be friendly even if guests were upset about something and tried to cash in their negative stamps on her. As a result, she began to collect quite a number of Gold Stamps, enough to fill a book which she cashed in to allow herself a free treat. For fifteen full books, she permitted herself a free trip away for a long weekend with a friend. Again, ''free'' means free of guilt; Diane had earned the right to these pleasant things.

All stamp collections, positive or negative, are eventually cashed in for a prize. A person who has a number of full books of negative stamps may do something to hurt himself or others, such as driving recklessly, committing an offense, insulting someone, quitting a job, or feeling sorry for himself. The Gold Stamp collector, on the other hand, may seek an opportunity to advance on the job, attend extra courses, read for pleasure, buy a long-denied bit of luxury, or have a dinner for a group of friends.

GAMES

The idea of playing interpersonal games was first brought to popular attention through Dr. Berne's book *Games People Play*.[7] Games are a special kind of transaction that requires two or more people (players), and there is always a payoff at the end. Such transactions differ from the complementary or crossed transac-

Figure 6.4
Basic ingredients for a game.

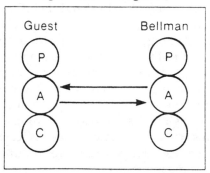

tions discussed earlier in that they operate at two levels, the social level and an *ulterior*, or psychological, level.

The game is always played at the hidden or psychological level, and it involves several steps that eventually lead to a payoff. The payoff comes when someone ends up feeling not-OK. Figure 6.4 shows the basic ingredients for a game. An arriving guest left her luggage with the bellman and, before checking in, spent some time in the cocktail lounge. She might signal the beginning of a game by asking a bellman, ''What did you do with my luggage?'' On the social level, this looks like an Adult request for information, aimed at the Adult in the bellman. But on the second, or ulterior, level, there is a double meaning implied by the words ''do with.'' This is a light accusation that the luggage is not available and perhaps was lost or misplaced, and, even better, that it was the bellman's fault. Figure 6.5 shows an ulterior message from the guest's Critical Parent aimed at ''hooking'' the bellman's Child.

Figure 6.5
''Ulterior'' aspect of a game.

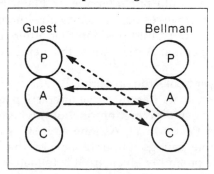

If the suitcase is really lost, rather than in the storage room behind the bellstand, we could observe two complementary transactions taking place at the same time, one at the social level, Adult to Adult, and the other at the psychological level, Parent to Child. Unless one player refuses to play the game, it can go on until the guest has collected enough angry stamps for a "free" complaint about poor service or even a letter to the manager. This may be something she wanted to do in the first place. The bellman, if he does not allow his Adult to analyze the situation, will add a stamp to his collection. He might walk away from the situation feeling inadequate. The next time a similar request is aimed at him, he might feel entitled to cash in his full book of stamps with an unsuspecting guest, a colleague, or his wife. This game is called NIGYSOB (Now I've got you, you S.O.B., also known as "bet you can't get around this one.") It describes a situation in which someone looks for people to make mistakes in order to give herself the justification for becoming angry and upset.

Each game has its own roles, number of players, level of intensity, length, and ulterior message. The ulterior message is a put-down of self or others. Games prevent honest and open relationships between the players. Yet we can easily recognize that many people play games. The games are ways of adding excitement to sometimes dull lives or situations; they are ways of obtaining strokes (even if negative); they are ways to confirm life positions ("See, I am not OK, nor are you"). Other games that might be played in a hotel situation follow.

"Yes, But . . ."

This game usually involves one person who makes suggestions to help another, only to have them rejected again and again. It is based on a childhood stance of "nobody can tell me what to do" and is the result of either always or never being told what to do. As a grown-up, such a person would play "Yes, but . . ." to confirm his basic not-OK position. To start the game, the player presents a problem and makes it appear that she is seriously asking for help and advice from one or more people. As soon as such help is offered ("Why don't you . . . ?"), the initiator discounts (negates) it with "Yes, but . . ." and gives all the reasons why such a suggestion would not solve the problem. Eventually, the "Why don't you . . . ?" person just gives up and leaves the initiator alone. This is then the payoff that proves to the Child position that others are stupid and parents don't have the answers either. A diagram of this game is shown in Figure 6.6.

The Child of the first player hooks the nurturing Parent in the other player. This is similar to the previous game in that the social interaction appears to be at the Adult-to-Adult level (seeking and giving information), whereas the ulterior transaction is at the Child and Parent level. As long as it stays at this double-complementary level, the game can go on until one of the players either switches into another ego state or simply gives up. It is the latter that the initiator looks for as a payoff.

Figure 6.6
The game of ''Yes, but . . . ,'' in diagram form.

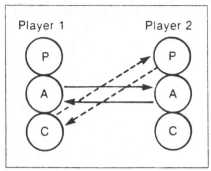

''Kick Me''

This game involves an initial player who does something to provoke another to put him down. Take the situation of a night auditor talking to his supervisor at 8:00 A.M. about an unbalanced night audit.

Night auditor: I had problems with my car last night and didn't get here till two in the morning. As a result, I haven't balanced the audit yet.

That is the social message from Adult to Adult. The ulterior message, from the rebellious Child to the supervisor's critical Parent, ''I'm a bad boy, unreliable and sloppy. Kick me.''

Supervisor: That's unfortunate. If you can't do the job in the allotted time, we'll have to let you go.

The social message at the Adult-to-Adult level simply informs the auditor of the facts of life. At the ulterior level, however, he is getting what he asked for: ''Yes, you were a bad boy and here is a kick—and a promise of more to come.'' Since game players are looking for this negative payoff, they may seek out people who are keen to play the complementary part in the game, people who are willing to ''kick'' them.

''See What You Made Me Do''

This is a common blaming game. The person who plays this game makes a mistake in the presence of another person and then blames the mistake on him or her. For example, a desk clerk posting a charge to a guest account makes a posting error. Just as another clerk looks over and notices the error, the first player tosses the account on the counter with a gesture of disgust and exclaims, ''See what you made me do! If you hadn't watched me I wouldn't have made this stupid mistake.'' Rather than taking responsibility, she blames the other for the mistake.

The initiator of this type of game tends to be a collector of angry stamps. She may feel inadequate about herself and her performance and may avoid accepting responsibility for mistakes by shifting it to others. This player may also have an arrogant stance of "I never make mistakes, but you do." In either case, it reflects a life position of not-OK. Initiators of this game often find themselves isolated from others and drifting from one job to another, usually referring to the last place of employment with feelings of hurt and resentment.

A line that helps to detect players of blaming games is the "If it weren't for . . ." sentence. This could be used by a guest when complaining about housekeeping service ("If it hadn't been for the maid coming into my room at 9:00 A.M., I would have enjoyed my stay here"), or by a fellow worker trying to explain why he left a large share of his work for the next shift ("If the assistant manager had given me a hand with the check-ins, I could have done my work on time").

"Blemish"

This game is often played in a work situation where one person tries to find something wrong with the work of another, however small the flaw might be. A senior clerk looking over the reservations taken by a new clerk may notice that the initials were placed in the wrong box on the form or that the date was written in numerals instead of numerals and words. Rather than acknowledging the overall good performance ("My, you did really well on your first day"), he will nitpick and find blemishes in the other's work. He might even communicate this in a backhanded compliment by saying, "You did really well on your first day. Unfortunately, I'll have to redo half of your work because the date is written out wrong." These put-downs may result in angry stamps being collected by the other player and may cause resentment and distrust among workers.

How Not To Play Games

There are a number of other games that can be played, all of which end with a negative payoff. You can avoid starting or being hooked into a game by recognizing that you are involved in a game or negative-stamp collecting. You must put your Adult to work to sort things out. Only your Adult can think; your Child and Parent can only react. Here is the Adult response in the example given earlier of the guest with the "hidden" suitcase:

Guest: What did you do with my suitcase?
Bellman: "Good afternoon. Did you check in with us? If I could have your name, please, I'd be glad to get it for you."

In this transaction, the bellman did not accept the ulterior implication that the suitcase might have been misplaced by the hotel staff. Instead, he first acknowledged the guest politely (positive stroke); he next clarified the Adult data regarding the guest's request to get possession of her suitcase; finally, he requested additional information so that he could attend to that request. Most likely, the response was accompanied by direct eye contact with the guest and an appropriate smile, showing businesslike attention to the person and her needs. By not allowing himself to be hooked by the ulterior transaction and by remaining at the positive (I'm OK, you're OK) level, the bellman invited the guest to respond equally positively and proceeded with the business at hand in a pleasant way.

APPLYING TA AT WORK

The goal of transactional analysis is to enable a person to have the freedom to change certain patterns of behavior and ways of reacting. Typically, people lose that choice as they adapt to the expectations of the world around them during childhood. Using TA, in particular the capacity of the Adult ego state, each person has the ability and freedom to overcome a not-OK life position. In addition to developing a strong Adult, this involves updating old Parent and Child information. This updating requires you to sort out which of the old "recordings" are still valid and appropriate in today's life. By sorting through the old recordings, you can discard as useless some childhood assumptions and produce new data for use today and in days to come. While it might have been a necessity of survival for the five-year-old Mike to believe everything others said about him, as a twenty-four-year-old person working at the front office, his early childhood recordings are no longer useful or appropriate to his day-to-day experiences. He has to unlearn old responses, sort out and discover new ones, and store them in his Adult for later use. This is, of course, the most difficult part. Most of us are quite comfortable with the things that worked in the past, even if they only resulted in negative strokes. At least we knew how they worked.

This resistance to change can be overcome in a systematic way, however. To start, you must listen to some of the old reliable Parent tapes to hear just what they are saying: "Keep a low profile" (that's what Uncle Al used to say); "Don't make waves" (it worked for Mom and for the little person within us); "Be humble" (another well-rewarded old saying); "Children should be seen and not heard" (certainly kept us out of trouble as little ones). These old tapes are examples of messages that are outdated for a grown person.

By continuously replaying these not-OK tapes and being guided by them in daily life, you severely restrict your growth and ability to change. These recordings keep you from moving towards an OK lifestyle. Having identified some of the old Parent tapes, you should determine the Parent words that you use to apply these old recordings. How do they appear in your daily routine interactions? Some examples follow:

Guest: I know it's late, but do you still have a room available?
Clerk: You should always make a reservation, especially during the summer!

Guest: Can you cash a personal check for me?
Clerk: We don't cash personal checks. It's a house policy. You should have
gone to the bank before 3:00.

Clerk A: I'm not happy with my day off next week. Can I switch with you?
Clerk B: Why do you always have to have your own way? Once the schedule
is up, it stays!

The old Parent tapes hidden in these responses should be fairly obvious. By
trying to apply some Adult questions to these old messages, you can determine
if they are still applicable today. Do they need to be adjusted, especially in a
service-oriented occupation? How valid are the tapes in your daily life? Through
this monitoring process of old Parent messages, you can sort out portions that
you want to keep in today's situations, those that you want to update so that
you can make full use of them, and those that you decide to discontinue because
they have become inoperative. Once alerted, you can monitor the use of these
old tapes in the new setting. If a discontinued tape surfaces (and it will, until
you have made the change completely), you can turn it off at will. Just as you
learned to adopt certain tapes as a child, you can discontinue them and switch
to new ones as a grown person.

Another aspect of your personality makeup that you have the power to
change is the Child. Most of us have learned, very early in life, certain not-OK
feelings about ourselves. We have a large collection of guilt, anxiety, frustration,
and fear recordings that frequently start playing in response to today's stimuli.
How do they appear in our daily interactions? One example is the following:

Guest: Why did you charge me for two? My wife checked out two nights ago.
This should only have been a single rate!

On the surface, this is an Adult-to-Adult message, with the possibility of an
ulterior message from the guest's Parent to the clerk's Child. Thus the clerk may
answer like this:

Clerk: ''How should I have known that? Nobody told me!''

The Child is hooked, and the clerk responds with an inappropriate defensive
statement that reflects a not-OK position. The real communication stops here.

By applying his Adult's computing ability, the clerk may hear an old Child
tape: ''I won't let them get me. Must make sure to have a good excuse handy.
They're always ganging up on me.'' Having identified the hurt and the source,
she can now separate this memory from the actual situation. Did the guest actually wish to ''gang up'' on the clerk, was he out to ''get me''? Most likely not.
The guest only expressed a reasonable annoyance at being billed for a double
instead of a single room and just happened to run into a clerk with a dirty-stamp
collection.

If this type of situation occurs frequently in a person's daily routine, some careful searching for the underlying Child message is called for. A decision can be made about what to do differently the next time a guest presents a similar hook. If you analyze one recurring instance at a time, you can become fast and efficient at recognizing similar situations and, using the computing Adult, avoid getting trapped. The alternative response to the same guest could go like this, "Mr. Smith, we seem to have made an error on your account. Your room rate was not adjusted after your wife's departure. I'm sorry about this. It'll just take me a moment to make an adjustment and reduce your bill." By accepting the complaint as fact (without assuming personal guilt), the clerk acknowledges the guest's Parental complaint, converts it into Adult information, and then deals with it in that fashion. The guest is told that he is in competent hands, thus reassuring his Child. Chances are, the guest will leave the hotel with an OK feeling about both having made a complaint and having been treated with respect and courtesy. The clerk, too, collects a positive stroke.

HOW TO STOP GAMES

Most people will recognize the games described earlier in this chapter. Yet they are often played without the awareness of the players involved. It is not until later that they may realize that they have gone through "the same old thing." This is the best time to stop game playing. Any game that is repetitive and therefore negative can be analyzed by the Adult. The details of the game can be computed, occasions and "favorite players" can be identified, and options can be considered. Rather than saying "Here I go again, I can't do anything about it," you can stop just at the beginning or part way into the game, switch to your Adult, and stop. Here are some basic approaches that have a high promise of success for the serious game-ender.[8]

Become Aware of Your Own Games

By using the Adult's analysis, you can see how and when you play games, and you can become alert to situations and people that are likely to trigger another game. Rather than trying to stop others from playing games, you can stop your own or refuse to be triggered into a game.

Refuse to Play Others' Games

It usually takes two or more to play transactional games. By either refusing to play the complementary hand or by responding in an unexpected manner to a hook, you can avoid giving or receiving the negative payoff. An example was the bellman who did not get hooked by the guest when she implied that her suitcase had been lost. Instead of responding from the (rebuked) Child, he applied his Adult and responded accordingly. Each game has its antidote.

Stop Discounting Others

Since the payoff of a game is usually a put-down, either of one's self or others, a good place to start ending games is with the put-down. By becoming aware of, and refraining from, discounting others or yourself, you can take control of games. In the game of "Blemish" discussed earlier, the put-down comes in the form of pointing out others' inadequacy and your relative supremacy. By not emphasizing other people's shortcomings and by stroking their strengths instead, you can stop this particular game. This technique still leaves you the option to share with the other player some Adult information about areas of her performance that are not appropriate or that need development. This can be done without an accompanying put-down. The following two techniques result from this approach.

Learn to Accept and Give Positive Strokes

People who are accustomed to giving and receiving only negative strokes may not be particularly happy, but at least they know they are receiving attention. By putting a stop to game playing, they would be deprived of these "plastic" strokes (fake ones are better than none). They therefore must learn to replace the old, negative stroking pattern with a new, positive one. This takes conscientious effort, but it is the only sure route to a more OK position.

Sometimes Leveling is Best

As was illustrated by the person who stopped playing the blaming game of "blemish," the basic reason for the encounter still remained: to inform the other person that part of his performance was not accurate or appropriate. The task is to give this information to the other person as openly as possible, without put-down or blaming implications. A clearly stated "I" message approach has the highest chance of being heard and appreciated.

You Can't Win Them All

Throughout this list of ways to stop game playing, I have taken the positive approach that, with some effort, games can be stopped by the players involved. But you will not always be able to bring about the changes. Be careful to avoid playing yet another game when you try to stop others, that of "Psychiatrist." Your aim should be to take responsibility for your part in the game playing; you should try to change and control your actions, not point out to others what is wrong with them. Sometimes you must accept the idea that people are responsible for their own actions, and you should not try to change others against their will. Instead, give yourself a positive stroke for recognizing your limits and for not succumbing to the temptation of blaming others for your failings. Not everyone has learned about TA.

KEY TERMS

Transactions   Ulterior transactions

Ego states   Probability estimating

Parent   Games

Adult   Trading stamps

Child   Stamp collections

Complementary transactions   Strokes

Crossed transactions   Discounting

NOTES

1. Maurice E. Villere, Thomas S. O'Connor, and William J. Quain, "Games Nobody Wins: Transactional Analysis for the Hospitality Industry," *The Cornell Hotel Restaurant Administration Quarterly*, November 1983, pp. 72–79.

2. Dorothy Jongeward, *Everybody Wins: Transactional Analysis Applied to Organizations* (Reading, Mass: Addison-Wesley, 1976), p. 2.

3. Eric Berne, *Games People Play* (New York: Grove Press, 1964).

4. Thomas A. Harris, *I'm OK—You're OK* (New York: Avon Books, 1969), p. 89.

5. Adapted from *Tact: Transactional Analysis in Customer Treatment* (New York: American Airlines, 1971).

6. Jongeward, *Everybody Wins*, p. 5.

7. Berne, *Games People Play*.

8. Jongeward, *Everybody Wins*, chapter 3.

9. Eric Berne, *Transactional Analysis in Psychotherapy* (New York: Grove Press, 1961).

ACTIVITIES

These can be done alone, in teams of two, or in slightly larger groups of five to six participants. Follow your instructor's guidelines. Subsequent discussion could involve the entire class.

1. Develop a list of three phrases for each of the ego states that are typical of guest service situations.

2. Write two messages you might send from your Critical Parent to a guest and two you might send to a fellow worker.

3. Read your critical messages to a partner and have him or her talk about how it feels to be on the receiving end. Work together to rephrase the messages to make them more Adult.

4. Write down three things you do in class or on the job that you can trace to your Natural Child. Discuss when such behaviors seem appropriate in either setting, and when they might get you into trouble.

5. How do you use your Little Professor (at work, at home, with friends, at school)?

6. What kinds of behaviors earn positive strokes in your present working environment? List three situations and explain to your group.

7. How do you give strokes to others? Recall three instances from recent interactions. What type of strokes did you give?

8. Think of the last time you *discounted* yourself or another person. Write down the details of both situations. Discuss with your partner what happened, how it felt, and how you could rewrite the scenario for a more accepting exchange of words.

9. Think of four situations in which you could apply specific aspects of TA (home, school, play, or work).

10. Do this exercise first in writing, then discuss it with your partner. Assume that a new clerk has made an error that caused a guest to write a letter of complaint. You have been asked to discuss the letter with the clerk. What would you say, depending on your predominant ego state (Parent, Adult, Child)?

GLOSSARY

Account settlement.   The payment, by cash or credit card, of outstanding balances on a guest folio or city ledger account.

Adjoining rooms.   Rooms next to each other without a connecting door.

Advance deposit.   A payment received by the hotel, prior to the guest's arrival. If accepted, the hotel is obligated to hold the reservation regardless of the arrival time.

Allowance.   A posting to a guest folio to adjust for unsatisfactory service or a posting error. Also called a rebate.

Amenities.   A term first used in the early 1980s to denote ''extras'' placed in guest rooms, such as shampoo, shower cap, and hair dryer. Since then it has come to refer to the wide range of products and services that distinguishes one property from its competitors, such as concierge service, complimentary shoe-shine service, use of hotel limousine during business hours, 24-hour room service.

American plan (AP).   A rate that includes the room price and certain meals. In North America, it includes a full breakfast, lunch, and dinner; in Europe, continental breakfast, table d'hote lunch, and dinner.

ASTA.   American Society of Travel Agents: A trade association of travel agents, tour operators, and vendors with worldwide membership.

AMEXCO.   The American Express Company: a major credit card and traveler's check issuer.

Audit.   Verification of all accounts, to ensure that all guest accounts for the day have been posted correctly and all records are in balance.

Audit trail. The paper trail that allows the tracing of a posting back to the original source.

Authorization code. The code received from a credit card company that allows the hotel to process a charge that is over the hotel floor limit.

Average rate. Two measures are used to express room sales: (1) The average room rate: total room revenue from one night divided by the total number of rooms occupied. (2) The average rate per guest: total room revenue divided by the total number of guests.

Back office. The support and managerial services that assist the guest services departments.

Back-of-the-house. Locations and departments not normally in direct contact with the guest. Examples: accounting, personnel, training, engineering. By contrast: *Front of the house.*

Block. To assign a specific room or group of rooms to individual reservations or group reservations before arrival, thus limiting the clerk's discretion in assigning rooms and ensuring the availability of promised room types.

Book. To sell hotel space, either to an individual or group.

Bucket. The file holder for guest accounts (folios), in order of room number.

Budget. An estimate of income and expenses for a given time period.

Call accounting. A computerized system that will cost local and long distance phone calls and pass charges to the electronic guest folio.

Cancellation. A guest's request to void a reservation previously made.

Cancellation bulletin. A report issued by credit card companies; another name for *Warning bulletin.*

Cancellation report. A summary report of all guests who held reservations and subsequently cancelled them.

Card-recovery bulletin. A report issued by credit card companies; another name for *Warning bulletin.*

Carrier. Any organization that transports passengers or goods.

Cash flow. The time between the sale of a good or service and the receipt of payment.

Cash out. The procedure the cashier follows at the end of the shift to balance the transactions of the day.

Cash sheet. The departmental control sheet maintained by the front-office cashier on which all cash transactions are recorded.

Check-in. The procedures involved in receiving the guest and completing the registration sequence.

Check-out. The procedures involved in departure of the guest and settlement of the account.

Charge record. A listing of all the transactions to a specific account or department.

City account. An account receivable for those other than guests registered in the hotel.

City ledger. A collection of city accounts and any other nonguest accounts (such as credit cards and advance payments).

Commercial rate (COMM). A reduced room rate given to selected business persons to promote occupancy.

Commission. A fee paid to a travel agent or other third party for business brought to the hotel. This is normally a percentage of the room rate the guest pays.

Complimentary rate (COMP). Accommodations and occasionally meals provided by the hotel without charge to the guest.

Concierge. A staff member who provides for guests' needs and special requests, usually involving an outside company for information or services.

Conducted tour. A prearranged escorted travel program, usually for a group, or a sightseeing program conducted by a guide.

Confirmed reservation. A reservation confirmed by the hotel, either over the phone (and in conjunction with a credit card), or in writing (with a confirmation card).

Connecting rooms. Two rooms, usually side by side, with an internal door that can be unlocked to connect the rooms.

Continental plan (CP). A room rate that includes a continental breakfast, which, in North America, usually consists of little more than a hot beverage and a sweet roll.

Correction report. A form used for NCR 4200–type posting machines to record corrections of posting errors. Used by the night auditor to balance the night audit.

Coupon. A form issued by travel agencies to their clients and used by the clients to settle their hotel accounts.

Courier. A professional travel escort or tour manager.

Credit.   (1) A posting used to indicate a decrease in the guest account (balance owing). (2) The time extended for payment of an account.

Credit card voucher.   See *Sales draft.*

Credit check.   A procedure performed by the front-desk staff to determine a guest's ability to pay.

CRT (cathode ray tube).   A video terminal as part of a computer work station.

Cut-off time.   (1) The time after which all nonguaranteed reservations are released for sale. (2) The hour by which a guest with a nonguaranteed reservation must register or risk forfeiting the reserved room.

Day rate.   A reduced charge for occupancy of a room for less time than overnight. It is used when the guest arrives and departs the same day, normally between the hours of 10:00 A.M. and 4:00 P.M.

Debit.   Sometimes called a charge. A debit posting is used to indicate an increase in the guest account.

Demi-pension.   In North America, room plus full breakfast and dinner; in Europe, room plus continental breakfast and either table d'hote lunch or dinner. Also called *Modified American plan.*

Departmental journal.   A form used by each department to control and maintain all vouchers and checks. Used to balance the transactions at the end of the shift or day.

Deposit.   The total monies of the cashiers' daily transactions minus their float. This would be deposited into a safe place at the end of each shift or day.

Desk agent.   A job title used by some hotels to replace the traditional "desk clerk."

Did not arrive (DNA).   A guest who made a reservation but did not arrive at the hotel to claim it or call to cancel.

Did not stay (DNS).   A guest who, immediately after check-in, returns to the desk and checks out without using the assigned room.

Discounting.   Giving reduced room rates to special groups.

Display terminal.   Another word for the *CRT,* or video screen attached to a computer.

Double.   A room with a large bed, suitable for two people.

Double-double.   A room with two double beds, suitable for up to four people.

Double occupancy.   Usually expressed as a percentage; the number of rooms occupied by more than one person.

Due out. A guest who is expected to depart from the hotel on a given day or during a given time period.

Due back. A situation that occurs when, during a cashier's shift, more money is paid out than is received, leaving the float short.

Dump. Computer talk for the process of making a back-up copy. This is done periodically to store data, either to free-up storage space in the computer or to make a second copy in case the main system malfunctions.

Duty manager. Title assigned to a member of the management staff whose turn it is to be on duty. Such person may have to be called in the evenings or on weekends to handle emergencies, complaints, or authorizations.

Energy management system. A computerized system to control environmental conditions in guest rooms. Example: Turns off air conditioning, heating, and lights when a room is vacant.

European plan (EP). A quoted room rate, usually in connection with package tours and travel agents, that includes only the room, no meals.

Familiarization tour. A complimentary or reduced-rate travel program for travel agents, travel writers, or airline employees, designed to acquaint them with a destination. Also called a "fam tour" or "fam trip."

Family plan. A special room rate that allows children to occupy their parents' room at no additional charge.

FIT (Foreign Independent Travel). Prepaid, unescorted trips designed to specifications of individual clients.

Flag. A signaling device used on the room rack to indicate the status of a guest room.

Float. The amount of cash and change in the cashier's drawer at the start and end of a shift.

Floor limit. (1) A dollar amount set by the credit card company. It limits the amount a hotel may accept on a card before obtaining a special authorization. It is unrelated to the limit the cardholder has arranged with the card issuer. (2) The amount a guest may charge before the hotel requires payment or a raised credit card authorization. Also called *House limit*.

Folio. A form used to record the details of all transactions between the hotel and each individual registered guest.

Forecast. A projection of business volume.

Forfeited deposit. A reservation deposit kept by the hotel when a "no show" fails to cancel the reservation.

Franchise. An independently owned hotel or motel that is part of a chain and pays a royalty for a number of privileges of affiliation.

"Front!". The call to the next bellman eligible for a rooming assignment or other errand that may result in a gratuity.

Front-of-the-house. The parts of the hotel in direct contact with the guests. Examples: front desk, restaurant, health club. By contrast: *Back-of-the-house.*

Full house. A hotel in which all rooms available for sale are occupied.

Full-service hotel. A hotel that provides a complete line of services and departments. These may include restaurant, lounge, room service, entertainment, recreation facilities, and various shops.

GIT (Group Inclusive Tour). A prepaid tour of specified minimum group size, components, and value.

Gratuity. A gift, usually of money, given in return for services rendered. See *Tip.*

Graveyard shift. The midnight to 8:00 A.M. shift.

Ground operator. A company or individual that provides such services as accommodations, sightseeing, transfers, and other related services, exclusive of transportation to and from a given destination.

Group booking. A situation in which one person reserves a block of rooms for a number of people. This may include special discounted rates, meals, and functions for all guests.

Guaranteed reservation. A reservation in which payment for the room is promised even if the guest fails to arrive.

Guest. A term commonly used to describe anyone using the services of a hotel. In legal terms, a person who is in a contractual relationship with the hotel.

Guest account. See *Folio.*

Guest check. The bill presented to persons utilizing a hotel's dining rooms or bars and often used as a department voucher.

Guest cycle. A sequence of transactions in the rooms business, from reservation through registration to account settlement.

Guest history file. A record of a guest's visits, including rooms assigned, rates, special needs, and credit rating.

Guest services. In general terms, the services offered to the guests of a hotel. Specifically, a section of the desk that looks after guests' special requests, frequently staffed by the *Concierge.*

Hard copy.   A printout of computer information. By contrast: *Soft copy*.

High-balance report.   A listing of all the in-house guest accounts that exceed the house limits set for cash, credit cards, and billing.

Hospitality suite.   A facility used for entertaining, usually at conventions, trade shows, and similar meetings.

Hot list.   Another name for *Warning bulletin*.

House count.   The number of registered guests in a hotel.

Housekeeping report.   A report of the status of all the guest rooms, compiled by the staff of the housekeeping department. Used by the front office to verify the accuracy of the *Room rack*.

House limit.   A dollar amount set by the hotel for guest account balances. When an account exceeds the specified dollar amount, the guest's credit worthiness is checked. Also called *Floor limit*.

IATA (International Air Transport Association).   An organization whose members include most of the world's international scheduled airlines. IATA suggests fares for government approval.

Inclusive tour.   A tour in which specific elements, such as air fare, accommodations, and transfers are provided at a flat rate.

Inclusive Tour Charter (ITC).   A tour that provides basic transportation by chartered aircraft.

Information rack.   An alphabetic listing of all registered guests, cross-referenced by room number.

Internal controls.   A means of checking work (completed and in progress) to make sure that proper procedures are being followed.

Journal.   A record of financial transactions. See *Departmental journal*.

Key rack.   A storage unit (rack, shelf, drawer) for guest room keys. Often combined with a *Mail rack*.

Land arrangements.   All services provided to a traveler (except ongoing transportation by public carrier) after reaching a destination.

"Last!"   A call to the bellman who most recently completed a "Front" call. He is assigned a task for which there will be no gratuity.

Late charge.   A department charge that arrives at the front desk after the guest has checked out.

Lock out.   Denying guests access to their room, usually because of an unpaid bill. Also called "double locked."

Mail rack.   A set of small shelves at the front desk where guest mail is stored, in order of the alphabet for "hold" mail and in order of room number for registered guests.

MCO (miscellaneous charges order).   A document issued by an airline or travel agent requesting that a ticket be issued or services be provided to the person named in the order.

Management contract.   An arrangement under which a hotel is owned by a single company or individual and is managed under contract by another.

Minibar.   A refrigerated unit in a guest room, containing snacks, alcoholic and nonalcoholic drinks. Guests are given a key to the minibar when they receive their room key. An inventory is taken daily, and stock consumed is replaced and charged to the guest's account.

Modified American plan (MAP).   A method of quoting room rates in which the charge includes breakfast and dinner as well as the room. Also called *Demi-pension*.

Multiple occupancy.   A room rented to more than one person at a time.

Murphy bed.   A bed that folds into the wall or appears to be a sideboard when stowed away.

Net wholesale rate.   A rate usually slightly lower than the group rate, offered when a hotel or motel is specifically mentioned in a tour folder.

Night audit.   A daily reconciliation of accounts receivable that is completed during the *Graveyard shift*.

Nonguaranteed reservation.   A room held for a guest until a stated cutoff time. If the guest does not arrive by that time, the room may be sold.

No-show.   A reservation that fails to arrive.

Occupancy.   A numerical expression of the number of people staying in a room, such as double, single, or triple occupancy. Not to be confused with the type of bed in the room, such as single, double, twin, or double-double.

Occupancy percentage.   The ratio between the number of rooms sold and the number available for sale.

Official airline guide (OAG).   Any of the several passenger and cargo air service manuals in general use throughout the world. Principal ones are the *North American Quick Reference Edition* and the *International Quick Reference Edition*.

On change.   The status of a guest room recently vacated but not yet ready for a new guest.

Out of order (OOO). The status of a guest room that is not available for sale because of planned work or an unexpected problem.

Overbooking. Committing more rooms to possible guests than are actually available.

Over/short. A discrepancy between the cash on hand and the amount that should be on hand.

Package tour. A saleable travel product offering, at an inclusive price, several travel elements that would otherwise be purchased separately by a traveler. Any or all of the following may be included: lodging; sightseeing; attractions; meals; entertainment; car rental; transportation by air, rail, water, bus, or private vehicle. May include more than one destination.

Paid in advance. A room charge that is collected before occupancy.

Paid occupancy percent. A ratio relating the number of rooms occupied, minus complimentary rooms, to the total rooms available for sale.

Paid out. Money paid on behalf of guests to settle tips for service staff, COD charges for deliveries, or payment for goods obtained in a concession store located in the hotel. This money is recovered when guests settle their account.

Parlor. (1) A sitting room that is part of a suite. In emergencies, parlors can serve as extra bedrooms. (2) A guest room with a hideaway bed, giving the room the appearance of a sitting room.

Payment. Money received from the guest. May be in the form of cash, check, or credit card.

(PABX) Private automatic branch exchange. A state-of-the-art switchboard.

(PBX) Private branch exchange. A traditional name for a manually operated switchboard installation.

Petty cash. Small cash disbursements out of the cashier's drawer, usually for house use with a manager's approval.

Pickup. (1) The procedure used with front-office posting machines to accumulate the folio balance by entering the previous balance into the machine before posting the new charges; the figure so entered. (2) Part of a group reservation is "picked up" when a guest belonging to that group contacts the hotel to make a reservation.

Point of sale (POS). A remote sales location linked to the central computer. In front-office accounting, this allows for entry of guest charges from the dining room or other areas directly to the electronic folio.

Point-of-sale terminal. (1) Automatic credit card authorization terminal. (2) Keyboard and screen set located at various points throughout the hotel. Charges to guest accounts are entered directly onto the electronic folio.

Post. To place or enter a charge into the guest account. Can be done manually or by machine.

Posting machine. A mechanical or electronic machine used to post debits and credits to front-office accounts.

PPPN. Per person, per night.

Preregistration. A method of speeding registration used for large groups, steady customers, or VIP's. On the morning of arrival, the required rooms are blocked off and keys are sorted out for each arriving guest. When the guests arrive, they need only sign their names to be roomed.

PRPN. Per room, per night.

Rack rate. The standard rate quoted from the room rack; the published rate that is posted in each guest room.

Rate. The price charged for a hotel room.

Rate type. A code assigned to a discounted rate, used for tracking purposes. Examples: corporate, government.

Rebate. See *Allowance.*

Recap. A summary of the transcript sheets used to obtain the day's grand totals. Short for *recap*itulation.

Reception. Another term for the front desk originally used in Great Britain and now also used in North America.

Receptionist. A term favored by some organizations as a job title over ''desk clerk.''

Referral chain. A chain made up of independently owned and operated properties. Provides standardized quality, shared advertising and joint reservation systems.

Refusal report. A record of all guests who were denied accommodation on a given day.

Registration. The procedure by which incoming persons become guests by completing and signing the registration card.

Registration card. The form completed by the guest upon arrival, giving name, address, company, and method of payment.

Relocation. A situation that arises when a guest arrives at the hotel with a confirmed reservation and finds that there is no room waiting. Alternate accommodation must be arranged, by the hotel. See *Walking a guest*.

Remind-O-Timer. A clock that can be set at 15-minute intervals, used mainly to time guests' wake-up calls.

Reservation. A mutual agreement between the guest and hotel. The guest agrees to take accommodation at a given time for a given period, and the hotel agrees to furnish the accommodation.

Reservations department. The office within the hotel that performs the functions of responding to reservation requests quickly and accurately. Maintains records of all pertinent data for new reservations, and charts reservations by date of arrival and departure.

Reservations status. The terms agreed upon by the guest and the hotel. The terms *Advance deposit, Guaranteed payment,* and *6:00 P.M. hold* are used.

Revenue report. The figures compiled by the night auditors, consisting of total departmental sales for one day. This includes total sales figures for all departments and room statistics. Also called the night auditor's report.

RNA (Room not available, or, Registered but not assigned). A guest has registered but is waiting for a specific room, which is assigned at the time it becomes ready for occupancy. This usually happens when new guests arrive before the current guest checks out.

Rollaway. A spare bed that can be wheeled into a room.

Rooming. The procedure by which the guest is greeted by the front desk staff, a room is assigned, and the guest is shown to the room. Also called *Room assignment*.

Rooming list. The names furnished by a buying group in advance of arrival and used by the hotel to preregister and preassign the party to rooms.

Rooming slip. A form issued by the front desk to the bellman and left by the bellman with the guest for verification of name, rate, and room.

Room inventory. The number of rooms in a hotel. Sometimes refers only to rooms available for sale.

Room rack. A piece of front-office equipment that visually represents the guests rooms: shows their relative location, type, rate, and current status.

Room status. The current condition of a guest room: vacant, occupied, checkout, or out-of-order.

Run of the house. Any room assigned from those available; may be at a prearranged rate, regardless of type and location.

RVNB (room vacant, no baggage). The guest has left the hotel but not formally checked out. Further investigation is needed to determine whether this guest has left with intent to defraud the hotel. See also *Skip.*

Sales draft. A three-part form supplied by credit card companies, used to record credit card transactions.

Self-registration. A procedure by which guests can use a machine to complete check-in procedures without staff assistance. A credit card is used as identification and the guest interacts with a computer by means of a touch-screen.

Selling up. A technique by which an arriving guest is encouraged to take a higher-priced room than had been planned or reserved.

Skip. A guest who departs secretly, without intention to pay.

6:00 P.M. hold. A reservation status for a room that will be held only until 6:00 P.M. The guest is not expected to pay if he fails to arrive. The guest who arrives after 6:00 P.M. will be accommodated only if there are vacancies at that time; no promises are made.

Sleep out (S/O). A room sold but not used.

Sleeper. A departed guest whose records have not been processed, giving the appearance of an occupied room.

Soft copy. A display of information on the computer screen, in contrast to *Hard copy.*

Source codes. A means of tracking how reservations were made or how a guest arrived at the hotel.

Special-interest tour. A tour designed to appeal to persons with a curiosity or a concern about a specific subject.

Statistics (stats). A collection of operating figures compiled to assist clerks and managers in decision making and planning.

Stayover. A guest extending a stay beyond the expected check-out day.

Stock card. A colored card of plastic or laminated cardboard, containing all the information relevant to a room. For each room in the hotel, there is a corresponding stock card.

Telephone call sheet. A form used to record room number, name and time of all guest wake-up requests. The sheet is then used to call the guests the next morning.

Telephone management system. A computerized system with such features as local phone charges, maid status, phone restrictions, message lights, and some features of *Energy management.*

Time-date stamp machine. An electric clock with a mechanism that prints date and time when a piece of paper is inserted.

Tour. Any prearranged (but not necessarily prepaid) journey to one or more destinations and back to point of origin.

Tour leader. A person with special qualifications to conduct a particular travel group. Not necessarily a professional tour escort or courier.

Tour vouchers (tour orders, coupons). Documents issued by tour operators to clients to be exchanged for lodging, meals, sightseeing, etc.

Transfer. (1) In accounting, a technique used to move a figure from one form to another, usually between folios. (2) In the travel industry, local transportation or porterage from one carrier to another, from a terminal to a hotel, or from a hotel to a theater or other attraction.

Transient guest. A short-term guest, one who stops while en route to other destinations.

Transposition. A transcription error caused by reordering the sequence of digits. For example, 432 written as 423.

Trial balance. A listing of all accounts payable and receivable, checked for arithmetic accuracy. Part of a *Night audit*.

Turn-away. To refuse walk-in business because no rooms are available.

Turn down. A special service rendered by the housekeeping department during the early evening hours. Used bathroom towels are replaced, garbage is removed, the room and bathroom are tidied, curtains are drawn, ice in the minibar is replenished, and the bed is prepared for the night.

Twin. A room with two one-person beds.

Unexpected arrival. A guest who arrives before the stated reservation date.

Unexpected departure. A guest who checks out before the anticipated departure date.

Upgrade. To move a guest into a higher-priced room category, while still charging the lower rate.

USTS (United States Travel Service). A U.S. Department of Commerce agency whose task it is to stimulate and encourage travel to the United States and its possessions from abroad.

Vacant room. A room that is ready to sell, has been cleaned by the housekeeping department, but is not yet occupied.

Valet. Special services, such as dry cleaning, ironing, and mending.

VIP (very important person).   A reservation or guest who warrants special attention and handling.

Voucher.   The sales record that authenticates a charge or credit to a guest account.

Walking (a guest).   Turning away a guest who holds a confirmed reservation because of the lack of available rooms. This may involve paying for the guest's accommodation at another hotel.

Walk-in.   An incoming guest without a prior reservation.

Wait list.   Names and telephone numbers of guests who wish to make a reservation for a sold-out date. If a vacancy occurs, the guest is contacted.

Warning bulletin.   A periodic publication issued by credit card companies. It contains numbers of cards that have been cancelled for various reasons, including loss or theft. No inference as to credit rating is to be drawn from the appearance of a number in this bulletin. Also called *Cancellation bulletin* or *Card recovery bulletin.*

Zero out.   To reduce an account to a zero balance.

APPENDIX A

IN CASE OF FIRE . . .

From time to time, hotels are in the news for the wrong reasons: hotel fires. Most regions have adopted stringent fire laws as a direct result of the 1981 and 1982 tragedies in Nevada (MGM Grand in Reno, where 84 persons died and 769 were injured) and in New York (Stouffer's in White Plains, where 26 business executives perished).[1] Among the new rules:

- Buildings that rise higher than 55 feet (about five stories) above the lowest fire department access must have automatic sprinklers installed in each guest room and exit corridor.

- The air supply to guest rooms must come from a source other than the exit corridors.

- A voice communication system must allow for at least one-way contact between guests and hotel staff.

- Hotels and motels must post a map on the back of guest room doors, showing all fire exits and escape routes.

- Improved emergency lighting, smoke detectors, fire alarms, sprinkler systems, and directional signs in public areas are mandatory.

- Hotel employees must be designated as fire safety directors and deputies must be certified to conduct fire drills and evacuations and to organize, train, and supervise an in-house fire brigade.

Several organizations offer training seminars, instructional materials, and handbooks for lodging operators, meeting planners, and guests.[2] The basic guidelines for staff members are summarized here:

Emergency Procedures for Employees at Large Properties

1. Pull the fire alarm box. Know where these boxes are located and how they work—before the emergency. Check to see whether the alarm au-

215

tomatically reports to the local fire department. A follow-up phone call is the recommended procedure in any case.

2. Notify the switchboard operator. Until the emergency is over, the operator must remain at the console and perform important coordinating functions. The switchboard operator must contact the fire department and designated management personnel.

3. Extinguish the fire with the nearest fire extinguisher. This requires familiarity with the available equipment and the methods for dealing with different types of fire.

4. If the fire spreads, guests and staff must be evacuated and the area closed off to prevent the further spread of the fire.

A detailed discussion of fire-fighting procedures is beyond the limitations of this book. Each hotel should establish fire regulations, conduct regular training sessions, and periodically check on the human and physical resources. Unfortunately, too many hotel operations pay only lip service to fire procedures. For the sake of the protection of property and human life, it is therefore up to each hotel employee, desk clerks in particular, to develop fire knowhow, including the ability to

- Describe fire precaution rules.

- Describe fire-fighting procedures.

- Know the exit routes and doors from every conceivable part of the hotel.

- Identify fires by type.

- Operate fire-fighting equipment.

- Inform the fire department.

- Inform the guests in a manner that avoids panic and maintains order.

- Verify that guests and hotel employees are out of potential danger zones.

- Assist in the evacuation of guests.

- Assist the fire brigade.

Desk staff must be able to explain to guests what precautions to take and how to behave in case of a fire. The basics, found in a booklet entitled "What if . . . there is a fire?" are condensed here.[3]

A guest just arrived should:

- Look outside the room and locate at least two exits, walk to them, and remember their location.

- Count the number of doors between his room and the nearest fire escape route.

- Find the nearest fire alarm box and fire extinguisher.
- Locate the "off" switch on the room's air conditioner to be able to turn it off in an emergency and prevent smoke from being sucked into the room.

In case of a fire, guests are advised to:

- Pull the nearest fire alarm.
- Close doors around the fire to prevent it from spreading.
- Phone the switchboard or the local fire department for help.
- Fight only small fires with available fire extinguisher and flee the area if the fire is not small.

If guests hear an alarm, they must:

- Take their room key.
- Test the room door before opening it. If it is cool, open the door carefully, look outside for smoke, and slam it shut if there is thick smoke in the hallway.
- Leave the room if there is little or no smoke outside and make their way to the nearest exit. The suggested procedure is to stay close to the walls and, if lights are out, to count the number of doors to the exit. Most hotels post maps in each guest room, showing the exact location of each guest room in relation to others and the exit routes.
- Guests should consult these before venturing out.
- Avoid using elevators and smoke-filled stairwells.
- Stay calm, do not hurry, and *think*.

If guests find their exit routes blocked, they are advised to:

- Return to their rooms (the safest place to be in such a situation) or go to the next available exit.
- Make their way to the roof for possible rescue by ladder or helicopter.
- Remember that the danger is almost always less than imagined.

Should guests determine that they have to remain in the room, their best moves are to:

- Shut off the air conditioner.
- Stuff wet towels, sheets, or blankets over the cracks of the door and air vents to prevent the entry of smoke.

- Remove all drapes to prevent the spread of fire should it enter through the window.

- Fill the bathtub and use an ice bucket or waste basket to carry water to remoisten the wet cloth to keep out smoke.

- Phone the desk, switchboard, or fire department and advise them of their presence in the room.

Clerks must know these rules and, ideally, have had practical experience in simulated training sessions. Fire departments are always willing to come to the hotel to demonstrate fire-fighting equipment and to let staff members operate extinguishers in controlled fires outside the hotel. Companies who service the fire extinguishers also cooperate in letting staff use the equipment before refilling. Regular drills, discussions, and tests must be used to keep old and new staff members current in their knowledge of procedures and ability to perform the steps outlined here.

NOTES

1. J. P. Jeffries, *Hotel Fires* (New York: The Educational Institute of The American Hotel and Motel Association).

2. Direct inquiries to the National Fire Protection Association, Batterymarch Park, Quincy, MA 02269; and the American Hotel and Motel Association, 888 Seventh Avenue, New York, NY 10019.

3. Direct inquiries to the National Fire Academy, U.S. Fire Administration, Washington, DC 20472.

APPENDIX B

"A ROOM AND A BATH FOR A DOLLAR AND A HALF":*

Major Events in the History of American Hotel Keeping

1794. The 73-room City Hotel opens as the first U.S. structure specifically intended as a hotel. Up to this date, innkeepers operated in converted homes. Described as an "immense establishment," it became the social center of the thriving town of New York, with its 30,000 residents.

1829. The Tremont House, the largest and costliest building of its kind, opens for business in Boston. While the typical inn of the day consists of a few rooms, each containing up to ten beds, the Tremont is the first to offer private single and double rooms, each with a lock on the door. Other firsts include: every room has a bowl, pitcher, and free soap; indoor plumbing is available for guests' use; French cuisine is featured in the restaurant; bellhops carry luggage and messages; an annunciator, an early version of the room telephone, reaches every guest room.

1859. Seven years after its invention, an elevator is installed in the six-story Fifth Avenue Hotel in New York.

1881. Electric lights are installed in the Prospect House in Blue Mountain Lake, NY.

1908. Ellsworth Statler opens the Buffalo Statler. His "invention" of the modern commercial hotel is likened to Henry Ford's invention of the modern automobile. Statler's attention to detail, resulting in features later taken for granted, included: fire doors protecting the two main stairways; guest room door locks with the keyhole above the knob for easy locating in the dark; a light switch immediately inside the door to eliminate groping in the dark; a private bath,

---

*Slogan used by the Buffalo Statler in 1908.

219

full-length mirror, and circulating ice water for every room; a free morning newspaper for every guest.

1910. The American Hotel Association is formed for the purpose of "apprehension and punishment to the fullest extent of the law, of professional deadbeats, check forgers, dishonest and undesirable employees, crooks of all description, and such other matters as may commend themselves to the consideration of the members."

1927. The Hotel Statler in Boston becomes the first to offer radio reception with a central control room from which broadcasts are piped to individual guest rooms.

1929. The Oakland Airport Inn in California opens as the first lodging operation specifically geared toward air travelers.

1933. Overexpansion: more hotels were built in the previous 10 years than ever before (or since), and the Depression causes the lowest ever average occupancy percentage: 51 percent. The Great Depression causes 85 percent of the nation's hotels to go into receivership or similar forms of liquidation.

1946. Inter-Continental Hotels signs the first hotel management contract, a new way of doing hotel business.

1946. With the post-war boom in the economy, the hotel industry records an all-time-high occupancy rate of 95 percent.

1947. The first television sets are installed in 40 guest rooms at the Roosevelt Hotel in New York.

1951. The "motel," largely a no-frills, family-operated creature, is first mentioned as a separate category in the annual Harris Kerr Forster lodging survey. The traveling public begins to switch from railroads, the predominant mode of transport in the '30s, to the automobile in the '40s and '50s.

1952. Kemmons Wilson starts Holiday Inns, which eventually becomes the world's largest hotel chain.

1962. The American Hotel Association, recognizing that they are more than "poor cousins" and a "passing fad," adds 209 motor hotels to the membership and changes its name to the American Hotel & Motel Association, (AH&MA). Smart operators realize that hotels and motels have become parts of the same industry. Eventually, the distinction further blurs: hotels offer drive-in registration and free parking, and motels install room service and restaurants.

1962. The 2,000-room Americana in New York opens as the tallest hotel in the world.

1965. Eighty of 557 Holiday Inns are linked by Holidex, IBM's computer reservations system.

1967. The hotel industry's battle to be exempted from the minimum wage laws finally ends.

1967. TraveLodge guests can now telephone ahead, free of charge, to reserve rooms at other inns of the chain.

1970. The three-story Pet Lodge in New York's Manhattan district offers accommodation to 100 cats and dogs.

1970. For the first time, women are admitted as students at the Culinary Institute of America.

1971. After 50 years of production, the NCR company officially ceases to manufacture the NCR 2000 front-desk posting machine.

1973. The number of motel rooms rises above that of hotel rooms, a statistical fact still true today.

1974. As part of a national energy conservation drive, many hotels reset thermostats to 68 degrees and turn the heat off in vacant rooms. One hotel even refunds guests for gasoline expenses.

1975. After losing 6,600 rooms in 1974, New York City's hotel industry removes 1,000 more from the over-saturated market.

1976. The Bellevue Stratford Hotel in Philadelphia closes after 72 years of operation, following the negative publicity resulting from Legionnaire's disease, which killed 29 banquet guests.

1979. OPEC announces increases in crude-oil prices and lodging operators cope with energy cost increases of up to 20 percent.

1979. The first woman is appointed general manager; appropriately enough, to the Queen Mary Hyatt in Long Beach, CA.

1980. Lodging operators are advised to watch these market trends: baby boomers, younger executives, female travelers, guest with special physical needs, the exercise craze, health-conscious diners, an aging population, emphasis on quality and value.

1980. The MGM Grand hotel fire in Las Vegas causes the death of 84 guests, due mainly to panic caused when lethal fumes and gases filled the building. The hotel was not equipped with sprinklers, and the ventilation system recycled the poisonous fumes. Retroactively purchased fire insurance and lengthy court battles eventually result in damage awards totaling several million dollars.

1980. A fire at the Stouffer Hotel in Harrison, NY kills 26; locked emergency doors and poorly marked exits contributed to the disaster.

1981. The Las Vegas Hilton fire is the third in a hotel in three months. Eight persons perish, 242 are injured, and property damage reaches $10 million. The lack of fire detectors, the absence of sprinklers, and failure of alarm systems are contributing factors.

1982. The 686-room Barbizon Hotel In New York accepts male guests for the first time.

1982. The amenities battle picks up tempo as hotels compete to provide guests with items other than clean rooms and friendly service: different soaps, shampoo, hand lotion, shower cap, bath oils, bath robes, lint remover, shoeshine mit, swimsuit bag, stationery, sewing kits, engraved pens and pencils, and whatever else guests might want to use (and take home).

1983. Fire protection information is routinely placed in guest rooms, alongside the Bible and room service menu.

1983. Chicago's Midland Hotel is the first to install computer terminals in 100 guest rooms.

1983. Chains introduce "brands" of hotels, such as Howard Johnson's Plaza hotels and Marriott's Courtyard concept.

1984. Guests at the Richmond Hotel in Chicago can take advantage of a $50 insurance policy to guarantee a room, however short the notice.

SOURCES

G. W. Lattin, *Modern Hotel & Motel Management*, 3rd ed., (San Francisco: W. H. Freeman 1977), pp. 3–15.

The Cornell Hotel and Restaurant Administration Quarterly, May 1985, pp. 38–89.

INDEX